DATE DUE			

MESSIAEN

MESSIAEN

Robert Sherlaw Johnson

University of California Press

Berkeley and Los Angeles   1975

UNIVERSITY OF CALIFORNIA PRESS
Berkeley and Los Angeles, California

ISBN 0 520 02812 0

Library of Congress Catalog Card Number:
74 81434

© Robert Sherlaw Johnson 1975

Printed in Great Britain

This book is set in 10 point Times New Roman

Contents

Acknowledgments

The author and publishers would like to thank the following for permission to quote extracts or music examples from copyright material:

FABER AND FABER: *Wagner's Ring and Its Symbols*, Robert Donington; RENÉ JULLIARD, Paris: *Rencontres avec Olivier Messiaen*, Antoine Goléa; PIERRE BELFOND, Paris: *Entretiens avec Olivier Messiaen*, Claude Samuel; LIBRAIRIE DELAGRAVE, Paris: *Encyclopédie de la Musique et Dictionnaire du Conservatoire Vol. I* (Tableau des 120 deçî-tâlas) and music examples 11 (jâti only), 39(a), 68 (jâtis); ERNST EULENBURG LTD: *Tristan und Isolde*, Eulenburg Miniature Score No. 905; UNIVERSAL EDITION (LONDON) LTD: from Stockhausen's article 'Music and Speech' in *Die Reihe Vol. VI*; *Messiaen's Cantéyodjayâ and Constellation-Miroir*, Pierre Boulez; music examples 7, 25, 27, 28, 30, 64, 65(c), 66; EDITIONS SALABERT, Paris: extracts from the text of Messiaen's *Cinq Rechants*, and music examples 1 (Duparc only), 11 (*Cinq Rechants* only), 62, 63, 64, 65(b); ALPHONSE LEDUC, Paris: music examples 8, 12(a)–2, 13, 16, 19, 20, 21, 24, 34, 35, 36, 37, 38, 39(b), 39(c), 65(d), 69, 70, 71(b), 72(b), 73, 74, 75, 76, 77, 78, 79, 80, 81, 82, 83, 84; EDITIONS DURAND, Paris: music examples 2, 3, 4(b), 5, 6, 9, 10, 12(b)–2, 14, 15, 17, 18, 22, 23, 26, 29, 31, 32, 33, 40, 42, 43, 44, 45, 46, 47, 48, 49, 50, 51, 52, 53, 54, 55, 56, 57, 58, 59, 60, 61, 64, 65(a), 67, 68 (Île de Feu), 71(a), 72(a).

Author's Foreword

Any study of a composer's music while he is still living must remain incomplete and even, in some respects, tentative. It has not been my aim in this book to present a highly critical study of Messiaen's music but to present his attitudes and his musical thought through a study of his major works. I have tried, on the whole, to let his music speak for itself; criticisms, if they are to be made, can be left to others—no two people anyway will agree about the nature of the criticisms which can be made about his music.

In his attitude to sources outside his own music, such as Indian rhythms, Peruvian folklore (in *Harawi*) and Hindu religion, Messiaen is not concerned with their scholarly accuracy. What he reads about these matters itself provides the artistic impetus for a major part of his music. His knowledge of Sharngadeva's rhythms, for instance, was initially derived from the table given in Lavignac's *Encyclopédie de la Musique et Dictionnaire de la Conservatoire* and does not arise from a critical study of Indian music at its primary source. Much less does it mean that his music has been influenced by the essential ethos of Indian music. Similarly, in his use of Peruvian mythology in *Harawi* it is of less importance to ask whether the symbolism he uses is accurate than to consider what use he makes of it, misconceived or not. The consideration of a work such as *Harawi* in relation to Peruvian folklore could form a fascinating study in itself but is outside the scope of this book. In addition, the degree of 'scientific' accuracy in Messiaen's use of birdsong is not something which affects the artistic integrity of his works which use birdsong and, again, more properly forms the basis of a separate study. (See Trevor Hold's article on 'Messiaen's Birds' in *Music and Letters*, April 1971.)

The author wishes to thank Olivier Messiaen for his help with, and for his comments on, certain portions of the book, and especially for the background information relating to *Méditations sur la Mystère de la Sainte Trinité*.

Grateful thanks are also due to Mr D. W. Snow of the British Museum (Natural History) for information relating to some of the more obscure birds listed in Appendix III.

THIS BOOK IS DEDICATED TO MY WIFE
AND TO NOELLE BARKER

1
Life and Early Influences

Olivier Messiaen was born on 10 December 1908 at Avignon. His father, Pierre Messiaen, was a teacher of English and a Shakespearian scholar, best known for his critical translation of the complete works of Shakespeare. His mother, the poetess Cécile Sauvage, had a profound influence on her son's artistic development and character; during her pregnancy she wrote a book of poems called *L'Âme en bourgeon* (The Flowering Soul), which Messiaen claims has had a particular influence on his character and his whole destiny.[1]

During the First World War, Messiaen lived with his mother and grandmother at Grenoble while his father was in the army. Grenoble is situated near the mountains of Dauphiny, which also had a great influence on him. It is these mountains in particular which he had in mind in 'Montagnes', the third movement of his song-cycle *Harawi*, or in 'Les Mains de l'abîme' from *Livre d'Orgue*, or in 'Chocard des Alpes' from *Catalogue d'Oiseaux*. They also strongly affect the character of the orchestral work *Et exspecto resurrectionem mortuorum* which he describes as 'being intended for performance in vast spaces: churches, cathedrals, and even in the open air and on high mountains. . . .'[2]

It was while he was living at Grenoble that he first taught himself the piano, and in 1917 he wrote his first composition, *The Lady of Shalott*, for piano, based on the poem by Tennyson. It was also at this time that he became aware of the theatre through his readings of Shakespeare and through his discovery of Mozart's *Don Giovanni*, Berlioz's *La Damnation de Faust* and Gluck's *Alceste*.

After the war his family moved to Nantes, and it was there that he received his first formal tuition in piano and harmony. His harmony teacher introduced him to a score of Debussy's *Pelléas et Mélisande* when he was still only ten years old; this was to become yet another major influence on his development as a composer. Besides the influence of the theatre, many other extra-musical influences have affected his musical development—nature, birdsong, his literary background and especially Catholic theology. In spite of his early introduction to opera and Shakespeare's plays, he has never himself written for the stage, these theatrical influences being absorbed into his music in

9

other ways. The reason for this is probably due to the fact that he never had a chance to see performances of any of these works at that time, their realization existing only in his imagination.

In 1919 he entered the Paris Conservatoire, where he studied until 1930. He first received piano lessons from Georges Falkenberg. Later he studied harmony with Jean Gallon, organ with Marcel Dupré, history of music with Maurice Emmanuel, percussion with Joseph Baggers and composition with Paul Dukas. His career at the Conservatoire was distinguished with first prizes in fugue (1926), accompaniment (1929), organ and improvisation (1929) and composition (1930). It was from Maurice Emmanuel and Marcel Dupré that he first received his knowledge of Greek rhythms, and, at about the same time, he discovered the table of 120 Indian 'deçî-tâlas'—that is, rhythms of the Indian provinces—listed by Sharngadeva in his treatise *Samgîta-ratnâkara* and reproduced in Lavignac's *Encyclopédie de la Musique*.[3] Some debt to Greek rhythms is present in his early works, but the more important Indian influences did not appear in his music until *La Nativité du Seigneur* in 1935.

In 1931, at the age of 22, he was appointed organist of the church of La Sainte Trinité, Paris. Although his duties there have involved him closely with the Roman liturgy, he has written little of importance for actual liturgical use. Instead, he has preferred a more meditative form of composition for organ, suitable for the accompaniment of certain parts of Low Mass, or other liturgical functions, at specific seasons of the year.

After the First World War, through the influence of Satie and Cocteau's manifesto 'Le Coq et l'Harlequin', the main trend in French music was away from the impressionism of Debussy towards a music devoid of romantic or pictorial associations. This music found its expression in small forms and in an eclecticism which drew its influences from (amongst other things) eighteenth-century dance movements and twentieth-century jazz, as well as from any other fashion which came to hand. At its best it could be witty, at its worst trivial, but it was mostly undistinguished and lacking in purpose. It was partly in reaction to this artistic climate that Messiaen and three other composers—Jolivet, Daniel-Lésur and Baudrier—joined together in 1936 to form the group known as 'La Jeune France'. They presented a concert of their music in Paris and printed in the programme their own manifesto which reacted against the tendency of the life of the time to become increasingly hard, mechanical and impersonal. They sought to restore to music a more human and spiritual quality, combined with a seriousness of intention so sadly lacking in much of the French music of the inter-war years.

It was in this same year (1936) that Messiaen married the violinist Claire Delbos, to whom he dedicated his first major song-cycle, *Poèmes pour Mi*, a work primarily concerned with the sacramental and spiritual aspects of marriage. This was followed in 1938, after the birth of their son Pascal, by a further song-cycle, *Chants de terre et de ciel*, which treats the subject of parenthood in a similar manner.

When war broke out, Messiaen joined the army and served as a hospital attendant until 1940 when he was taken prisoner. He spent two years in Stalag VIII at Görlitz in Silesia, during which time he wrote the *Quatuor pour la Fin du Temps*, for clarinet, violin, cello and piano. This work was first performed in the prison camp on 15 January 1941.

Before the war he had taught ensemble work and sight-reading at the piano at l'École Normale, and organ and improvisation at the Schola Cantorum in Paris, but after his repatriation in 1942 he was appointed Professor of Harmony at the Paris Conservatoire—a progressive move on the part of the director, Claude Delvincourt. Although at first Messiaen was not able to teach composition there, he started private composition classes in 1943 at the house of a friend, Guy Delapierre. It was in these classes that he first came into contact with his more illustrious pupils: Yvonne Loriod, Pierre Boulez and Karlheinz Stockhausen. He gave up these private classes in 1947 on being appointed Professor of Analysis, Aesthetics and Rhythm at the Conservatoire. His classes now virtually became composition classes, although he held no official appointment as Professor of Composition at the Conservatoire until 1966.

The early 1940s were an important formative period for Messiaen's composing. His contact with the pianist Yvonne Loriod prompted him to write his major works for piano, *Visions de l'Amen*, *Vingt Regards sur l'Enfant-Jésus* and, later, *Catalogue d'Oiseaux*. The piano, hitherto somewhat neglected by Messiaen, also features as a prominent instrument in many of his orchestral works after this time. Ever since then, Loriod has remained the foremost interpreter of his piano music, and her long association with Messiaen resulted in their marriage in 1962, his first wife having died in 1959 after a prolonged illness.

The most important musical event after his return from Germany was the performance on 1 April 1945 of *Trois petites Liturgies de la Présence divine*. This work aroused a great storm of controversy among the critics. Almost overnight, Messiaen became a composer who was condemned, on the one hand, for his vulgarity and lack of good taste, and praised, on the other, for a vivid imagination and true creative genius. The work was disliked by the avant-garde of the day for what they regarded as his reactionary harmonies, reminiscent of the nineteenth century, and it shocked the conservatives because of its unusual instrumentation [4] and treatment of voices, and because of the peculiar dissonances which, by this time, had become a feature of Messiaen's style. The non-Christian was out of sympathy with the religious sentiments expressed, while the traditional Catholic was displeased by the apparently vulgar treatment of sacred ideas. It is the mark of a truly original work that it tends to set off a very deep controversy, and it would be no exaggeration to say that the *Trois petites liturgies* is one of the most original works of its genre which had been written up to that time. It cannot be classed either as an oratorio or as a cantata because the treatment of the subject matter is symbolistic and not dramatic. It sets out, in fact, to transfer

11

something of the substance of the Church's liturgy to the concert-hall, an operation which is discomfiting to the non-believer as well as to the conservative Catholic.

Notwithstanding all the adverse criticism which he received, Messiaen's reputation as a composer was now secure. Commissions followed—not least the commission from Koussevitzky which resulted in the composition of the *Turangalîla-Symphonie* and invitations to give classes in composition and analysis all over Europe and in America. The *Turangalîla-Symphonie* was first performed in Boston in 1949 under the direction of Leonard Bernstein, and in the same year Messiaen also gave a composition course at the Berkshire Music Center in Tanglewood, USA. In the following year he gave a course in rhythmic analysis at Darmstadt and the same course at Sarrebrück in 1953.

The period from 1943 to 1950 was to be one of developing crisis, both for Messiaen and for post-war music in general. As early as 1944, Messiaen had stated, in his classes, his dissatisfaction with the purely pitch-based serialism of Schönberg and Berg, at the same time putting forward the possibility of a series of durations, a series of intensities and a series of timbres.[5] This was to result eventually in the composition of *Mode de valeurs et d'intensités* (1949) in which he adopted these types of series while retaining a primarily modal outlook. Although Messiaen himself did not develop this particular device in his compositions, it had a particular influence on Boulez's approach to serialism (see Chapter 14).

In more recent years, Messiaen has not only been as far afield as Japan (where *Turangalîla* was performed in 1962) but he has also had performances of his works in Eastern European countries. His influence on others, both directly as a teacher and indirectly, has been substantial. Although at the time of writing he is still productive as a composer, it is nevertheless possible to assess his achievement and to give some account of his place in contemporary music.

Notes on Chapter 1

1. *ROM* * p. 19 (one of the poems from *L'Âme en bourgeon* is quoted on pp. 20–2).
2. The preface to the score.
3. Vol. I (Editions Delagrave, 1924). The full title is *Encyclopédie de la Musique et Dictionnaire du Conservatoire*. The name 'Sharngadeva' exists in two or three different English transliterations. The French transliteration used in the Encyclopedia is the one adopted by Messiaen: 'Çârngadeva' (the 'ç' is pronounced 'sh'). In order to avoid confusion, the French transliterations of the names of the rhythms and jâtis have been adopted throughout this book.
4. See Chapter 8, pp. 66–7.
5. *ROM* p. 247.

* Abbreviations used in the notes:
  ROM = *Rencontres avec Olivier Messiaen*—Antoine Goléa
  EOM = *Entretiens avec Olivier Messiaen*—Claude Samuel
  TLM = *Technique de mon langage musical*—Olivier Messiaen

2

The Development of Messiaen's Musical Language

In order to understand the way in which Messiaen developed as a composer, it is necessary to bear in mind that he has his musical roots in the anti-symphonic outlook of Debussy rather than the nineteenth-century symphonic tradition. His training at the Conservatoire was a conventional one. He was taught the traditional musical forms, including fugue and sonata, but the approach to these forms apparently laid more stress on their sectional structure than on their organic content. In 1942 Messiaen published his theoretical treatise *Technique de mon langage musical* in which he sets out the essential features of his early musical language. His sectional rather than organic conception of traditional forms, especially of sonata form, is revealed in his discussion of his own procedures which are derived from them. The situation could hardly be otherwise, as traditional symphonic procedure arose from a harmonic practice which depended on progression and on the tensions and relaxations created by the principle of dissonance and resolution. For Messiaen, on the other hand, harmony is decorative rather than functional, and tonality becomes absorbed into a broader conception of modality. This lends his music a static rather than a dynamic quality, his harmony existing in a state which is neither tension nor relaxation—the mood of the moment is captured and transfixed in a timelessness which is implied by the structure of the music itself. The result is a harmony in which part-writing has no real function, a harmony that is totally vertical rather than horizontal. For most of the time, constructional harmonic relationships play no part in Messiaen's music, except at certain points in some works where simple dominant-tonic or subdominant-tonic relationships become evident.[1] The suspension of psychological time in his music is particularly apt for the works which involve religious symbolism. It would be a mistake, however, to regard the artistic vision as being anything other than a unified concept, the idea and its means of expression being conceived together.

The precedence for this conception can, of course, be found in the French tradition of the early part of this century. In his Prelude 'Voiles', for instance, Debussy uses, for the most part, a single whole-tone scale, creating a sense of movement only within an absolutely static framework. Before this, Duparc

13

created a similar situation in his song 'C'est l'extase'. The resemblance between the melody of the piano introduction and a passage from the climax of the 'Liebestod' of *Tristan und Isolde* is striking, but whereas in Wagner this phrase has the function of carrying the music on over the climax of Act III, in Duparc it represents one ecstatic moment, captured and held immobile, as it were, in eternity.

Ex.1

Duparc:'C'est l'extase'

Wagner:*Tristan und Isolde*
(col 8 . . .)

Harmony

Messiaen derives his harmonic vocabulary from a number of different sources. One of the most basic aspects of his harmony is the principle of the added note. In addition to the classical added sixth, seventh and ninth, he quotes a special case in Chapter XIII of *Technique de mon langage musical* which is an important feature of his style. He says: 'In the resonance of a low C, a very acute ear hears an F sharp (the eleventh harmonic). Therefore we are justified in treating this F sharp as an added note in the basic triad, to which a sixth has already been added.' Because of this acoustical relationship, Messiaen then argues that the appropriate resolution of this F sharp will be C:

Ex.2

Viewed in classical terms this appears to be a very odd argument in favour of a resolution which does not behave as such. Not only does the 'dissonant' note fall through an augmented fourth, but it does not create a sense of movement, or of tension and relaxation, since there is no necessity for the F sharp to resolve at all. It nevertheless fits into the context of Messiaen's harmonic language and it is only the use of the word 'resolution' which can really be questioned.

   Another procedure is quoted in Chapter XIV of *Technique de mon langage musical* which involves added notes in a different way. Messiaen cites what he calls 'the chord on the dominant'. This chord contains appoggiaturas which

14

can be resolved in the normal way (ex. 3a); he then adds further appoggiaturas so that the chord on the dominant becomes a resolution of a more complex dissonance (ex. 3b); finally he adds the notes of resolution into the new dissonance to produce a chord which cannot be resolved because it collapses the duality of dissonance and resolution into a single moment.

Ex.3

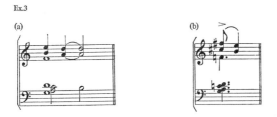

As in the case with the use of the word 'resolution' in connection with example 2, the term 'chord on the dominant' is a little misleading also. This chord does not normally have a 'dominant' function in Messiaen's music. The use of the term is derived by analogy with the process of building up diatonic dissonances in thirds on the dominant in classical harmony, until one reaches the dominant thirteenth which, like Messiaen's chord, can incorporate all the notes of the diatonic scale. It can be used either in the form quoted above or in any of its inversions, as at the beginning of 'Résurrection' from *Chants de terre et de ciel* where three different forms of the chord are used in the piano part in bar 3.

Precedent for the incorporation of resolutions into dissonant chords can also be found in Debussy. At the beginning of the Prelude 'Feuilles mortes', he uses a chord which is also to be found in Act II Scene 2 of *Tristan und Isolde*, but treated in a different manner. In Wagner, the chord appears over a pedal-note and the top note is treated as an appoggiatura resolving down a tone in the usual way. Although the note of resolution—D flat—is present throughout, it is placed in a much lower register and, as such, does not interfere with the process of resolution. Debussy lays the chord out differently and brings the appoggiatura and its resolution into close proximity in the middle of the chord. It now becomes impossible to resolve the appoggiatura, and the effect created is that of a chord which combines both dissonance and resolution. It is interesting to observe that the appoggiatura note F sharp does move down a tone, as in Wagner, but the whole chord moves with it, so intensifying the static effect.

Ex.4

(a) Wagner: *Tristan und Isolde*

(b) Debussy: 'Feuilles mortes'

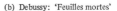

Messiaen cites other devices and processes in Chapter XIV of his treatise by means of which his harmonic vocabulary is further extended. Two of these are worthy of particular mention: the use of the 'modes of limited transposition' and 'added resonance'.

The modes of limited transposition are described fully by Messiaen in Chapter XVI and they form the basis of melody as well as of harmony. Their chief interest lies, however, in the variety of harmonic colour which they provide. They are artificial modes, having no connection with the modes of folk-music or plainchant. They are based on the equal-tempered chromatic scale and they divide the octave into two, three or four equal intervals, each interval being subdivided into the same relationship of tones and semitones. The first mode forms an exceptional case, being the whole-tone scale, dividing the octave into six equal divisions. Because of its use by previous composers, notably Debussy, Messiaen tends to avoid it unless it is well concealed in the texture.

Ex.5

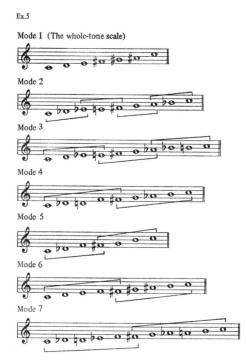

Mode 2 is the one which he uses most. An examination of it reveals that each three-note cell, being identical, can only exist in three transpositions. Beginning on D flat or D produces two different sets of notes from the above example, but an attempt to begin on E flat would simply produce the same set of notes again. Similar considerations apply to the other modes. The initial notes of these modes as given above are not intended to be 'finals' or tonics; no note takes precedence over any other in this respect. The modes themselves do not imply a particular tonality, but they can be made to slip easily from one tonality to another without any real sense of modulation.

Modes 4, 5 and 6 appear to be truncated forms of mode 7 since their notes are all present in some transposition of mode 7. Although Messiaen specifically excludes other truncated modes (examples 341–4 of his treatise), there is some point in listing modes 4 to 6 as distinct from 7 since they give rise to particular characteristic harmonies which occur in his music. He quotes some of these as examples 346 (mode 4), 349 (mode 5) and 351 (mode 6).

Two particular chords derived from these modes are of especial interest. The first is the 'chord of resonance', derived from mode 3, so called because it contains a fundamental note and all its odd harmonics up to the fifteenth. The other is the chord of fourths, consisting of all the notes of mode 5.

Ex.6

(a) Chord of resonance

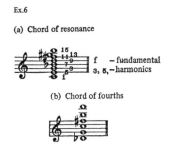

f — fundamental
3, 5, — harmonics

(b) Chord of fourths

The device of 'added resonance' is probably the one which has the most far-reaching implications both for Messiaen and younger composers. It can take the form either of a note or chord played quietly above a louder principal note or chord, or of a chord played loudly in the bass register of the piano against other material (inferior resonance). This device is used constantly from the time of the piano *Préludes* (1929) and examples are quoted in *Technique de mon langage musical*.[2] Some of the most striking uses of the device are to be found in works subsequent to the publication of this treatise. In *Neumes rythmiques* for piano, for example, he makes use of upper and lower resonances simultaneously, and in *Catalogue d'Oiseaux* there are many examples of birdsong coloured with either upper or lower resonances, or both (see ex. 72b).

Ex.7 [3]

Neumes rythmiques

The sound of the resonance notes should be absorbed as much as possible into the sound of the principal notes, so that the device becomes essentially a modification of timbre rather than a straightforward harmonic device. In *Couleurs de la Cité céleste* Messiaen achieves a real modification of timbre by this means. At figures 40, 57 and 87 in the score, low notes in the trombone are associated with a quiet chord played in the upper middle register of the clarinets. When well balanced, the clarinet notes are not heard in their own right, but they merge with the timbre of the principal note.

Ex.8

Traditionally, harmony and timbre are quite separate concepts, but the use of added resonance brings the two together in a way which enables harmony to function as timbre. This concept pervades much of Messiaen's harmonic thought, particularly in his later music. His chords become 'sound entities', complete in themselves, and the listener should not be aware of the individual notes which constitute a chord. Messiaen frequently marks the melodic line to be played louder than the associated chords, but this merely emphasizes their unified nature and timbre-like quality. Previously Debussy had used sequences of identical chords in 'La Cathédrale engloutie' as a thickening of a melodic line, rather than a harmonization. Messiaen extends the principle by changing the structure of each chord for each melody note, thus simulating a constant change of timbre, as in the sixth movement of the *Turangalîla-Symphonie*.

Ex.9

Melody: Onde Martenot *f*, Vlns.I (con sord.) *p*

Chords: Strings (con sord.) *p*

The unity of harmony and timbre is important in the work of some post-war composers, and especially in electronic music where the nature of the sound medium makes it impossible to distinguish between the different constituents of a sound-complex unless they are also differentiated in timbre. Messiaen's harmonic vocabulary as a whole could be conceived as a continuum, ranging from the most consonant to the most dissonant harmonies.

Because every chord arises from the same global considerations there is never any question of inconsistency in his harmonic language.

Messiaen has been criticized for harmonic inconsistency in the way he juxtaposes harsh or complex dissonances in the same piece as consonant-sounding harmonies. This criticism is misconceived because, however consonant or dissonant the harmony, Messiaen always thinks of it in terms of timbre or colour.

Messiaen has frequently spoken of colour-associations in his music.[4] He is not the first composer, of course, to associate colours with sounds but, whereas others have done so in a somewhat arbitrary or oversimplified way by associating colours with particular notes or keys, it is quite evident from Messiaen's discussion of the matter that he perceives colour-sound relationships in a much more complex way than this. He speaks with absolute conviction, and it is quite apparent that the association of colour and sound is a valid experience for him. Mode 2 of limited transposition, for instance, suggests certain shades of violet, blue and purple, and mode 3 brings to mind orange, with red and green and spots of gold, and also a milky-white with iris reflections like an opal. Many examples occur in *Catalogue d'Oiseaux*, such as the chords associated with sunrise or sunset [5] and the reflection of the colour of a bird's plumage in the presentation of its song.[6] It is not only harmonies and modes which give rise to colour associations, however, but the totality of the music 'with its melodies, chords, rhythms and complexes of sounds and complexes of durations'.[7]

As a consequence of these associations, one can speak of 'colour' chords, and a melody which has harmonies associated with it could be said to be 'coloured' by these harmonies, rather than 'harmonized' in the classical sense. Messiaen himself talks of harmonies in this way in connection with *Chronochromie*, where a series of durations in Strophes I and II is 'coloured' by harmonies in the strings.[8] Also in *Sept Haïkaï* and *Couleurs de la Cité céleste* he goes so far as to name colours in the score in connection with particular chords.

A harmonic system which is static and not dynamic raises acute problems of formal structure in his music. The sense of growth and development which was so important to the structure of the classical symphony is lost. Messiaen became fully aware of this problem, even in his earliest period. In *Technique de mon langage musical* he says: 'Is a dissonance possible with our complicated chords? Among this accumulation of "added notes" what becomes of the classical inessential notes: the pedal, passing-note, ornament and appoggiatura? They are indispensable to the expressive and contrapuntal content of the music: let us retain them while enlarging them.'[9] He goes on to speak of the 'pedal-group' replacing the pedal-note, the 'passing-group' replacing the passing-note, the 'ornament-group' replacing the ornament, and the 'anacrusis—stress—désinence' [10] replacing the dissonance with its preparation and resolution.

These devices are, of course, to be found in the nineteenth century, the ostinato being an example of a 'pedal-group' and the cadenza of an 'ornament-group'. There is, however, a fundamental difference between Messiaen's use of them and their traditional usage: previously they played a role subsidiary to the basic harmonic structure and form of a piece, whereas in Messiaen they are fundamental (as he admits) in providing the means whereby a movement may be extended or developed. In symphonic music, any accumulation of tension with its consequent resolution could be called 'anacrusis—stress—désinence', the accumulation of tension being achieved through the use of dissonance as well as dynamic accent and rhythm. Since a dissonance is not possible for Messiaen (in the classical sense), he is thrown back entirely on dynamic accent, rhythm or, in some cases, melodic contour in order to define this device. None of these devices in themselves were sufficient to overcome the latent moribundity which threatened many of the works of the early period (1928–43) and it was largely the rhythmic system which he developed in his second period (1935–48) which enabled him to extend and develop his works to significant proportions.

Melody

Certain features of Messiaen's melodic style correspond very closely to aspects of his harmony, notably the frequent use of the tritone and the descending major 6th which he mentions in Chapter VIII of *Technique de mon langage musical*. Many of his melodic shapes, however, have resulted from a parody of melodic fragments of other composers, of plainchant, of the Indian *jâtis* or—in his later music—of birdsong. He cites certain fragments which have influenced him particularly; the opening of Mussorgsky's *Boris Godunov*, a phrase from Grieg's 'Solveig's Song' and a fragment from Debussy's 'Reflets dans l'eau', for instance. These derivations remain essentially fragmentary in Messiaen's work, and it is not impossible to find a number of different derivations being used in the same movement, but always transformed into his own characteristic modality and style.

Ex. 10

(a) Mussorgsky: *Boris Godunov*

(b) Messiaen: 'Arc-en-ciel d'innocence'

com-me u-ne ma-je - scu - le de vieux mis-sel

(Further examples, and examples of derivations from other sources, are given in *Technique de mon langage musical*, exx. 75–89.)

The melodic derivations from the Indian *jâtis* are of some importance, as they form a distinct melodic type from the above examples. The word *jâti* means 'birth' or 'origin', and in the music of medieval India the term was applied to melodic formulae which were the foundation or origin of the more complex *râgas* of later music. A number of these jâtis are quoted in the article on Indian music in Lavignac's *Encyclopédie de la Musique* (Vol. I), and some of these provide the basis of examples such as the following in Messiaen:

Ex.11[11]

Jâti 'ândhri'

Cinq Rechants V

The most important sources of Messiaen's melodic patterns are plainchant and, since 1941, birdsong (see Chapter 11). He transforms the intervallic structure of plainchant to conform to his own modal system while retaining its essential melodic shape and rhythmic character. He gives an example of the derivation of a theme from the first movement of *La Nativité* from the Introit for the third Mass of Christmas (exx. 108 and 109). In addition, he discusses in Chapter XII the influence of antiphon melodies, Alleluias, psalmody and Kyries on particular melodies of his own. Although he does not specify the precise sources of these melodies, some of them are in fact striking examples of the transformation of actual plainsong into his own melodic style. The first movement of *Les Corps Glorieux* is derived from the solemn *Salve Regina* melody [12] and the last movement from Kyrie IX in the Roman Gradual. The opening of 'Résurrection' is related to the Alleluia from the Mass of the Easter Vigil. Another example, in a work written after *La Technique de mon langage musical*, is to be found in the opening of 'Regard de l'Esprit de Joie' from *Vingt Regards*. This is based on the Gradual *Haec dies* for Easter Sunday.

Ex. 12 (a) 1. *'Salve Regina'* / 2. 'Subtilité des Corps Glorieux'

Sal - ve Re - gi – na, ma - ter mis - se - ri - cordi – ae.

Bien modéré

(b) ·1. *'Haec dies'* / 2. 'Regard de l'Esprit de Joie'

Haec di · - es, quam fe - cit

Presque vif

(col 8) (chord)

staccato

Form

Up to the time of *Technique de mon langage musical* Messiaen regarded melody as the most important element in his music. In Chapter I he says: 'Melody is the point of departure. May it remain supreme! And whatever complexities there may be in our rhythms or harmonies, they shall not dominate it, but, on the contrary, they shall be subject to it like faithful servants.'

It is therefore no accident that most of the forms to be found in his music up to the time of the *Turangalîla-Symphonie* arise from melodic considerations and not from harmonic ones. This is not really surprising as it has already been established that Messiaen's harmony, being essentially colouristic and not structural, cannot generate the form of a piece. There are three basic forms which Messiaen cites in Chapter XI of his treatise: the binary sentence, the ternary sentence and the song sentence, which he describes as follows:

Binary sentence
1. Theme—commentary—open cadence
2. Theme—commentary—closed cadence

Ternary sentence
1. Theme and consequent
2. Commentary on the theme and its consequent
3. Repetition of the theme and its consequent

Song sentence
1. Theme and consequent
2. Middle period (with a movement towards the dominant)
3. Final period arising from the theme but not an exact repetition of it

The commentary is defined as a melodic development of a theme in which fragments are repeated on different degrees and varied rhythmically, melodically and harmonically. Elements which are foreign to the theme may be introduced and developed also, but these will be similar in style to the theme.

Even the more complex forms which Messiaen derives from sonata form and from other sources are melodically orientated. The most important derivation is the 'development-exposition' form: a development of a theme followed by its statement. In Chapter XII of his treatise Messiaen says: 'All instrumental forms derive more or less from the four movements of the Sonata. "The Allegro with two themes" synthesizes the whole Sonata. Having written absolutely strict "Allegros with two themes", we find that there is one thing obsolete in this form: the Recapitulation.' He then goes on to say that the most useful aspects of the sonata for him are the central development, with its continual modulation and feeling of unrest, and the terminal development (the coda), with its implied dominant and tonic pedals.

It is clear from this analysis that he is thinking of the sonata sectionally rather than organically, and, as a result, the forms which he derives from it have very little to do with its real spirit. The nature of the sonata is such that one could not detach parts of it in the way he does and still retain the essential element of organic growth and development. Messiaen's developments (in the 'development-exposition' form) are only parody developments insofar as they use a process of motivic fragmentation and are tonally undefined. He uses the 'development-exposition' form in four works written between 1929 and 1939. These are 'Cloches d'angoisse et larmes d'adieu' from the *Préludes* (1929), *Dyptique* for organ (1930), 'Le Verbe' from *La Nativité du Seigneur* (1935) and 'Combat de la Mort et de la Vie' from *Les Corps Glorieux* (1939). The development sections of *Dyptique* and 'Le Verbe' do not succeed, the first being too four-square in its phrase structure and too static in its harmony and the second, although more flexible from the rhythmic point of view, lacking power and intensity. A better sense of progression and climax is obtained in 'Cloches d'angoisse', but the most successful of the four is 'Combat de la Mort et de la Vie' (see Chapter VI). Because of its artificiality, the form is not capable of the immense variety which was possible within the true sonata form, and it is significant that, having written one excellent example, Messiaen does not return to this form again.

Other forms to be derived from the sonata are of lesser importance as they are only used once in each case. Messiaen mentions in Chapter XII of *Technique de mon langage musical* a form which is described at some length as 'Development of three themes, preparing for a final theme growing out of the first'. This forms the basis of the last movement of *La Nativité*—'Dieu parmi nous'. An example of a movement based on the 'terminal development' of sonata-form with its implied pedal-points is 'Enfants de Dieu' from the same work.

Another source of musical form mentioned in *Technique de mon langage musical* and used only once is the liturgical Sequence. This gives rise to the second part of 'Le Verbe' from *La Nativité* (see Chapter 6).[13] The other plainchant 'forms' described in Chapter XII are melodic rather than formal processes, and have already been mentioned under the heading of Melody on page 21.

More important than any of these is the form described as 'Variations of the First Theme separated by Developments of the Second'. This appears for the first time in the seventh movement of the *Quatuor*, and it forms the basis of couplet-refrain and other strophic forms to be found in Messiaen's later music. The significant point about this is the fact that it is a compositional procedure rather than a form and so allows of a great deal of variation and flexibility in its application. By alternating the treatment of two different musical ideas Messiaen achieves a sense of continuity and growth across the contrasting sections of the form. Furthermore, the principle can be extended to embrace any form which involves different treatments of different material, such as *Neumes rythmiques* (see Chapter 10), or any movement involving a refrain, whether this refrain is altered or not.

Messiaen has been criticized because of his use of sectional forms. It is true that sectionalization has been the weakness of a number of early works, but it is clear that in his later works his musical thought often *demands* a sectional treatment. The stark juxtaposition of ideas in earlier works eventually becomes sophisticated in the '40s with superimposition as well as juxtaposition being involved. The eventual outcome is a refined collage structure such as is used in *Couleurs de la Cité céleste*, where not only melody and harmony but also rhythm and timbre interact to form the total collage.

Notes on Chapter 2

1. See 'Le Verbe' from *La Nativité du Seigneur* (Chapter 6) and 'Regard de l'Esprit de Joie' from *Vingt Regards* (Chapter 8).
2. Ex. 217—upper resonance. Exx. 218–20—inferior resonance.
   Ex. 221—resonance intermingling at the same pitch as the principal chords.
3. Messiaen's use of accidentals, although logical, is very complex. Without changing the nomenclature of any notes, the author has taken the liberty of simplifying his notation in this and subsequent examples mainly by omitting superfluous naturals. Every note is assumed to be natural until it is altered by a flat or sharp, or by a key-signature. Each accidental is regarded as applying throughout the bar, but at the same register and on the same stave only. Nevertheless, accidentals are sometimes repeated within a bar for the sake of clarity.
4. A full discussion of this question can be found in Chapter 2 of *EOM*.
5. 'Le Traquet Stapazin' pp. 8–10, 25–6. 'La Rousserolle Effarvatte' pp. 10–15, 38–40.
6. For example—the blue rock-thrush centres on A major in both 'Le Merle bleu' and in 'Le Traquet rieur', suggesting the association of this key with this particular shade of blue.
7. *EOM* p. 38.
8. *EOM* p. 160.
9. *TLM*, Chapter XV.
10. *TLM* ex. 302, 305–10.
    The word *désinence* means 'termination' or 'ending', neither of which is a strictly accurate translation in this context. For Messiaen it implies the falling away from a climax rather than something final; 'cadence' would be a better description, but its use could be confusing in this context. The original French word is preferred.
11. This jâti is quoted by Messiaen in his treatise (ex. 111) but he gives no melodic derivation from it, nor from his ex. 112. He also quotes a phrase from *Les Corps Glorieux* (his ex. 113) which is not related to either of these, but is derived from the jâti 'shâdjî' (see Chapter 6, ex. 39(a)). Messiaen erroneously refers to these jâtis as râgas in his treatise (Chapter VIII).
12. *Vesperale Romanum* p. 25 (1924 edition) and *Liber Usualis* p. 276 (1935 edition).
13. The second movement of the *Trois petites liturgies de la Présence divine* is described in the title as a Sequence, although its musical structure only slightly resembles it (see Chapter 8).

3
Early Works

Before going on to discuss the questions of rhythm and symbolism in Messiaen's music, a glance at the early works will be useful in order to illustrate the use of harmony, modes and characteristic forms, and in order to reveal the crisis in his music which led to the rhythmic development of the late '30s and early '40s.

In the list of works which appears at the end of *Technique de mon langage musical*, Messiaen marks with a star those works which he considers to be typical of his musical language, while those which he considers especially typical receive two stars. The 'two-star' works all date from 1935 onwards, when rhythmic considerations come to the fore in his compositions, while most of the 'one-star' works date from the early period. The first work to be starred is also his first published work, *Le Banquet céleste* for organ, written in 1928. Although *Le Banquet* was written when he was a student and is a short work, its rhythmic structure and modal characteristics are of great interest in the light of later developments. Like many later pieces, it is in the 'Binary Sentence' form described in Chapter 2 (p. 22). In the first section, the theme (bars 1–4) is repeated and extended by a commentary which grows directly out of the theme (bars 5–11). The second section repeats the opening (with a decorative passage added in the pedals) and is followed immediately by a more extended commentary towards the climax of the piece. These two commentary passages introduce a dynamic element into what would otherwise be a static and uninteresting form. The expanded repetition of the opening idea in the first section gives rise to a double structure with one function overlapping the other. Besides being in binary form, therefore, the piece falls into three periods of four, seven and fourteen bars respectively. The first period is the statement of the theme, and the other two are its repetition with separate commentaries. The binary structure is defined by the addition of the pedal part in the second half. In spite of the inherently static nature of the harmony, a feeling of expansion is achieved by means of these extended repetitions.

Binary structure	I		II
Rhythmic structure	1st period bars 1–4	2nd period bars 5–11	3rd period bars 12–25

Mode 2 (of limited transposition) is used almost throughout *Le Banquet céleste*, but constantly shifts from one transposition to another. Like all the modes of limited transposition, it does not in itself define a tonality for the piece as a whole. Neither is it strictly possible to describe the piece as being in F sharp major, although it has a key signature of six sharps with a strong suggestion of F sharp major. This is only one of the factors contributing to a richer modal flavour, a mode which it is impossible to name or even describe in terms of a scale because it depends on the intermingling of the various transpositions of mode 2 and the harmonies derived from it, and on the F sharp 'tonality'. The ending on the dominant seventh of F sharp becomes logical when viewed in this light as it is the logical *modal* ending of the piece. A glance at the opening reveals that this chord is more strongly implied in the first and third bars than in the second which is modally less 'pure' because of the presence of an E sharp, foreign to the 'note-set' used in this bar. In a sense this E sharp could be regarded as a dissonant factor which resolves on the dominant seventh in the third bar, but it is also one of the notes which, along with the C sharp below it, defines this same dominant seventh at the conclusion of the piece.

Ex.13

* E♯, foreign to the mode

The *Préludes* for piano (1929), also written while Messiaen was a student, are not all as successful as *Le Banquet céleste* in coping with the problem of form. Only the fourth, 'Instants défunts', and the sixth, 'Cloches d'angoisse et larmes d'adieu', anticipate future developments. There are eight preludes altogether; some of the titles are reminiscent of Debussy with an occasional touch of surrealism. This is evident, for example, in the sharp contrasts of the second, 'Chant d'extase dans un paysage triste' or in the dreamlike quality of the fifth, 'Les sons impalpables du rêve. . . .'

Each Prelude exhibits a unique form. The first, 'La colombe', is a binary sentence, but without the double structure of *Le Banquet*. Both 'Chant d'extase' and 'Les sons impalpables' use a symmetrical rondo form: ABACDCABA in the case of the former and ABACABA + coda in the latter. In addition to the perfect symmetry of 'Chant d'extase', a sense of growth and asymmetry is introduced by varying the *A*-section in a cumulative way, each time it returns, towards a point of climax at the beginning of its fourth appearance about two-thirds of the way through the piece. This is followed by a 'désinence' throughout the following *B*-section, so that the final appearance of *A* also functions as a coda. As in *Le Banquet céleste*, a double structure is evident, but achieved in a different way. The form of 'Les sons impalpables', on the other hand, remains entirely sterile as there is no attempt to break the symmetry. The middle section does at least move towards a climax just before the return of the next *A*-section, but this is insufficient to counteract the tediousness of the over-repetition of *A* in its original form.

Both the third Prelude, 'Le nombre léger', and the last, 'Un reflet dans le vent', also suffer from the sterility of overformalization. 'Le nombre léger' is a short *moto perpetuo* in binary form, but with the second appearance of the theme presented rather unconvincingly in the dominant and treated in canon in the coda. 'Un reflet dans le vent' conforms to the sectional structure of sonata form, but unfortunately the form is imposed on the material and does not, as it would in the classical sonata, grow logically from the thematic and harmonic processes of the piece.

The remaining preludes are more successful from the formal point of view. The fourth, 'Instants défunts', although slight, uses two distinct musical ideas in alternation. The first occurs three times and is contracted at each reappearance, and the second appears twice, the second time expanded. As in 'Chant d'extase' and 'Les sons impalpables', the form arises from symmetrical considerations (A B A—B+A—— Coda) but the asymmetry introduced by the expansions and contractions retains the interest which is lacking in 'Les sons impalpables'. There is a striking resemblance between the form of 'Instants défunts' and a type of structure which is used by Messiaen in his later music: Strophe, Antistrophe and Epode. The Strophe and Antistrophe present contrasted material or treatments and may be repeated, while the Epode, which occurs only once, is different from both Strophe and Antistrophe and, like the *Epodos* in Greek poetry, has the function of rounding off and resolving the conflict of the previous sections.[1]

The sixth Prelude, 'Cloches d'angoise et larmes d'adieu', has already been mentioned in Chapter 2 as an example of 'development-exposition' form.[2] A sense of intensification, characteristic of classical development sections, is achieved in the first section by means of the simple device of contracted repetitions of the same material in successively higher keys. The piece begins with an additive rhythm (unusual for this period) on repeated Gs, suggesting the tolling of a bell:

Ex.14

Values (♪):1 2 2 2   3 3 5   5   (barlines omitted)

This is the only example of a rhythm of this type being applied to single notes until *La Nativité du Seigneur*, although it is obviously related to the principle of contraction and expansion of whole phrases which has already been found in *Le Banquet céleste* and some of the *Préludes* (including this one).

The seventh Prelude, 'Plainte calme', is in a simple ternary form with its first section repeated with 'open' and 'closed' cadences. It exhibits, there-

27

fore, a form combined from the binary and ternary sentences described in Chapter 2.

Most of the *Préludes* use the same mode of limited transposition throughout, although in different transpositions (as in *Le Banquet*). The first three are all based on mode 2, for instance, and the fourth on mode 7. 'Les sons impalpables du rêve' illustrates a more varied use of the modes. It opens with a polymodal passage consisting of a pedal-group of chords in the right hand in mode 3 and the main homophonic theme in the left hand in mode 2.

Ex.15

The second section is based partly on mode 2 and partly on a different mode, not of limited transposition; a passage in mode 6 leads back to the repetition of the first section. The middle section uses mainly mode 7. Each section, therefore, is identified by its mode or 'colour' as well as by its material.

Two devices used in the *Préludes* are of particular importance in view of later developments. One is the use of canon and the other of 'added resonance' (see Chapter 2). Thematic canons are used in the middle section of the second, the last section of the third, the repetition of the second section of the fourth, the middle section of the fifth, and the first section of the sixth Prelude. These are all typically static canons and, like the modes, are colouristic rather than structural. The extensive use of the device is noteworthy, however, as it anticipates the important use of mensural canons to be found in Messiaen's later music.

Two striking uses of added resonance are to be found in the *Préludes*. The first occurs at the end of 'La colombe' where a short melodic fragment is reproduced very quietly a diminished fifteenth above. The other, near the beginning of 'Cloches d'angoisse', involves the use of resonance homophony in mode 6 above the principal homophony in mode 2, the whole of which in turn add resonance to the chords in the lower and middle register of the piano.

In spite of their weaknesses, the *Préludes* remain an important early work in Messiaen's output, partly because of their use of the modes of limited transposition but mainly because of the formal processes involved in the second, fourth and sixth.

Les Offrandes oubliées, written in the following year (1930), shows a greater influence of Stravinsky than of Debussy. It was written for a normal orchestra, including triple wind and a small percussion section, and it has also been published in the composer's own piano reduction. The orchestration is, on the whole, relatively conventional. None of the colourful uses of percussion, so typical of later works, are to be found here. In the piano arrangement of the work the three movements are given titles: 'La Croix', 'Le Péché' and 'L'Eucharistie', and in both versions each movement is preceded by a short original text elaborating the theological background. The most interesting movement is the second, which follows a system of expansion and contraction of rhythmic cells reminiscent of Stravinsky's *Le Sacre du Printemps*. It was in 1930 that Messiaen first began to analyse this work, and it has often been the subject of analysis in his composition classes since then, as well as influencing some of his later rhythmic procedures (see Chapter 4). The last movement of *Les Offrandes* provides an example of 'added resonance' applied in an orchestral context. The principal theme is given to the first violins and is surrounded by a halo of harmonic colour on four solo violins and five solo violas. The fourth and fifth violas play in unison to reinforce the bass of the harmony.

A large number of minor works were written between 1928 and 1933, some of which have been published. Two vocal works were written in 1930— *Trois mélodies* and *La Mort du Nombre* (see Chapter 7)—and the *Dyptique* for organ (see Chapter 2, p. 23). The *Dyptique* is only important insofar as the second (and better) part of the work was later arranged for violin and piano to form the last movement of the *Quatuor pour la Fin du Temps*. All four works written in 1932 have appeared in print—the *Thème et Variations* for violin and piano, the *Fantaisie burlesque* for piano, *Apparition de l'Église éternelle* for organ and *Hymne au St Sacrement*. In addition, the last two are starred by Messiaen in his list of works in *Technique de mon langage musical*. The organ work is unusual for Messiaen in its predominant use of bare fifths in the harmony. It also makes use of expanding and contracting rhythmic cells similar to *Les Offrandes oubliées*, although the resemblance to Stravinsky's *Le Sacre* is less marked.

The main importance of the *Hymne au St Sacrement* lies in the uses of the modes of limited transposition for colour effects. In his note on the work [3] Messiaen speaks of the colour-chords of the opening theme and the juxtaposition of the colours of three different modes for the second theme. In the development section (based on the first theme) he goes on to talk of mixtures of 'gold and brown, with orange striped with red, then orange and milk white with green and gold'.

Both the *Fantaisie burlesque* and the *Thème et Variations* for violin and piano suffer from the same fault as the last Prelude: the application of forms dependent on harmonic progression to a conception of music in which this plays little part. The *Fantaisie* is a very formalized rondo, but without even the thematic interest of *Un reflet dans le vent*. The difficulties in the *Thème et Variations* are somewhat different. Although Messiaen successfully uses the principle of variation when applied to melody (as in the seventh movement of the *Quatuor*), his harmony does not form the suitable basis of a theme on which variations can be written. Classical variations depended on harmonic progression to unify the whole work, as well as to provide variety within each variation. The theme of Messiaen's *Thème et Variations* only provides unity at the risk of stagnation, because its harmony lacks the variety of progression. It is a measure of his ability as a composer that he is able to write a reasonably successful piece in this genre in spite of these obstacles, but it does not form a suitable point of departure for future work.

Of the three works written in 1933, two—the *Fantaisie* for violin and piano and the Mass for eight sopranos and four violins—remain unpublished. The third—*L'Ascension*—is Messiaen's most important work of his early period. The first version was written for orchestra, and it was arranged for organ in the following year—a process which Messiaen claims was so tiresome that he was obliged to rewrite much of it.[4] In fact the first, second and last movements remain substantially the same in both versions, but the third movement was entirely rewritten. The first movement, 'Majesté du Christ demandant sa gloire à son Père', is cast in the form of a song sentence (see Chapter 2). The rhythmic structure of the theme, consisting of a cell repeated in an expanded form, is related to processes already present in the best of his earlier works.

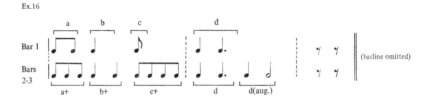

Ex.16

This movement mixes two modes of limited transposition (2 and 3) and the key of E major. The first phrase (bar 1) is in mode 2, ending with a cadence on the tonic of E; the second phrase (bars 2–3) is in mode 3, leading to an imperfect cadence on the dominant of E. These three elements are used throughout the movement in juxtaposition, one leading smoothly into the other.

The second movement, 'Alléluias sereins d'une âme qui désire le ciel', uses two principal melodies based stylistically on elaborate plainchant Alleluias. The first is in mode 3 and the second in mode 7 with some use of foreign notes. In his use of the modes of limited transposition, Messiaen occasionally slips in notes which are foreign to the mode, but in the case of mode 7 there are only two notes of the chromatic scale which are not used. Their introduction into the second Alleluia melody of this movement therefore involves using the total chromatic scale. In spite of this, the modal flavour is retained by restricting the melodic behaviour in a way which recalls the râgas of Indian classical music.[5]

The third movement of the orchestral version, entitled 'Alléluia sur la trompette, alléluia sur la cymbale', is untypical of Messiaen in some respects. Influenced by the dance rather than by the liturgy, with more than a suggestion of the influence of Villa-Lobos in its rhythm and orchestral colour, it is unique among Messiaen's output.

In the organ version, this movement is replaced by 'Transports de joie d'une âme devant la gloire du Christ qui est la sienne'. This is the first of a series of ecstatic movements which occur in many of Messiaen's main works between 1934 and 1948—'Dieu parmi nous' (*La Nativité*), 'Résurrection' (*Chants de terre*), 'Joie et clarté des Corps Glorieux' (*Les Corps Glorieux*) and 'Joie du sang des étoiles' (*Turangalîla-Symphonie*). It does not succeed, however, as well as these later pieces in creating the sense of ecstatic abandonment which was to reach its culmination in 'Joie du sang des étoiles'.

The last movement, 'Prière du Christ montant vers son Père', is an example of a ternary sentence. The opening series of chords in mode 7 lead to a dominant 7th chord of G major. As in *Le Banquet céleste*, the overall 'mode' of the piece results from a combination of the modes of limited transposition and a Mixolydian mode, since the piece ends on this dominant chord and not on the tonic of G.

On the whole, *L'Ascension* sums up the achievement of Messiaen's early period, at the same time bringing to a head the crisis caused by the inability of his harmonic language to create, on its own, sufficiently dynamic and extended structures. With the introduction of his rhythmic systems in *La Nativité du Seigneur* in the following year, the foundations were laid for a significant and coherent development in his musical thought.

Notes on Chapter 3

1. See also Chapter 13, p. 160.
2. p. 22.
3. Erato recording—STV 70 673.
4. *EOM* p. 173. The dates for the two versions of *L'Ascension* in *TLM* are given incorrectly as 1933 for the organ version and 1934 for the orchestral version. United Music Publishers' catalogue lists them correctly and the order of composition is confirmed by Messiaen in his conversations with Claude Samuel in *EOM* (p. 173).
5. See also the discussion of 'Antienne du silence' from *Chants de terre* in Chapter 7.

4
Rhythm

Messiaen's interest in rhythm dates back to his student days. It was his organ teacher, Marcel Dupré, and his tutor in the history of music, Maurice Emmanuel, who stimulated his interest in ancient Greek rhythms. After *L'Ascension* the deçî-tâlas of Sharngadeva [1] began to play a more important part in his music. A particular feature of many of these rhythms is their ametrical character, and it is this feature which becomes a basic characteristic of Messiaen's rhythm. The notion of a beat becomes replaced by a shortest note-value (the *mâtra* in Indian theory) from which a rhythmic pattern can be built up.

The importance of rhythm for Messiaen is emphasized in a lecture which he gave at the 'Conférence de Bruxelles' in 1958. During the course of this lecture he said: 'Let us not forget that the first, essential element in music is Rhythm, and that Rhythm is first and foremost the change of number and duration. Suppose that there were a single beat in all the universe. One beat; with eternity before it and eternity after it. A before and an after. That is the birth of time. Imagine then, almost immediately, a second beat. Since any beat is prolonged by the silence which follows it, the second beat will be longer than the first. Another number, another duration. That is the birth of Rhythm.'[2] It is clear from this statement that Messiaen regards rhythm as arising from an extension of durations in time rather than from a division of time.

One of the most important of Sharngadeva's rhythms is number 93: 'râgavardhana' (see Appendix 2). This frequently occurs in his music in retrograde form with the long note divided into three equal shorter values:

Ex.17

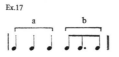

The second part of this rhythm (b) is a diminution of the first part (a) with the addition of a half-value on the second note. From this example Messiaen derives the principle of 'added values' either by the lengthening of a note, the addition of a short note-value, or by the addition of a short rest:

Ex.18

In the early works of the second period—*La Nativité du Seigneur, Poèmes pour Mi* and *Chants de terre et de ciel*—the effect of these added values is usually a stretching or contraction of the time-values in a passage which is basically metrical. This is the case in the first section of 'La Vierge et l'Enfant' and 'Les Bergers' from *La Nativité*. In the following example time-signatures have been inserted in order to clarify the underlying metre.

Ex.19

'La Vierge et L'Enfant'

The second section of 'Le Verbe' from the same work moves further away from a sense of metre. The slow melody is accompanied by chords of different durations, from three to six in each bar, which are only analogous to the beat of classical music insofar as they mark the flow of time.

Ex.20

Other passages from *La Nativité* foreshadow an independence of rhythm from metre which was to develop fully during the course of the next ten years. Such passages as the one at the beginning of 'Les Bergers' look forward to the more complex polyrhythms of the *Quatuor* or even the *Turangalîla-Symphonie*. The right hand plays a pedal-group of nineteen chords in quavers while the left hand—the principal part—plays a series of nine chords in an independent ametrical rhythm. The structure of this rhythm is interesting as it can be divided into a number of cells of two values, each preceded by a different value (the values themselves may consist of two or three chords).

Ex.21

Besides 'râgavardhana', Messiaen makes frequent use of two other Sharn-

33

gadeva rhythms, both displaying the same feature of inexact augmentation or diminution. These are number 105 'candrakalâ' and number 88 'lackskmîça'.

Ex.22

105 : candrakalâ   88 : lackskmîça

In 'candrakalâ', the note-values of the *b*-group are an augmentation of the *a*-group, with an added value at the end to make the augmentation inexact. In 'lackskmîça' the *b*-group is also an inexact augmentation of *a*. This gives rise to several methods of augmentation and diminution in Messiaen's music, the most straightforward being the augmentation of a series of note-values by a constant *proportion*.

Ex.23

Augmentation by the addition of a quarter of each value:

Augmentation by a constant *note-value* is also possible, as for instance in 'La Bouscarle' from *Catalogue d'Oiseaux*. The passage beginning on page 2, bar 8 is a mensural canon, the values in the left hand being one semiquaver longer than those in the right.

Ex.24

'La Bouscarle'

R.H.   etc. (barlines omitted)

L.H.   etc.

A more flexible treatment of augmentation can be found in the piano piece *Cantéyodjayâ*. In the passage called 'râgarhanakî' on page 5, the longer notes are augmented by increasingly longer proportions according to their length. The shortest note remains unchanged.

Ex.25

Values ( ):   4   6   10   8   4   7   13   10
                                          (+1) (+3) (+2)

Inexact augmentations and diminutions represent the freest treatment. In these cases a different proportion is added to each note-value, but not in proportion to its length, or some values remain constant while others are augmented. Messiaen quotes an example of this in his treatise (ex. 26) taken from 'Arc-en-ciel d'innocence' from *Chants de terre*. This shows two successively inexact augmentations:

Ex.26

+

(+ = added value)

A further step can be taken in manipulating rhythmic cells in this way. This is to apply both augmentation and diminution to the same rhythmic cell.

34

This is a practice not normally adopted by Messiaen (although example 21 above from 'Les Bergers' can be analysed in this way). It is more characteristic of Boulez, the following passage being taken from 'Constellation-Miroir' of his third Piano Sonata.

Ex.27

These two rhythms are superimposed and the resulting counterpoint is reduced to a single line. The effective lengths of notes can be shortened, but each one so treated is 'resumed' by a grace-note to mark the end of the duration.

Ex.28

A consequence of the addition and subtraction of rhythmic values to be found in Messiaen's later music (from the time of *Vingt Regards*—1944) is the type of rhythm which features progressively increasing or decreasing values. The opening and closing passages of 'Regard des prophètes, des Bergers et des Mages' and of 'Regard de l'Onction terrible' both provide examples of this type of rhythm. The first of these pieces begins with a series of durations in the left hand, diminishing from sixteen semiquavers in length to one semiquaver by the successive subtraction of one semiquaver from each value. At the beginning of 'Regard de l'Onction terrible' the same rhythm is superimposed on its retrograde. For Messiaen, the next step was to permutate a series of such values and to apply the same permutation cyclically until the original series returns once again (see Chapter 10—*Île de Feu II* and Chapter 13—*Chronochromie*).

The progressive augmentation or diminution of values is for Messiaen akin to manipulating living material, which accounts for his description of the device which he calls 'personnages rythmiques'. 'Let us imagine,' he says, 'a stage on which we place three characters. The first acts; he even acts brutally by striking the second. The second person is "acted" (upon), since his actions are dominated by those of the first character. Finally, the third character is present at the conflict and remains inactive. If we transfer this analogy into the realm of rhythm, we obtain three rhythmic groups: in the first the durations are always increasing—this is the attacking character; in the second the durations decrease—this is the character who is attacked; and in the third the durations do not change—this is the immobile character.' [3] Messiaen claims the derivation of his 'personnages rythmiques' from Stravinsky's *Le Sacre du Printemps*, especially from the 'Glorification de l'Élue' and the 'Danse sacrale'.[4] Stravinsky does not, of course, apply the principle in the clearcut and rigid way in which Messiaen sometimes uses it (as, for example, in the third movement of *Turangalîla*—see p. 92), but it is the expansion and contraction of rhythmic cells in *Le Sacre* which give rise to the general idea of 'personnages rythmiques', whether applied specifically in the way that Messiaen describes or in a more general way. 'Instants défunts' from the *Préludes*, cited in Chapter 3 (p. 27), is an example of its more general manifestation: the material of the first section contracts at each appearance, while the second section expands. The coda, which appears once and is unrelated to the other two sections, remains unchanged.

In the first chapter of *Technique de mon langage musical* Messiaen speaks of the 'charm of impossibilities' in music: modes which cannot be transposed more than a limited number of times without reproducing the original scale, and their counterpart in rhythm—rhythmic patterns which cannot be reversed because they are the same both forwards and backwards. These palindromic or 'non-retrogradable' rhythms (to use Messiaen's term) are found only in very simple cases in Sharngadeva's table or as parts of more complex rhythms:

Ex.29
51 : vijaya   27 : simhavikrīdita

The self-contained nature of these rhythms renders them incapable of entering into organic relationship with other rhythms. They are either used as rhythmic pedals or are augmented symmetrically around the central value.

Ex.30 *Cantéyodjayâ*. pp. 22 – 3.

Certain composite rhythmic patterns or *tâlas* appear in a number of different works in a number of different harmonic or melodic guises. The most important of these is made up from the three Sharngadeva rhythms quoted in examples 17 and 22 above—'râgavardhana', 'candrakalâ' and 'lackskmîça'. This and one other important rhythmic pattern are quoted in the following example and labelled 'Tâla 1' and 'Tâla 2' for future reference:

The use of Greek rhythms is less obvious in Messiaen's music of his first and second periods; they are not mentioned in *Technique de mon langage musical*, presumably because of their lesser importance at this time. It is the Indian rhythms which give rise to the most important devices of added values, inexact augmentation and diminution and of non-retrogradable rhythm, although some of these devices can be applied to Greek rhythms in their turn. One of the most outstanding examples is the use of a peonic or 'cretic' rhythm with augmentation and diminution in 'Joie et clarté des Corps Glorieux'.

Ex.32

A similar treatment of this rhythm can be found in 'Danse de la fureur' from the *Quatuor* (pp. 29–31) and in *Visions de l'Amen*, first and fourth movements (see ex. 44).

More important and striking uses of Greek rhythms are to be found in later works, notably the first movement of *Messe de la Pentecôte* and in *Sept Haïkaï* where they are modified freely in 'irrational values' (see Chapters 10 and 13).

During the course of Messiaen's second period, particularly from the time of the *Quatuor* (1941), rhythmic and pitch structures move increasingly along independent paths. Different sequences of harmonies may be used to 'colour' a particular rhythm in different contexts, or the same homophonic sequence may be used to colour different rhythms. The first movement of the *Quatuor* is most important in pointing the way to future developments: in the piano part, Tâla 1 (ex. 31 above), consisting of seventeen values, is combined with a sequence of twenty-nine chords so that the two overlap throughout the movement (see ex. 42).

Rhythmic canons are also a feature of the later part of the second period, sometimes being used with a different colouration for each part. In 'Regard du Fils sur le Fils' the two strands are differentiated by the use of a chord sequence in mode 6 for the upper strand and one in mode 4 for the lower strand. The rhythm used is Tâla 1, with its values increased by a half in the lower strand. A more complex example of rhythmic canon occurs in the last movement of *Harawi*. Again, two strands in mode 6 and mode 4 are used, but in this case the number of chords does not coincide with the number of values in the rhythm. A series of six chords overlaps with eleven values in the upper strand and seven chords with eleven values in the lower. The values of the lower strand are one-and-a-quarter times those of the upper.

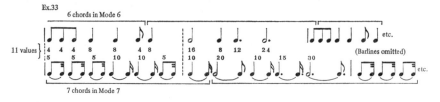

In this example the dynamic marking gives prominence to the lower strand so that the listener's attention is divided equally between the quicker moving values of the upper strand and the louder ones of the lower. The effect is one of two strands of music moving at different tempi, with the consequence that the functions of tempo and duration overlap in much the same way as the functions of harmony and timbre are made to overlap by the use of added resonance (see Chapter 2, pp. 17–18). The independence of rhythm and pitch which was becoming evident by this time led ultimately to a total independence of all musical elements—pitch, duration, intensity and attack (or timbre)—by 1949 with the composition of *Mode de valeurs et d'intensités*.

Messiaen's own discussions of rhythm concern themselves with the short duration of individual sounds rather than with phrases or whole sections of a piece. Nevertheless he has shown an awareness, even from the time of his earliest works, of the importance of manipulating the larger time-scale in a similar way to the individual rhythmic pattern. This is apparent in such works as *Le Banquet céleste* and 'Instants défunts' from the *Préludes* (see Chapter 2), just as much as in later works. Sometimes the sense of balance between the main sections of a piece can reach a high degree of sophistication, as in 'Par Lui tout a été fait' from *Vingt Regards sur l'Enfant-Jésus*. The overall shape of this piece resembles the rhythm 'râgavardhana'. The first main section is described as a fugue which is repeated exactly in retrograde form after a short central section. A stretto then leads to the climax and apotheosis of the movement. Even in its general outline, the resemblance to 'râgavardhana', with its non-retrogradable first cell and different second cell, is apparent. Closer examination reveals a more exact correspondence. The first section of the piece has three symmetrical sections, A–B–A, distinguished by a change of tempo for the middle section as well as by a different treatment of the material. These sections are 205½, 269 and 205½ quavers long respectively, at 160, 132 and 160 quavers to the minute. This gives an effective total duration of 1′ 17″, 2′ 2″ and 1′ 17″ approximately for each section. These durations are almost exactly in the proportions 2:3:2, which correspond to the first cell of 'râgavardhana'. Although the stretto and coda which follow are shorter than the main body of the movement, while the final duration of 'râgavardhana' is longer than the whole of the first cell, the accent provided by the climax in the coda of 'Par Lui tout a été fait' has its counterpart in the accentual effect of the last long value of the Indian rhythm.[5] Messiaen is not aiming for mathematical precision in the proportions of this movement but in a total structural balance suggested by the shape of 'râgavardhana'. *Reveil des Oiseaux* presents an analogous but rather different scheme of proportions between its sections (see Chapter 13).

Notes on Chapter 4

1. See Chapter 1, p. 10.
2. The text of this lecture is published by Leduc in French, English and German. It is interesting to compare the statement at the beginning of this passage 'Let us not forget . . .' with the statement from *TLM* quoted on p. 22: 'Melody is the point of departure . . .'.
3. *EOM* p. 72.
4. *EOM* p. 72. Boulez has published an extended analysis of *Le Sacre du Printemps*, based on Messiaen's approach, in his article 'Stravinsky demeure' (Vol. I of *Musique Russe*, Presses Universitaires de France, 1953). This article has been reprinted in *Relevés d'apprenti*, Éditions du Seuil, 1966.
5. Assuming the principle that in a rhythm where all notes are given equal stress the longer ones tend to sound accented.

5

Christianity and Symbolism

In his conversations with Claude Samuel, Messiaen refers to the importance which the Catholic faith has for him: [1] 'The first idea that I wished to express, the most important because it is placed above all else, is the existence of the truths of the Catholic faith. I have the good fortune to be a Catholic; I was born a believer and it so happens that the sacred texts have struck me even from my earliest childhood. A certain number of my works are destined therefore to highlight the theological truths of the Catholic faith. This is the main aspect of my work, the most noble, without doubt the most useful, the most valid, the sole aspect which I will not perhaps regret at the hour of my death.'

Because he is a Catholic, Messiaen attaches prime importance to the Christian symbolism which forms the subject of most of his works written between 1928 and 1944, and of some of his later works. He claims that the nature of his symbolism is not mystical, but theological.[2] Mysticism seeks the annihilation of being which, in its perfection, is the contemplation of ecstasy and unites man to the Godhead. Messiaen, on the other hand, is concerned with the truths of the Catholic faith which relate to God's act of redemption in the world by the Incarnation and Sacrifice of Christ. It is the expression of God's relationship with man that gives his music its theological, rather than a mystical, orientation.

In spite of this theological emphasis, certain movements tend towards a mystical expression within the theological framework of the whole. The second part of 'Combat de la Mort et de la Vie' (*Les Corps Glorieux*) and 'Je dors, mais mon cœur veille' (*Vingt Regards*), for example, are both mystical in character in the sense defined above. The latter movement is even described by Messiaen in his preface to *Vingt Regards* as a 'dialogue of mystical love'.

In *Harawi*, the *Turangalîla-Symphonie* and *Cinq Rechants* (1945–8), Messiaen turns to the subject of love and death, as symbolized by Tristan and Isolde, and from 1953 to 1961 he is especially attracted by nature and birdsong as the subject of his works. In Chapter 1 of *Entretiens avec Olivier Messiaen* he speaks of human love and the love of nature not as being opposed to his faith but as being complementary to it and implied in it. Concerning Tristan

40

and Isolde, Messiaen says: 'A great love is a reflection, a pale reflection, but nevertheless a reflection of the one true love, the divine love.'³ In the case of nature, Messiaen claims that he not only loves nature for its own sake, but because he sees in it, as God's Creation, a manifestation of the divine.⁴ He sums up his attitude to these three aspects of his work—the Catholic faith, the *Tristan* myth and nature—in these words: '. . . They are united in one and the same idea: divine love!'⁵ It can be said, then, that the whole of Messiaen's output is concerned either with the revelation of God through Christianity, the action of God in man in the form of love or, in the case of the pieces in which birdsong predominates, the action of God in nature.

In emphasizing the theological rather than the mystical aspects of religion, Messiaen is influenced by Western scholasticism which has been characteristic of Roman Catholic Christianity since the time of St Thomas Aquinas. Just as the scholastic mind preferred to define articles of faith in terms of self-contained ideas which can be understood in terms of human reason and logic, so Messiaen reflects this attitude by selecting specific theological ideas as the subject matter of specific movements. These ideas become separate entities in the separate movements of a work just as they form separate articles of faith within the Catholic religion as a whole.

Like the theologians of the Middle Ages, he also attaches symbolic importance to certain numbers. The numbers three and five are numbers of the divinity. Three is the number of the Trinity and five is the number of the Indian god Shiva who represents the death of death and is therefore a type of Christ.⁶ The number three forms the basis of the textural structure of 'Le Mystère de la Sainte Trinité' (*Les Corps Glorieux*), and 'Regard du Fils sur le Fils'.⁷ In connection with the latter piece, he speaks of 'three sonorities, three modes, three rhythms, three strands of music superimposed on each other'.⁸ There is also a duality of textures inherent in the piece—a rhythmic canon superimposed on the main theme and the contrast of the rhythmic canon with birdsong in alternate sections, as well as the duality of the two-part rhythmic canon itself, all of which can be taken as symbolic of the two natures of Christ—human and divine—inherent in one person.

There are also three movements in *Trois petites Liturgies de la Présence divine* and five in *Messe de la Pentecôte*. *Les Corps Glorieux* and *Visions de l'Amen* each have seven movements, the symbolism of which is explained in the preface to the *Quatuor*: 'Seven is the perfect number, the Creation of six days sanctified by the divine Sabbath: the "seven" of this (day of) rest is prolonged through eternity and becomes the "eight" of inextinguishable light, of perfect peace.' Both of these numbers are present in the *Quatuor*: there are seven movements relating to theological subjects, and one movement which is simply called 'Intermède', making eight in all.

In the preface to *La Nativité du Seigneur*, Messiaen again speaks of the numbers three and five. He mentions five principal theological ideas: (1) our destiny fulfilled by the Incarnation of the Word (III—'Desseins éternels'); (2) God living amongst us, God suffering (IX—'Dieu parmi nous', VII—

'Jésus accepte la souffrance'); (3) the three births: the eternal birth of the Word (IV—'Le Verbe'), the temporal birth of Christ (I—'La Vierge et l'Enfant') and the spiritual birth of Christians (V—'Les Enfants de Dieu'); (4) a description of some of the persons involved in the Christmas feast: the Angels (VI—'Les Anges'), the Magi (VIII—'Les Mages') and the Shepherds (II—'Les Bergers'); and (5) nine pieces altogether in honour of the motherhood of the holy Virgin.

He also cites five principal means of musical expression: (1) the modes, (2) expanded pedals, decorations and appoggiaturas, (3) added values, (4) progressive enlargement and contraction of intervals, and (5) the chord on the dominant. All these devices are described in *Technique de mon langage musical* except for the fourth, which is not of very great importance. Messiaen gives the following explanation in the preface to *La Nativité*: 'The parts proceed by direct, but not parallel, movement and pass successively through the interval of the augmented fourth, the (perfect) fifth, and minor sixth and the major sixth, for example.' An example of this occurs in the seventh movement, 'Jésus accepte la souffrance' (p. 6, bars 1–6 in the score). No attempt is made to link these means of expression with the five theological ideas; they merely illustrate the theological importance of number itself for Messiaen.

In many of the works written between 1943 and 1948 Messiaen makes use of cyclic themes, after the manner of Liszt. In *Vingt Regards* and the *Turangalîla-Symphonie* these themes have a symbolic function within the context of the work in which they occur, and one cyclic theme—the 'Thème d'amour'—is common to both works.

Apart from these cyclic themes, there is no symbolic significance in any of Messiaen's characteristic melodic shapes (such as those mentioned in Chapter 2). Neither the modes of limited transposition, nor particular types of chords or chord-sequences, nor (except in his most recent music) particular rhythms, have any symbolic significance in themselves. On the other hand, certain types of melody—those based on the plainsong Alleluias and birdsong—are associated with certain expressive ideas. The Alleluia-types are used to express the joy of praising God, as in the second movement of *L'Ascension* and in 'Résurrection' from *Chants de terre*, and birdsong expresses the experience of a more mystical joy, as in 'Regard du Fils sur le Fils' from *Vingt Regards* and 'Amour, oiseau d'étoile' from *Harawi*.

Certain keys in association with particular modes of limited transposition are also associated with expressive ideas. The key of F sharp major, together with mode 2, is used in a number of slow ecstatic movements, from *Le Banquet céleste* (1928) to 'Jardin du sommeil d'amour' (from *Turangalîla*, 1948), whenever it is a question of the mystical experience of a superhuman love. *Le Banquet céleste, O Sacrum convivium!* (a short motet written in 1937) and 'Le baiser de l'Enfant-Jésus' (*Vingt Regards*) express God's love for man in the Eucharist; 'Regard du Père' expresses God's love for his Son, and 'Regard du Fils sur le Fils' and 'Je dors, mais mon cœur veille' (*Vingt Regards*) all express his love for mankind through his Son. In the second part of 'Combat de la Mort et de la Vie' (*Les Corps Glorieux*) it is the fulfilment of divine love, victorious over death, which is being expressed; and 'Amour, oiseau d'étoile' (*Harawi*) and 'Jardin du sommeil d'amour' are concerned with the fulfilment of ideal human love as symbolized by Tristan and Isolde (see Chapter 9).

Another series of slow movements in the works up to 1944 are in E major. These are less mystical in character and usually imply an element of praise. The two slow movements from the *Quatuor*, 'Louange à l'Éternité de Jésus' and 'Louange à l'Immortalité de Jésus' fall into this category, as well as 'Desseins éternels' from *La Nativité du Seigneur*. It is interesting to note that 'Louange à l'Immortalité de Jésus' appeared in the earlier *Dyptique* for organ in a different key, but without the theological idea associated with it in the *Quatuor*. The element of praise inherent in 'Desseins éternels' is to be found in the quotation from scripture which is printed in the score: 'God, in his love, has chosen to be his adopted son, through Jesus Christ, to the praise and glory of his grace' (Ephesians 1: 5–6).

Other keys which provide links between certain specific movements, but also found in other contexts, are F major, G major and E minor. Both 'Les Anges' (*La Nativité*) and 'Antienne du silence' (*Chants de terre*) are centred on F. 'Antienne du silence' is dedicated to the feast day of the Guardian Angels, which links it to 'Les Anges'. Two movements in G major have for their subject the desire for the fulfilment of love: 'in 'Amen de désir' (*Visions de l'Amen*) it is a question of the desire for divine love, and in 'L'Amour de Piroutcha' (*Harawi*) the desire for the fulfilment of human love. The remaining key—E minor—is associated with mode 2 in 'La Croix' (*Les Offrandes oubliées*) and 'Jésus accepte la souffrance' (*La Nativité*) to express the suffering of Christ on the cross.

In his conversations with Claude Samuel, Messiaen mentions that he has never written any settings of the Ordinary of the Mass,[9] although he has written one short offertory motet for unaccompanied choir: *O Sacrum convivium!* His lack of interest in music intended for liturgical purposes appears to have stemmed from his desire to express his religion more freely, from the point of view both of the forces involved and of subject-matter. Neither of his works which involve voices and orchestra—*Trois petites Liturgies de la Présence divine* and *La Transfiguration*—comes strictly under the heading of oratorio or cantata, as their subject-matter is contemplative rather than dramatic. The use of the word 'Liturgies' in the title of the former work emphasizes the ritualistic rather than dramatic nature of this work. Messiaen himself says: 'I wished to accomplish a liturgical act—that is to say, to transfer a kind of divine office, a kind of communal praise to the concert hall.'[10]

The longer organ works—*La Nativité du Seigneur, Les Corps Glorieux* and *Messe de la Pentecôte*—could have a neo-liturgical function, 'capable of being performed during a Low Mass, respecting the main divisions of the Mass, and commenting on the texts pertaining to each mystery of Christ in the Proper of the Season, together with the Graces that flow from them'.[11] *Messe de la Pentecôte* specifically suggests this function as an 'organ mass' because of the titles given to each movement, which correspond to the main events of the Mass: 'Entrée', 'Offertoire', 'Consécration', 'Communion' and 'Sortie'.

A source of symbolism in Messiaen's more recent works has been some of the Sharngadeva rhythms. For many years he was unaware of the meanings of the names which Sharngadeva gave to these rhythms, and the first work to make acknowledged use of their symbolism was *Couleurs de la Cité céleste* (1963). A rhythmic *tâla* is used during the course of this work (see Chapter 13) which includes five Sharngadeva rhythms: 'tritîya' (3), 'gajalîla' (18), pratâpaçekhara' (75), 'vijaya' (51) and 'râgavardhana' (93). The general symbolism of the work is derived from the Apocalypse and centres upon the theme of the Holy City (Apoc. 21)—attainable only through the saving grace of Christ's Resurrection. In his second preface to the score, Messiaen implies that he has chosen these rhythms with their symbolism in mind. 'Tritîya' means 'a third' (it is the third rhythm on the table) and it can be taken as being symbolic not only of the Trinity but also of Christ's Resurrection on the third day. 'Pratâpaçekhara'[12] is a compound of two words—*pratâpa* meaning 'splendour', 'majesty' or 'dignity' and *çekhara* meaning 'best' or 'most beautiful'. The complete word—'most beautiful splendour'—can be applied to the Holy City as described by John in the Apocalypse (Chapter 21). 'Vijaya' means 'victory' and is therefore symbolic of the victory of Christ over death. 'Râgavardhana'[13] is also a compound word with different shades of meaning. *Râga* can mean 'colour'; it can also mean 'desire' or 'love'. *Vardhana* means 'increasing' or 'growing'. 'Râgavardhana' can therefore mean 'increasing in colour' or 'growing in love'. Both meanings are relevant to the work; the former meaning can be associated with the colour content of the piece and its resemblance (as Messiaen puts it) to a stained-glass window, and the latter meaning relates to its symbolism: the Holy City being the fulfilment of God's love for man and man's love for God.

'Gajalîla' has the most complex meaning of all. It means literally 'the game (or 'play') of the elephant'. In his conversations with Claude Samuel, Messiaen explains the mystic symbolism of this word:[13] 'The number of the elephant god, Ganesha, is the number four. "Gajalîla" has four durations, and the fourth, which is dotted, represents perhaps the "illumination of the mind".' It is appropriate that this rhythm, symbolizing divine enlightenment, should come at one of the climactic points in the work (fig. 69) in combination with two Alleluia melodies symbolizing the Holy City and two themes from the *Turangalîla-Symphonie* which, because of their association with this work, symbolize 'love' (see Chapter 9).

Notes on Chapter 5

1. *EOM* pp. 11–12.
2. Rostand: *Olivier Messiaen* p. 23.
   Goléa confirms this in his book (*ROM* p. 47): 'Messiaen himself has always claimed to write theological music, as opposed to "mystical" music, which he insists is not his affair.'
3. *EOM* p. 22.
4. *EOM* p. 26.
5. *EOM* p. 31.
6. See the preface to the score of *Et exspecto resurrectionem mortuorum*.
7. For a discussion of 'Le Mystère de la Sainte Trinité', see Chapter 6.
8. The preface to *Vingt Regards*.
9. *EOM* p. 13. This statement is not strictly correct, as an unpublished Mass for 8 sopranos and 4 violins was written in 1933 and is listed in *TLM*.
10. *EOM* pp. 13–14.
11. *EOM* p. 13.
12. Messiaen gives slightly different meanings for these words in his note on *Méditations sur le Mystère de la Sainte Trinité* (1969); 'pratâpaçekhara' is given as 'the power which emanates from the forehead (or countenance)' and 'râgavardhana' as 'the rhythm which gives life to the melody'.
13. *EOM* p. 85.

6
Organ Works 1935–1939

Among the works of the early (pre-war) part of Messiaen's second period, the two organ works, *La Nativité du Seigneur* and *Les Corps Glorieux*, best illustrate his new rhythmic techniques. Such is the importance of *La Nativité* that he precedes it with a preface explaining the basis of these techniques, as well as some of the modes of limited transposition and the general theological considerations mentioned in Chapter 5 (pp. 41–2). The discussion of rhythm differs in minor respects from his more detailed consideration of the subject in *Technique de mon langage musical*, and in addition to the two Sharngadeva rhythms 'râgavardhana' and 'candrakalâ' (see Chapter 4), which he discusses without naming them, he also cites number 33 on the table—'turangalîla'—which has a similar structure to these, in that the second half of the rhythm is a diminution of the first half. Messiaen renders the diminution inexact by the addition of a value, so making it conform to the characteristics of 'râgavardhana' and 'candrakalâ':

Ex.34

$\sqcap$ $\sqcap$. $\quad$ $\sqcap$ $\sqcap$ $\rfloor$ | (+ = added value)

La Nativité du Seigneur is divided into four books, the first consisting of three pieces, the second of two, the third of three, and the last of only one. Each piece is preceded by a quotation from scripture relevant to its theological content.

The first piece, 'La Vierge et l'Enfant', describes the rejoicing of the daughter of Sion (symbolic of the Virgin Mary) at the birth of the Saviour: 'Conceived by a Virgin a Child is born to us, a Son is given to us. Rejoice with all your heart, daughter of Sion! See how your king comes to you, with justice and humility.' The form is ternary with a shortened repetition of the first section and the mood of rejoicing is set by the decorated transformation of the Introit melody for the third Mass of Christmas: *Puer natus est nobis . . .*[1] ('A child is born for us, a Son is given to us: whose kingdom is upon his shoulder, and his name shall be the Angel of great council'). This melody is accompanied by an accompaniment in the left hand and on the pedals which

46

is rhythmically independent of it. The phrase-lengths of the melody (defined by the opening upward flourish which begins each phrase) are variable in length, while the rhythmic structure of the accompaniment is fixed in groups of eleven quavers by means of the chords in the left hand. The varied rhythm of the pedal-part fits into the same eleven-quaver groups with a certain degree of flexibility and independence towards the end of each half of the middle section (p. 2, bars 4–6; p. 3, bar 6; p. 4, bar 3). The essential feature of this passage—a principal part of flexible rhythmic structure accompanied by one or more rhythmic pedals—became a dominant feature of Messiaen's music later in his second period.

The second piece, 'Les Bergers', describes the shepherds praising and glorifying God as they return to their fields having seen the child Jesus in the manger. The form of the movement is very simple: an introduction, followed by a binary sentence (repeated) and a variation of the binary sentence (also repeated). The main theme of the movement, in its naïve simplicity, is strongly suggestive of a shepherd's pipe. There is a marked resemblance between the introductory section of this movement and the opening of 'Les sons impalpables du rêve' from the *Préludes* in the use of a pedal-group of chords in the right hand in mode 3 and a principal homophonic strand in the left hand in mode 2. The dream-like atmosphere of the opening suggests the shepherds contemplating the sleeping child in the manger. In addition there is also a general resemblance between this opening and the two-part homophonic rhythmic canon at the beginning of 'Regard du silence' (number 17 of *Vingt Regards*) which also describes the sleeping Christ in the manger.

The symbolic aspects of the tonality of the third piece, 'Desseins éternels', were discussed in Chapter 5 (p. 43). Its slow, ecstatic melody consists of a simple statement, eight bars in length, followed by a long commentary on it (nineteen bars).

The first book of *La Nativité* focuses on the Child Christ as the Son of the Virgin and the Son of God, through whom mankind has become the adopted children of God. The second book has as its subject Christ as the Word of God: the Word, 'begotten of the Father before the daystar' [2] ('Le Verbe'); the Word who has given power to those who receive him to become the children of God ('Les Enfants de Dieu'). 'Le Verbe' was mentioned in Chapter 2 (p. 23) as being an example of 'development-exposition' form, although not altogether a particularly successful example. In both the examples of this form which are successful—'Cloches d'angoisse' and 'Combat de la Mort et de la Vie'—Messiaen moves through a rising series of tonal centres, combined with some compression of the material, in order to intensify the climax. The 'development' section of 'Le Verbe', on the other hand, remains too firmly rooted on the 'chord on the dominant' on a pedal G so that there is no feeling of progression between the beginning of the piece and the end of the first section. The 'chord on the dominant' breaks off fourteen bars before the actual climax, which is preceded by a gradual crescendo throughout a polyrhythmic passage in the previous nine bars. This poly-rhythm combines two Sharngadeva rhythms—'turangalîla' (no. 33) and 'sârasa' (no. 103), consisting of ten and nine mâtrâs respectively. Each rhythm recommences as soon as it finishes so that the two rhythms are constantly shifting in relation to each other. The passage breaks off just before the point where the first beat of each rhythm is due to coincide once again.

Ex.35

This passage depends entirely on the crescendo to define the climax as the rhythmic pattern is too static to achieve any cumulative effect.

Although it has been stated (p. 15) that the chord on the dominant does not normally have a 'dominant' function, this movement is one of the few cases where Messiaen's harmony assumes a functional aspect. The G pedal-point on which the chord on the dominant is based becomes a *real* dominant in relation to the opening of the second section which starts on a chord of G major. The modal 'final' of the whole is not C, however, but G.

The second section of this movement is based on the form of a liturgical Sequence, as described in *Technique de mon langage musical* (Chapter XII). The feature of the fully-developed Sequences of the later Middle Ages was the repetition of a different musical phrase for each pair of stanzas. The musical form was therefore usually AABBCC . . . throughout. The Sequence which Messiaen has taken as his model for 'Le Verbe' is an early example of the form and has nothing to do with the Nativity.[3] Both the form and the melodic contour of his melody are derived from *Victimae paschali*—the Sequence for the Mass of Easter Sunday.

Just as the first part of 'Le Verbe' is based on the central development section of sonata form, so 'Les Enfants de Dieu' is based on the 'terminal development' (or coda) with its predominant use of dominant and tonic pedals. The motives of the opening two-bar phrase are developed over several pedal-points, mainly on the dominant, leading to a climax (mainly on the sub-dominant), based on the main theme, and a quiet coda section on the tonic. The piece is slight when viewed on its own, but has something of the character of a coda section to the first part of *La Nativité*.

Two out of the three pieces in the first and third books are concerned with the personalities surrounding the Nativity of Christ. In the first book we have the Virgin Mary and the Shepherds, and in the third book the Angels and the Magi. The remaining piece in the third book, 'Jésus accepte la souffrance', looks forward to the Passion of Christ—the sacrifice for which he was destined from the time of his birth. The sixth piece, 'Les Anges', is an excellent example of the transformation of the Sharngadeva rhythm 'vasanta' (no. 73) by means of augmentation, diminution and added note values.

Ex.36

(a) vasanta   (b) 'Les Anges'

added values

(The piece is based mainly on the original rhythm and the first of these two variations.)

Although the seventh piece, 'Jésus accepte la souffrance', is rudimentary in its structure, it illustrates a device which is important in Messiaen's music: the expansion of the duration of whole sections arising from the augmentation of the phrases which comprise each section. It consists of a main theme alternating with three episodes, the first two being related; the third episode, which is different, is based on the progressive enlargement and contraction of intervals described in Chapter 5 (p. 42). The opening two chords, answered by the 'Boris' theme [4] on the pedals, form the main theme. This theme is expanded at its third and fourth appearances by means of the repetitions of its two components:

(1) and (2) a – b
(3) a – b – a
(4) a – b – a – a – b

The expansion of the episode is accomplished by means of a rhythmic expansion of the components themselves as illustrated in the following example:

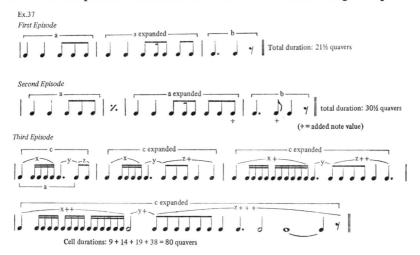

Ex.37

First Episode

a   a expanded   b   Total duration: 21½ quavers

Second Episode

a   a expanded   b   total duration: 30½ quavers
(+ = added note value)

Third Episode

c   c expanded   c expanded

c expanded

Cell durations: 9 + 14 + 19 + 38 = 80 quavers

The eighth piece, 'Les Mages', with its long slow melody on the pedals (4' and tierce), and the regular punctuation of semiquaver chords, suggests the slow journey of the Magi to Bethlehem. Although the key is F sharp major, mode 2 plays no important part in this piece, so that it does not form part of the group of 'mystical' slow movements described in Chapter 5 (pp. 42–3).

The single piece which forms the fourth and last book, 'Dieu parmi nous', theologically sums up the whole work. The first of its three themes is based on two Sharngadeva rhythms. The descending chords in mode 4 in the first bar are based on 'lackskmîça' (no. 88) and the answering phrase in the pedals in the second bar on 'râgavardhana' (no. 93).

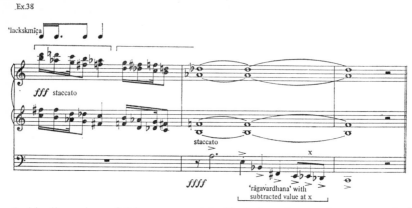

Ex.38

In his discussion of this movement in *Technique de mon langage musical*, Messiaen says of this theme: 'Like the organ chorale by Bach, " Adam's Fall", like the descent of Ariane-la-Lumière into the darkness where Bluebeard's wives languished (in Paul Dukas's opera, *Ariane et Barbe-bleue*), this passage combines rhythmic precipitation and the movement from treble to bass with the idea of the fall. The fall referred to here, however, is the glorious fall of the second person of the Holy Trinity into human nature.' [5] The second theme is strongly contrasted with the first and expresses the love of Christ for the communicant, the Virgin and the whole Church. The third theme is a 'Magnificat' of praise in 'birdsong style' (as it is described in Messiaen's treatise). This is the first instance of the use of the term *style oiseau*. The melody itself is not based on any birdsong, so that the description refers rather to the florid, jubilatory style of the melody and not to its derivation.

These three themes are developed in the manner described by Messiaen in Chapter XII of his treatise and lead eventually to a powerful toccata section based on the descending phrase in the pedals in the second bar of the piece. A new motive based on the rhythm 'candrakalâ' (no. 103) answers the statements of the principal theme in this section so that all three of the, for Messiaen, most important Sharngadeva rhythms—'râgavardhana', 'candrakalâ' and 'lackskmîça'—are present in this piece.

'Dieu parmi nous' is not only the most powerful piece in *La Nativité* but it is also Messiaen's most successful single piece to be written up to that time. His rhythmic procedures are not yet fully developed and his handling of form is still somewhat lacking in assurance. *Les Corps Glorieux*, written four years later, does not break new ground, but represents a greater maturing and integration of his methods than either *La Nativité* or the intervening song cycles (see Chapter 7).

One feature of *Les Corps Glorieux* which is lacking in *La Nativité*, but which was to become characteristic of several later works, is a symmetrical relationship between the movements. There are seven movements arranged in three books: three pieces in the first and third, and one in the second book. The first and last movements are thematically related, as are the third and fifth, while the first and fifth movements are related texturally, being monodic, and the third and seventh are polyphonic. These relationships of themes and texture form a cross-symmetry around the long central movement.

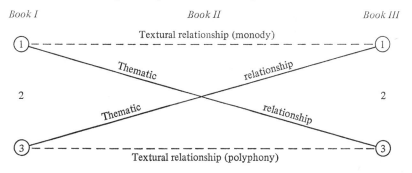

Book I   *Book II*   *Book III*

The melody of the first movement and the principal melody of the last movement are both derived from plainsong sources (see Chapter 2, p. 21); both are based on mode 2 and both have similar cadences at the end of each phrase. The melodies of the third and fifth movement, on the other hand, are both derived from the *jâti* 'shâdjî'.

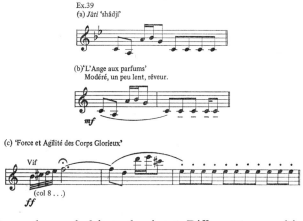

As in earlier works, mode 2 is predominant. Different transpositions of it are used in the first piece, 'Subtilité des Corps Glorieux', interspersed with passages in mode 3 and more chromatic passages.

The second piece, 'Les eaux de la grâce', makes use of the modes of limited transposition in order to define the ternary form of the piece. In the first section the right hand plays the homophonic theme, which is in mode 2, and the pedals play an inner part (4′) in mode 1 (the whole-tone scale). The two modes combine to form the notes of mode 7, which is the mode of the semi-quavers in the bass, played by the left hand. In the middle section, mode 3 in the manuals is combined with mode 2 in the pedals, their transpositions changing with each phrase of music. The third section returns to the material and the modes of the first.

The main feature of 'L'Ange aux parfums'—the third piece—are the varied reappearances of the opening '*jâti*-based' theme (ex. 39 above). It is stated unaccompanied, as a monody, at the beginning, and after an episode it is restated against a sequence of chords on the manuals. It is then immediately developed in two-part polyphony. The episode consists of three-part polyphony with two homophonic strands in rhythmic crab canon against a monody in the pedals which uses a non-retrogradable rhythm derived from the canon. The rhythm of the canon combines two Sharngadeva rhythms: 'catustâla' (no. 69) and 'râgavardhana' (with its last value contracted). The episode is repeated in a more concentrated form after the development of the opening theme, and it leads to a short fragmentary coda.

In his book *Penser la musique aujourd'hui*, Boulez speaks of polyphonies of monodies, polyphonies of homophonies, or of monodies combined with homophonies. He defines these terms in their most general sense—a monody being a structure of single notes, and a homophony a structure of chords without melodic implication. Although Messiaen's homophonies in *Les Corps Glorieux* still have melodic implications and his monodies are still melodic, 'L'Ange aux parfums' looks forward to the more general conception of textural combinations as envisaged by Boulez and as found in Messiaen's later works. Superimpositions of a homophony on another homophony have already been found in Messiaen's earlier work ('Les sons impalpables du rêve' and 'Les Bergers'), but this is the first piece to exploit different combinations of homophony and monody to produce textural contrasts in its various sections.

'Combat de la Mort et de la Vie'—the long central movement—has already been cited as Messiaen's most successful application of the 'development-exposition' form. The first part of the movement begins and ends with the same material, but the intensification of the opening theme which takes place during the intervening development enables it to return in a more powerful and exciting form than before. In spite of the latent inertia in Messiaen's harmony, the impression at this point in the movement is one of genuine conflict which has increased throughout the section. The final reiteration of thick added-note chords on the full organ sums up the power of the whole section.

This point of maximum conflict gives way suddenly to the release of tension at the beginning of the slow section: 'Extrêmement lent, tendre, serein (dans la Paix ensoleillée du Divin Amour).' It is this juxtaposition of opposites—extreme dissonance and consonance, conflict and peace—which makes the second section of this movement more intensely ecstatic than *Le Banquet céleste*, which it resembles in key, mode and form.

52

Both the fifth movement, 'Force et agilité des Corps Glorieux', and the sixth, 'Joie et clarté des Corps Glorieux', make much use of the Greek 'cretic' or 'peonic' rhythm (see Chapter 4, p. 37). In the sixth movement it also appears in augmented form as well as forming part of the main rondo theme and the accompanying chords of the two episodes.

The last movement, 'Le Mystère de la Sainte Trinité', is the most remarkable in the work. The choice of registration creates a most ethereal effect and enhances the mystery of the movement. The principal melody—derived from the Roman Kyrie IX—symbolizes God the Son and is played on an 8' Flute on the Choir (Positif). The chromatic melody on the pedals (Subbass 32', coupled to Swell) symbolizes the Father. It consists of the rhythm of 'Tâla 1' (ex. 31) stated at various points in the movement. Intertwining these two melodies on a 16' Bourdon and 2' Piccolo on the Swell (Récit) is a 'quasi-atonal'[6] melody symbolizing the Holy Spirit. Its rhythm is free, and it consists of phrases based on the extended-appoggiatura principle ('anacrusis—stress —désinence'), alternating with variations of an undulating phrase terminating in a chromatic descent.

Number symbolism pervades the whole structure of the movement. The number 'three', symbolic of the Trinity, permeates each part of the piece as well as the three-part polyphonic texture of the whole. There are three 'accents' or climactic points in the Swell melody, the principal melody is based on a nine-fold Kyrie, and there are three different Sharngadeva rhythms used in the pedal-part. Melodic links unite the three melodies, but each is rhythmically independent, having a different number of phrases of different lengths. There are seven phrases in the Swell melody, nine in the principal melody and five in the pedals. 'Seven' is the perfect number (see Chapter 5, p. 41) and the number of gifts bestowed by the Holy Spirit.[7] 'Five' is a divine number in Hindu mythology, being the number of the god Shiva (see Chapter 5, p. 41).

As in the previous major organ works, each movement is preceded by a short quotation from scripture relating to the theological content of each movement. The first piece in each of the first and third books deals with the promise of the resurrection of man. The second and fourth pieces are concerned with the power of the Saviour to lead mankind to eternal life. The remaining pieces express the fulfilment of the resurrection. 'L'Ange aux parfums' is preceded by a quotation from the Apocalypse: 'The aroma of incense, the prayers of the saints, will rise up from the hand of the angel in the presence of God' (8: 4). The sixth piece expresses the joy of the saints in the kingdom of the Father, and they are finally united to the Trinity of the last piece through the Resurrection of Christ.

In all the organ works since *L'Ascension*, Messiaen's use of the organ is as highly colourful as his orchestration and even his piano-writing were to be in the works of the next decade. Just as later on he was to talk of the 'piano-orchestre'—a conception of piano-writing which was to exploit its timbre to the full, just as if it were an orchestra—so one could describe his organ writing as being equally inspired by an orchestral conception of timbre. The way in which he sets off sharply contrasting timbres one against another—as in 'Le Mystère de la Sainte Trinité'—resembles the handling of orchestral forces which was typical of Debussy and Ravel.

No further organ works were to be written during his second period; after 1940 he turned his attention to piano and orchestral compositions and to his sole chamber work of significance: *Quatuor pour la Fin du Temps*.

Notes on Chapter 6

1. See Chapter 2, p. 21.
2. Ps 109 (Vulgate), Ps 110 (Hebrew).
3. All the Christmas Sequences were removed from the Roman liturgy by the Council of Trent in the sixteenth century.
4. The thematic shape derived from the opening of Mussorgsky's *Boris Godunov*—see Chapter 2, p. 20.
5. *TLM* pp. 41–2.
6. Messiaen describes the descent from the accents of this melody as being 'quasi-atonal' (*TLM* p. 57) but the term could be applied to the whole melody.
7. The gifts of the Holy Spirit are Wisdom, Understanding, Counsel, Fortitude, Knowledge, Piety and Fear of God.

7

Messiaen the Poet: the Early Song Cycles

It is not surprising that Messiaen, coming from a literary background, should wish to write his own poems to set to music rather than to draw on the work of others. In Chapter 6 of *Rencontres avec Olivier Messiaen*, Goléa describes how Messiaen's critics have denigrated his poems, and even his admirers have only rarely paid tribute to them;[1] yet the texts, whatever their literary merits, are an integral part of the composer's thought in the song cycles *Poèmes pour Mi* (1936), *Chants de terre et de ciel* (1938), and *Harawi* (1945), as well as in the choral works *Trois petites Liturgies de la Présence divine* (1943) and *Cinq Rechants* (1948). No criticism of the poems is relevant apart from the music, as they were written at the same time as the music and often conceived simultaneously with it.[2]

The early song cycle, *Trois Mélodies* (1930), is a slight work, hardly typical of Messiaen's mature harmonic style. The poems for the first and last songs, 'Pourquoi?' and 'La fiancée perdue', are his own, and that of the middle one, 'Le sourire', is by his mother. Musically and poetically, the first and third songs are immature. The second is the best and more typical of Messiaen's harmonic language, being based on various transpositions of mode 2 with no particular tonal implications.

La Mort du Nombre—a short chamber cantata for soprano, tenor, violin and piano, written in the same year (1930) as *Trois Mélodies*—is better, although still not entirely representative of the composer's methods. The tenor sings the role of the 'Second Soul', close to death and weighed down by earthly ties; while the soprano, the 'First Soul', sings of hope and encouragement. The idea is similar to Bach's Cantata *O Ewigkeit, du Donnerwort*, where the soprano sings the part of 'Hope' and the tenor the part of 'Fear'.

Harmonically, *La Mort du Nombre* is reminiscent of Ravel, but particularly recalls Wagner's *Tristan und Isolde* in the final section, to the extent of reiterating the same harmonies that are used in the 'Liebestod' (E major and B major), with a final progression through E minor to B major. The whole of this final section is the idea of the 'Love-death' translated to the religious plane. The soul, released from physical works by death, enters into eternal union with God. The influence of the music of *Tristan* anticipates Messiaen's

55

later interest in the Tristan myth in *Harawi, Turangalîla* and *Cinq Rechants* (see Chapter 9).

The more important song cycles, *Poèmes pour Mi* and *Chants de terre*, both deal with different aspects of the sacrament of marriage. 'Mi' was Messiaen's familiar name for his first wife, Claire Delbos, and *Poèmes pour Mi* praises the sacrament of marriage and the various spiritual states arising from it for the husband. *Chants de terre* comments further on this theme in relation to parenthood and the innocence of childhood.

The first of the two cycles consists of nine songs grouped into two books, four in the first and five in the second book. The first song, 'Action de grâces', is an act of thanksgiving for God's gifts to man: the gift of nature, of woman's love ('un œil près de mon œil, une pensée près de ma pensée . . .'),[3] of an immortal soul, and of a body which will rise again. It gives thanks for the gifts of truth, of the Spirit, and of grace, but above all for the gift of God himself as a sacrifice on the Cross and in the Eucharistic bread. The neo-liturgical nature of this song is emphasized by a vocal line which is reminiscent of a liturgical rather than an operatic recitative. Each phrase is centred on a reciting note (or 'tenor') which rises in pitch throughout the song. Each comma of the text is marked by an inflexion of the melody and each full stop by a more elaborate phrase suggesting the behaviour of the prayer or lesson chants at Mass. Messiaen himself draws a parallel between this passage and psalmody, with its melodic cadences and the practice of decorating particular words with a long vocalise in certain types of plainchant.[4] The song ends with seven 'Alleluias' sung to an elaborate melismatic melody recalling the plainchant Alleluias at Mass. As with these liturgical Alleluias, Messiaen extends the final 'a' by means of an extended concluding melisma or *jubilus*.[5]

The poem of the second song, 'Paysage', displays the influence of the French symbolist poets of the late nineteenth century:

Le lac comme un gros bijou bleu.
La route pleine de chagrins et de fondrières,
Mes pieds qui hésitent dans la poussière,
Le lac comme un gros bijou bleu.
Et la-voilà, verte et bleue comme le paysage!
Entre le blé et le soleil je vois son visage:
Elle sourit, la main sur les yeux.
Le lac comme un gros bijou bleu.

('The lake like a large blue jewel. The road is full of pitfalls and quagmires. My feet falter in the dust. The lake like a large blue jewel. And there she stands, green and blue like the countryside! Between the corn and the sun I see her face: She smiles, her hand up to her eyes. The lake like a large blue jewel.')

The repetition of the first line and the contrast of the calm beauty of the lake with the difficulties and pitfalls of the road suggest the contrast between the troubles and difficulties of life and the security offered by a permanent relationship with the beloved. Both this song and 'La Maison' which follows are musically very simple and rely to a certain extent on a *parlando* style of vocal writing reminiscent of Debussy or Ravel, rather than on liturgical recitative as in 'Action de grâces'. *Parlando* style is used in several of the songs from *Poèmes pour Mi*, but in the later song-cycles it gives way to a more lyrical style, except in certain parts of *Harawi* where it is used to suggest an incantation (see Chapter 9).

The last song of the first book, 'Épouvante', is violently contrasted in its quasi-surrealistic vision of hell. In theology, hell is the total loss of God's love, and just as the love between man and woman is 'a reflection, a pale reflection, but nevertheless a reflection of the one true love, the divine love',[6] so the loss of this love, or even the fear of losing it, reflects the pain of loss of the divine love in hell.

In spite of the appropriateness of the imagery raised by the poem of 'Épouvante' in the context of the cycle as a whole, it is important not to lose sight of the necessity for a *musical* contrast in the work at this point. For Messiaen, in fact, this is the first consideration, and the poetic and theological considerations flow from it.

Marriage is a vocation, on the other hand, and totally committed love between a man and a woman is the mark not of the devil but of the Holy Spirit. The vocational nature of marriage is emphasized in the refrain of the fifth song, 'L'Épouse'—'Va où l'Esprit te mène' ('Go where the Spirit leads')—and it provides the remedy for the despair of 'Épouvante'.

Whereas the songs of the first book relate to the preparation for marriage, those of the second deal with its fulfilment, 'L'Épouse' forming the link between the single and married state. The next three songs symbolize the consummation of marriage and its sacramental aspects. 'Ta voix' begins: 'Fenêtre pleine d'après-midi Qui s'ouvre sur l'après-midi, Et sur ta voix fraîche (Oiseau de printemps qui s'éveille)'. ('Window full of afternoon, Which opens on the afternoon, And on your fresh voice (Awakening bird of spring).') There is a suggestion here of a poetic link with the sixth movement of the *Turangalîla-Symphonie*—'Jardin du sommeil d'amour'. The garden, drowsy in the heat of the afternoon, symbolizes the world of the lovers, for whom the entry into the experience of marriage is like a bird awakening in the springtime and breaking into song. For Messiaen, birdsong is symbolic of joy, but in 'Ta voix' the bird is mentioned only in the poem; there is no attempt at birdsong in the piano accompaniment as in various movements of *Harawi* or as in 'Jardin du sommeil d'amour'.

United in one flesh, the lovers become 'Les deux guerriers', the title of the seventh song; they gather strength from the sacramental nature of their vocation in order to overcome the difficulties of life and to advance to the gate of the heavenly city. Their unity is vividly expressed in the phrase: 'Je suis tes deux enfants, mon Dieu!' ('I am your two children, O my God!'). The sacramental nature of their union is expressed in the sentence that follows: 'En avant, guerriers sacramentels!' ('Forward, sacramental warriors!')

The significance of the next song, 'Le Collier', is to be found in the last line: 'Ah! mon collier! Tes deux bras autour de mon cou, ce matin' ('Ah! my necklace! Your two arms around my neck, this morning'). Awakening from sleep to find her arms around his neck, the husband addresses his wife as a necklace of springtime ('renouveau'), or of delight ('sourire') and of grace. The piano accompaniment, with its rotation on three chords in the right hand, translates the necklace into musical terms.

The final song, 'Prière exaucée', balances 'Actions de grâces' at the beginning. The husband's prayer is granted, his loneliness is over ('Ébranlez la solitaire, la vieille montagne de douleur'), joy has returned in a day of glory and resurrection ('Voici ton jour de gloire et de résurrection! La joie est revenue'). The union of man and woman symbolizes the union of Christ and the Church,[7] and the joy of marriage anticipates the joy of the day of resurrection, when man is finally and eternally united to God.

Although *Poèmes pour Mi* uses, to some extent, Messiaen's new rhythmic procedures, they are applied somewhat less systematically than in *La Nativité*. His next work, *Chants de terre et de ciel*, also has greater rhythmic flexibility and the piano has a more important role in relation to the voice, anticipating to some extent its more virtuosic role in *Harawi*.

Poèmes pour Mi was arranged for soprano and orchestra in 1937; this version adds distinctly more colour to the accompaniment because of the greater range of timbre available. Neither *Chants de terre* nor *Harawi*, on the other hand, has been orchestrated, although the piano writing is more orchestrally conceived. It is this very fact which makes their orchestration unnecessary, because in them Messiaen exploits the colour possibilities of the piano more fully and uses a greater variety of piano timbre. An orchestral arrangement, therefore, would have little to add.

The first movement of *Chants de terre* links the cycle to *Poèmes pour Mi*. Its title is 'Bail avec Mi', which can be translated as 'Life with Mi'. The song is dedicated to Messiaen's first wife, Claire Delbos, and it unites the idea of physical love with its more spiritual aspects. The physical nature of love is suggested by the repetition of the word 'terre' in the poem: 'Ton œil de terre, mon œil de terre, mes mains de terre . . .' and the spiritual in the second half: 'Étoile de silence à mon cœur de terre, à mes lèvres de terre.' 'Étoile de silence' ('star of silence') is a symbol which is frequently used by Messiaen; the star is symbolic of anything to do with the spiritual as distinct from the physical and the 'silence' is the silence of heaven, or 'Le silence harmonieux du ciel' as Messiaen describes it in the preface of *Quatuor pour la Fin du Temps*.[8]

'Antienne du silence' is dedicated to the feast of the Guardian Angels (2 October). The poem is written in the form of a particular kind of liturgical antiphon with one alleluia in the middle and one at the end. These antiphons are found associated with the canticles of Lauds and Vespers in Paschaltide (for example, *Pax vobis, ego sum, alleluia: nolite timere, alleluia*) and their musical setting is very simple and syllabic in treatment. The alleluia sections of 'Antienne du silence', on the other hand, are melismatic and, like the alleluias at the end of the first movement of *Poèmes pour Mi*, are influenced by the Alleluias of the Mass with their long final *jubilus*. The texture of the movement is four-part polyphonic with one part in the voice and three in the piano (all monodies). The modal characteristics of the two principal lines exhibit an interesting extension to the modes of limited transposition. The mode of the main part in the piano is based on the same version of mode 7 that is used in the second theme of the second movement of *L'Ascension* (see Chapter 3, p. 30). Not all of the notes of the mode are used, however. The octave above the tonic is omitted and two notes are added on in the upper octave, one of which (G sharp) is foreign to this particular transposition of mode 7.

Ex.40

This same scale forms the basis of the mode for the soprano line, but a distinction is now made between the function of the D flat which is used only in descending phrases and its enharmonic equivalent C sharp which, in nearly every case, rises a minor third to E. The melodic behaviour of the various notes of the mode becomes specialized so that the mode is best described by a melodic formula rather than by a scale. In this respect it resembles the modes of plainsong, where melodic formulae can be crucial in defining the mode, and the *râgas* of Classical Indian music.

Ex.41

Melodic formulae for the soprano part of 'Antienne du silence'

Phrases 1–4

5th Phrase:

Termination

By means of the transposition, combined with the distortion of melodic formulae, it is possible for Messiaen to use nearly the whole chromatic scale, in the setting of the second alleluia, without destroying the character of the mode.

The next two songs are dedicated to Messiaen's son Pascal (called 'bébé-Pilule' in the title). In 'Danse du bébé-Pilule' he is depicted at play and in 'Arc-en-ciel d'innocence' he is asleep. Both songs emphasize the innocence of childhood in sharp contrast to the fifth song, 'Minuit pile et face' (dedicated to the faithful departed). In *Technique de mon langage musical* [9] Messiaen describes the opening of 'Danse du bébé-Pilule' as an artificial folk-song with an onomatopaeic refrain: 'Malonlanlaine, ma'. Like certain parts of *La Nativité du Seigneur*, the rhythm of this opening suggests an underlying metre (in this case $\frac{2}{4}$), which has been stretched and compressed by added and subtracted values. The rhythmic structure becomes fully ametrical as the song proceeds, leading to polyrhythmic passages in the middle section. The rhythm of 'Arc-en-ciel d'innocence' is less complex, but is noteworthy for the fact that it is in this piece that Tâla 1 (Chapter 4, p. 37) makes its first appearance.

In 'Minuit pile et face' it is the awareness of the child's innocence that emphasizes for the parent the weight of his own sinfulness. Like 'Épouvante', it is a surrealistic nightmare in which past sins appear before the sinner, dancing in mockery of him in a 'Carnaval décevant des pavés de la mort' ('Deceitful carnival from the pavements of death'). Messiaen indulges in a rather obvious but nevertheless effective bit of word-painting here. At the words 'Ils dansent, mes péchés dansent!' he begins a five-part fugal exposition as each phantom of the past commences its terrifying dance—like the fragments of broomstick in Dukas's *L'Apprenti sorcier*. At the climax of the movement, a passionate appeal to the Trinity, 'the Father of light, Christ the Vine of love, and the Spirit, the Comforter with seven gifts', banishes the nightmare, leaving only the innocence of the sleeping child, 'his hand under his ear, clothed in a tiny nightdress'.

Just as *Poèmes pour Mi* ended with references to the resurrection of man, *Chants de terre* ends with a movement called 'Résurrection' on the subject of Christ's resurrection. It is dedicated to Easter day, the festival of the Pasch from which the name of Messiaen's son, Pascal, is derived. Not only is the opening based on the Alleluia of the Easter Vigil (see Chapter 2, p. 21), but the melodic style of plainchant pervades the whole song, and it also influences the modal character of the second part of each section ('Je suis ressuscité . . .') which is in the seventh Gregorian tone. The movement as a whole is in binary form with a tremendous tension established in the first half, followed by an enormous resolution in the second. Examination of the harmonic structure of the piece reveals important differences in chord-structure between the two halves. There is a greater sense of stability in the second half, with its greater dependence on less complex added-note chords rooted on the tonic C sharp.

Notes on Chapter 7

1. *ROM* pp. 120–1.
2. *ROM* p. 120.
3. 'an eye close to my eye, a thought close to my thought . . .'
4. *TLM* p. 45. A portion of the song is quoted in example 176 in *TLM*.
5. The *jubilus* is the melismatic extension of the final 'a' of the Alleluia sung between the Epistle and Gospel of the Roman Mass.
6. *EOM* p. 22; see also Chapter 5, p. 41 of this book.
7. Ephesians 5.
8. 'The silence of heaven' is derived from Chapter 8 of the Apocalypse: 'The Lamb then broke the seventh seal, and there was silence in heaven for about half an hour' (8: 1).
9. p. 33.

8
The Works of the War Years

Quatuor pour la Fin du Temps (1940–41)

Messiaen was captured by the Germans in 1940 and taken to a prison camp in Görlitz in Silesia. There he found himself in company with a cellist, a violinist and a clarinettist. The Germans had been helpful in supplying him with writing materials and manuscript paper, and had presented the cellist with a cello which unfortunately had one of its strings missing. The clarinettist and the violinist had been allowed to retain their instruments which they had brought to the camp. It was for these players that Messiaen first wrote a short trio which was later to become the fourth movement of the *Quatuor*. In spite of the fact that a piano was not available at this time, he continued with the composition of the rest of the work, and it was not until after its completion that a piano was brought into the camp. This piano was far from ideal: it was an upright, out of tune, and many of its keys refused to function properly.

The first performance of the work took place in the camp on 15 January 1941 in front of an audience of 5,000 from all walks of life—peasants, workers, intellectuals, doctors, priests and many others. 'Never,' says Messiaen, 'have I been listened to with such attention and understanding.'[1]

The combination of clarinet, violin, cello and piano is doubtless not one which Messiaen would have normally chosen if it had not been for the restrictions which circumstances had imposed upon him. The group of instruments is too large to allow the piano to express itself freely, yet too small to obtain the variety of timbre which is a feature of his organ and orchestral writing. In spite of these limitations, Messiaen obtains from his instruments the maximum variety of which they are capable, not only from the individual instruments but also by using them in various different combinations in each movement.

The point of departure for the work was the vision of the Angel in the Apocalypse 'who lifted up his right hand towards heaven, and swore an oath . . . that there should be no more Time' (Apoc. 10: 5. 6). In his conversations with Goléa[2] Messiaen emphasizes that, in spite of its initial connection with the Apocalypse, the work is not intended to be a commentary on it. He also points out that the title—'Pour la Fin du Temps'—has a double meaning, for it also expresses his desire for the end of musical time based on the equal durational divisions of classical music,[3] a tendency already discernible in previous works.

Prior to the *Quatuor*, all the works written from 1935 onwards involve either a solo instrument or voice and piano. It is characteristic of the early song-cycles that, for the most part, the piano and voice are rhythmically interdependent and are virtually treated as one instrument.[4] Neither these nor the organ works, therefore, display polyrhythms of a complex nature. Because four instruments are involved, the *Quatuor* is the first work of Messiaen's second period to employ the polyrhythmic structures which were to become characteristic of his later work. The first movement, 'Liturgie de cristal', is the most important from this point of view, since it superimposes two independent rhythmic pedals, played by the cello and piano, on two independent birdsongs, played by the violin and clarinet. The piano's rhythmic pedal consists of a repetition of the seventeen durations of Tâla 1 (see Chapter 4, p. 37), coloured by the repetition of twenty-nine different chords. The resulting overlap of chords and durations is reminiscent of the *color* and *talea* of the medieval isorhythmic motet. Messiaen himself emphasizes the importance of the dissociation of rhythm from harmony and melody in this work 'in the manner of Guillaume de Machaut whose work I did not know at the time'.[5]

Ex.42

The rhythm of the cello part is non-retrogradable. It forms a continuous rhythmic chain which is non-retrogradable from centre to centre, as well as from end to end. There is in reality no true beginning or end to this rhythm.

Ex.43

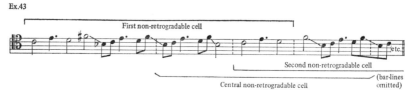

Neither of these rhythmic pedals are in any way related to the birdsong, nor do they determine the duration of the movement. The shape of the movement is determined by the free course of the birdsong and the rhythmic pedals are cut short arbitrarily at the end of the movement. These rhythmic pedals, therefore, function in a similar way to the modes of limited transposition in other contexts in providing a 'colouration' of a movement (or in other cases a section of a movement), rather than defining its structure. In these circumstances one can talk of a 'modal' use of rhythm and the extension of 'mode' into the rhythmic domain, which was to foreshadow its later extension into the domains of intensity and timbre in *Mode de valeurs et d'intensités* (1949).

Like *Les Corps Glorieux*, the *Quatuor* displays thematic and textural relationships between the movements, which shape the work as a whole, as shown in the following diagram.

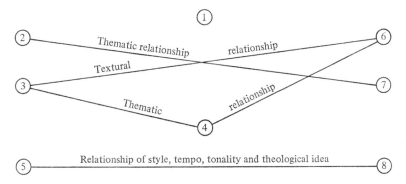

The second movement, 'Vocalise, pour l'Ange qui annonce la fin du Temps', is linked thematically to the seventh movement, 'Fouillis d'arc-en-ciel, pour l'Ange qui annonce la fin du temps': the opening idea of the second movement represents the Angel 'who announces the end of Time', and it returns to be developed in alternate sections of the seventh movement. Both movements state two principal ideas. The contrasting idea of the second movement, which follows immediately on the opening theme, is transformed and extended in the second section of the piece as a long sustained melody in the strings against independent cascades of chords on the piano representing 'Les harmonies impalpables du ciel'.

The importance of the seventh movement, described by Messiaen as 'Variations of the First Theme, separated by Developments of the Second', has been referred to in Chapter 2 (p. 23).

The third and sixth movements are both monodies; the third is for clarinet alone and the sixth is for all four instruments playing in octaves. In addition, both movements are thematically related to the fourth 'Intermède', which omits the piano. The third movement, 'Abîme des oiseaux', describes the 'abyss of Time, its sadness and its weariness', but contrasting with this are the birds, who are 'the opposite of Time; they are our desire for light, for the stars and for the things of heaven'.[6] The sixth movement is entitled 'Danse de la fureur, pour les sept trompettes'—the seven trumpets sounded by the seven angels of the Apocalypse (8:2). In the preface, Messiaen claims that this is the most rhythmically characteristic movement in the work, with its use of added values, augmentations and diminutions, and particularly in its use of a series of non-retrogradable rhythms in the middle section, forming the rhythm described as Tâla 2 in Chapter 4 (p. 37).

Both the fifth and eighth movements are related in style, tempo (slow), tonality (E major), instrumentation (solo stringed instrument and piano) and theological idea. The fifth movement, 'Louange à l'Eternité de Jésus' for cello and piano, is a homage to Jesus as the eternal Word of God. The eighth movement, 'Louange à l'Immortalité de Jésus' for violin and piano, is addressed to Jesus as Man, risen to immortality. The derivation of this latter movement from the early organ piece *Dyptique* has already been mentioned (Chapter 3, p. 29). The fifth movement also appears in an earlier work—*Fête des belles eaux* written for six Ondes Martenots (q.v.) for the Paris Exhibition of 1937. This work is of no particular importance, except for this one section, although at this stage no theological idea is attached to it.

Visions de l'Amen (1943)

After his repatriation, Messiaen came into contact with the pianist Yvonne Loriod through his composition classes at the house of Guy Delapierre. The immediate result of this contact was a large work for two pianos, *Visions de l'Amen*, which was first performed by Loriod and the composer in Paris on 10 May 1943. The only piano works to appear between this work and the *Préludes* of 1929 were the *Fantaisie burlesque* (1932), *Pièce pour le Tombeau de Paul Dukas* (published in the *Revue musicale*, May–June, 1936) and a *Rondeau* for piano (1943). All these works are of only minor importance and receive no star in the list in *Technique de mon langage musical*.

Visions de l'Amen is the first of Messiaen's works to employ the piano, as it were, in an orchestral manner, on a grand scale: a conception which was already emerging in the piano part of *Chants de terre et de ciel* (especially in 'Résurrection'). Although the two piano parts in *Visions de l'Amen* are of equal difficulty, they are distinct in character. The first piano has all the passages of rhythmic or harmonic complexity, while the second has the principal themes.

It is also the first work to employ a cyclic theme—an important feature in other works of the mid-'40s. The use of cyclic themes in this and other works establishes a continuity of musical thought and provides a focus for the symbolic content of the work. The procedure is reminiscent of Liszt, but, for Messiaen, the cyclic theme does not form the symphonic basis of all the thematic material in the work. In *Visions de l'Amen* the cyclic theme symbolizes the 'Amen' of the divine will. It is stated in the first movement, 'Amen de la Création', it is transformed in the fifth movement, 'Amen des Anges, des Saints, du chant des oiseaux', and is extended to form the theme of the last movement, 'Amen de la Consommation'. Fragments of it appear at the end of the third movement, 'Amen de l'Agonie de Jésus', to symbolize Jesus' acceptance of the divine will in the Garden of Gethsemane, before his Passion. It does not feature at all in the second movement, 'Amen des étoiles, de la planète à l'anneau', in the fourth movement, 'Amen de désir', or in the sixth, 'Amen du Jugement'.

The 'Amen' of the title has a four-fold significance. It is the creative act ('Amen de la Création', 'Amen des étoiles'), it is the acceptance of the divine will ('Amen de l'Agonie de Jésus'), it is the desire for union with God ('Amen de désir') and it is the expression of 'that which will be'—the divine judgement ('Amen de Jugement') and the eternal consummation of Paradise ('Amen des Anges', 'Amen de la Consommation'). In all these aspects it embodies the power and finality of the divine action on the cosmos.

Rhythmic pedals are used more extensively in this work, appearing in every movement except the sixth ('Amen du Jugement'). Tâla 1 (ex. 31) makes its appearance again in no less than three of the movements: 'Amen des étoiles', 'Amen de l'Agonie' and in canon in 'Amen de la Consommation'; Tâla 2 (ex. 31), which previously appeared in 'Danse de la fureur' from the *Quatuor*, is used in 'Amen des Anges'.[7] The first of these tâlas uses Sharngadeva rhythms, the second uses Messiaen's own non-retrogradable rhythms, and a third, a double rhythmic pedal, which appears in the first and fourth movements, is based on Greek rhythms. The latter is mainly based on variations and augmentations of 'cretic' feet, but one of the parts also employs the composite 'Aristophanian' metre and its retrograde.

Ex.44

Piano 1
R.H.: Variations of Cretic feet.

The most interesting passage from the rhythmic point of view occurs in the second movement, 'Amen des étoiles, de la planète à l'anneau'. This is one of Messiaen's 'cosmic' movements in which the stars, and in this case Saturn (the 'planète à l'anneau'), symbolize the divine action in the cosmos. The stars can be symbols of eternity in a passive way (as in 'Amour, oiseau d'étoile' from *Harawi*), but he refers again to an 'active' cosmic symbolism in the poem of *Trois petites liturgies* (third movement) and in 'Répétition planétaire' and 'Katchikatchi les étoiles' from *Harawi*, as well as in 'Joie du sang des étoiles' from *Turangalîla* (see Chapter 9). The form of 'Amen des étoiles' is ternary with a three-fold development of the main theme as the middle section. The third of these developments presents three different treatments of the first five notes of the main theme superimposed upon each other, together with a chord-sequence in mode 7. The duration of the passage is determined by the interaction of the first five notes of the theme with Tâla 1 in the left hand of the first piano. The tâla consists of seventeen durations so that five repetitions of the tâla coincide with seventeen repetitions of the melodic figure. The melodic figure is transposed down a semitone at each repetition and is so constructed that the first note of its first appearance and the last note of its final appearance is B (the dominant of E, which is the tonic of the piece). The right hand of the first piano is in birdsong style and defines a series of contracting durations by its phrase-lengths: 12 – 12 – 12 – 11 – 7 – 5 – 6 (crotchets). The chord-sequence in the right hand of the second piano and the development of the theme in the left hand both fall into independently expanding phrase-lengths: 5 – 5 – 5 – 5 – 7½ – 12½ – 5 – 25 (crotchets) for the chord-sequence and 10 – 13 – 17 – 26 for the development of the theme. The combination of all these rhythmic movements corresponds to the three elements of 'personnages rythmiques' (see Chapter 4, pp. 35–6) which more usually occur in juxtaposed rather than superimposed form. The two parts of the second piano form the active, expanding elements, the right hand of the first piano is the element which is acted upon (or contracting element), while the rhythmic pedal in the left hand is the passive element which does not change.

Although there are no new departures in *Visions de l'Amen*, techniques which have gradually emerged in Messiaen's earlier music become more crystallized. The rhythmic structure of the work is more complex than before, owing to the more extensive use of rhythmic pedals and canons, and the effects of harmonic resonance are extended, particularly in the last movement where the main theme and harmony on the second piano are clothed in upper and lower resonances simultaneously on the first piano to create the effect of a jubilant peal of bells.

Trois petites Liturgies de la Présence divine (1944)

Although, in his earlier orchestral works, Messiaen employs his forces in a way which enhances his feeling for harmonic colour and resonance, it was not until the composition of the *Trois petites Liturgies* that he exploited new sonorities either by the use of unusual instruments or by new combinations of more familiar instruments. A feature of his orchestration from this time is the use of the piano in a semi-solo capacity. The majority of his later orchestral works include it at least as a prominent orchestral instrument and in some cases (in *Reveil des oiseaux* and *Oiseaux exotiques*, for instance) as a *concertante* soloist. Its use arises not so much from a desire to exploit it as a virtuoso instrument but because of the particular timbres and colours which it has to offer to the orchestral whole. In *Trois petites Liturgies* it is associated with the celesta and vibraphone to form a group which Messiaen describes as evoking the sounds of the Balinese 'gamelan' orchestra. In *Turangalîla* this group is amplified by the addition of a glockenspiel and metal percussion instruments to form 'a small orchestra within the large orchestra, the sonority and function of which are reminiscent of the Balinese gamelan'.[8] This feature is found again in later works—*Sept Haïkaï* (1962) and *Couleurs de la Cité céleste* (1963)—where this section is even further augmented by the use of cencerros,[9] gongs, tam-tams and other metal percussion. In *Trois petites Liturgies* and in *Turangalîla*, Messiaen also makes use of a new timbre in the form of the Ondes Martenot. This is an electronic instrument (formerly referred to as 'electrophonic') invented by Maurice Martenot in 1928.[10] Messiaen was not the first composer of importance to use it orchestrally, as Varèse had previously used it in *Ecuatorial*, written ten years before *Trois petites Liturgies* in 1933–4. Messiaen himself had used the instrument in three earlier minor works: *Fêtes des belles eaux* for six Ondes Martenots (1937), *Deux Monodies en quarts de ton* (1938) and *Musique de scène pour un Oedipe* (1942) for solo Ondes Martenot. The first of these pieces was written for the Paris Exhibition of 1937 as a show-piece for the Ondes Martenot. It is of no great significance, except for the fact that the fifth movement of the *Quatuor* is derived from it.

Another innovation in the orchestration of the *Trois petites Liturgies* is the arrangement of the instruments on the concert platform as prescribed in the score. The work is scored for strings, Ondes Martenot, piano, celesta, vibraphone, maracas, Chinese cymbal, tam-tam and a choir of eighteen women's voices. Messiaen directs that the strings should be placed at the back on either side of the choir and the remaining instruments (including the percussion) at the front. In taking the strings away from their customary dominant role in the orchestra, Messiaen follows a practice previously adopted by both Stravinsky and Varèse. This is also characteristic of his later orchestral works, even the *Turangalîla-Symphonie*. Although this latter work uses a large body of strings in their customary position on the platform, the handling of the orchestral forces as a whole reduces their importance to one of strict equality with the rest of the orchestra.

It was observed in Chapter 5 that the *Trois petites Liturgies* is a ritualistic rather than a dramatic work. Although there is no action in this work (action being an essential part of liturgical ritual), the essence of ritual is retained by means of the text and the musical form, with its dependence, once again, on number symbolism.

The titles of the three movements of the work are: 'Antienne de la Conservation intérieure' (Dieu présent en nous . . .), 'Séquence du Verbe, Cantique Divin' (Dieu présent en lui-même . . .) and 'Psalmodie de l'Ubiquité par amour' (Dieu présent en toutes choses . . .). The use of the terms 'antiphon' (*antienne*), Sequence and psalmody in the titles suggests a connection with the liturgy. The form of the first movement is ternary with, in fact, a psalm-like chant for the middle section, preceded and followed by the same text and music (the repetition has some additional material superimposed). This reflects the practice in the Roman rite of preceding and following a psalm-chant with a short versicle or antiphon in free musical style as distinct from the formal repetitions of the psalm-tone. 'Antienne de la Conversation intérieure' partially resembles the shape of a Gregorian psalm-tone in having a reciting note followed by an elaborate ending (see also 'Actions de grâces', p. 56).

A different form of psalmody—responsorial psalmody—is to be found in the last movement. In the liturgy, this involves the repetition of a short 'response' after each line of a psalm. There is no attempt to simulate a psalm-tone in this case. Part of the text is simply spoken rhythmically and followed by a repetitive melodic figure. This occurs four times in the first and third sections of the movement, followed by a refrain (or response) with the same music and similar text each time ('Posez-vous comme un sceau sur mon cœur', 'Imprimez votre nom dans mon sang', 'Mettez votre caresse tout autour') ('Set yourself like a seal upon my heart', 'Imprint your name on my blood', 'Place your caress all around').

Although the second movement is described as a Sequence, the form of the text and the melodic line has a closer resemblance to an extended responsory than to a liturgical Sequence. The essential musical feature of the Sequence is the use of different music for each pair of successive stanzas (see Chapter 6, p. 48). In 'Séquence du Verbe' the text which opens the movement is repeated as a response after successive 'versicles', and the melody of both versicle and response is the same throughout. The decorative material in the orchestra, however, is varied at each repetition, and in this respect the structure of the movement is derived from the Sequence. Melodic development in the original liturgical form becomes decorative development in 'Séquence du Verbe'.

The text, which is by Messiaen himself, is surrealistic in nature—in spite of being Christian at the same time.[11] This is especially apparent in the last movement where he speaks of:

> 'Temps de l'homme et de la planète,
> Temps de la montagne et de l'insecte,'

and

> 'De la profondeur une ride surgit,
> La montagne saute comme une brebis
> Et devient un grand océan.
> Présent, vous êtes présent.'

('Time of man and of the planet, time of the mountain and the insect. . . . From the depths a ripple arises, the mountain leaps like a sheep and becomes a great ocean. You are present, really present.')

The reference in this extract is to the different durations of time: the very long time-scale of the cosmos, the long time-scale of the mountains, the relatively shorter time of man and the very short time of the insect. The imagery of the mountain which leaps like a sheep is derived from Psalm 113 (114 in the Hebrew) where 'the mountains skipped like rams, and the hills like lambs . . . at the presence of the God of Jacob'.

There is no cyclic theme as such in *Trois petites Liturgies*, but there is a

motivic connection between the principal themes of each movement, based on
a rising second and a falling perfect fourth, or some permutation or inversion
of the three notes defined by these intervals.

Ex.45

Besides the themes based on the perfect fourth, each movement has a
second theme in which the tritone features prominently. In medieval symbolism the tritone was the 'devil' in music and the perfect intervals symbolized
the divinity. This distinction is not one which is valid in Messiaen's music, but
the juxtaposition of the two intervals in this context suggests the contrast of
the worldly and the divine which is the subject of the work.

Ex.46

The contrast of the Godhead and the world is also symbolized by the role
of the numbers 3 and 4 in the form, rhythm and thematic structure of the
work. 'Three' is the number of the Godhead and 'four' is its extension into
nature, symbolizing the world,[12] the creation of the Godhead. There are three
movements: the first and last are in ternary form, and the third movement has
a coda, making a fourth section. There are three groups of vocal or instrumental timbres: voices, strings and percussion. The percussion is divided into
two groups of three instruments each: pitched percussion comprising the
piano, celesta and vibraphone, and unpitched percussion consisting of
maracas, Chinese cymbal and tam-tam; a total of six instruments. Associated

with the five-part strings is the Ondes Martenot, making six parts in all. The choir consists of eighteen sopranos (3×6) who sing either in unison or divide into three parts. In certain passages their number is reduced to twelve, to six, or to a solo voice.

The numbers three and four can also be found in the thematic structure of the work. In the first movement the three statements of the opening motives (based on the perfect fourth) are extended into a fourth subsection by means of the contrasting theme, based on the tritone. The middle section consists of four statements of a tripartite AAB form. In the second movement, the response theme consists of three phrases and appears six times throughout the movement, and in the last movement there are four repetitions of a section which is itself divided into three parts: the opening psalmodic chant, a repetitive melodic figure and the short refrain.

Trois petites Liturgies is unique among Messiaen's output of this period in providing no obvious uses of Sharngadeva rhythms. Even Tâla 1 (ex. 31), which appears in every major work between 1938 and 1949, only appears in a degenerate form in the first movement.

Ex.47

A study of the broad outline of the first section of the first movement, however, reveals a dependence on the shape of the rhythm 'râgavardhana' in a general sense. The rhythm of the vocal part of the first three sub-sections is as follows:

Ex.48

It can be seen that the durations of the actual melodic phrases, excluding the rests, form three non-retrogradable cells of three values each: $7 - 8 - 7$, $7 - 10 - 7$, $7 - 12 - 7$ (values in quavers)—a characteristic of the first cell of 'râgavardhana'. In addition, the total durations of each of these three sub-sections, including the rests, together with the longer duration of the fourth sub-section, define the total shape of 'râgavardhana'. The relative proportions are by no means exact in their correspondence to the Indian rhythm, but they expand and contract by analogy to it:

Durations of sub-sections in quavers: $40 - 54 - 52 - 80$
Durations of the values of 'râgavardhana': $2 - 3 - 2 - 12$

A similar awareness of the 'macrocosmic' rhythmic structure of the work, as distinct from its 'microcosmic' or small-scale structure, can be found in other places in the work. The middle section of the first movement presents an interesting combination of rhythms defined by the phrase structure of the voice, solo violin and Ondes Martenot parts. Each enters at a different point with its own independent material, although the violin and Ondes Martenot parts have the same phrase structure on different time-scales:

Vln:		45	—	45	—	67	—	105	45	—	60	45	—	45	—	67	—	137
Sops:	51	—	51	—	84	51	—	51	—	84	51	—	51	—	72	51	—	51	—	65
Ondes Mt:						28	—	28	—	42	—	43	29	—	43	—	23	—	23	—	83	—	113

[Values in semiquavers; the vertical alignment after the beginning of each part is not intended to be exact.]

Vingt Regards sur l'Enfant-Jésus (1944)

The unique rhythmic and ritualistic qualities of *Trois petites Liturgies de la Présence divine* make it stand apart from Messiaen's other works of this time. In the work which followed, *Vingt Regards*, he returns to the same rhythmic and symbolic characteristics of previous works. Because it was written for solo piano, however, it does not present the same opportunities for complex superimposition of rhythmic structures as the *Quatuor* or *Visions de l'Amen*.

The sources of religious inspiration are varied. Some of the pieces are purely descriptive rather than symbolic in a ritualist sense, being inspired by various forms of visual art. 'Première Communion de la Vierge' (no. XI) is based on a painting showing the Virgin kneeling in contemplation, worshipping the child in her womb; 'Le baiser de l'Enfant-Jésus' (no. XV) is derived from an engraving of the child Jesus leaving his mother's arms to embrace St Thérèse of Lisieux; and 'Regard de l'Onction terrible' (no. XVIII) is inspired by a tapestry representing Christ, the Word of God mounted on a horse. He is revealed in battle, but only his hands are visible on the hilt of a sword, which he wields in the midst of flashes of lightning.

The work in general was influenced by various theological writers: St Thomas Aquinas, St John of the Cross, St Thérèse of Lisieux, the Gospels, the Roman Missal and especially Dom Columba Marmion's *Christ and his mysteries* and Maurice Toesca's *Les Douze Regards*. These last two writers have spoken of the 'Regards' of the shepherds, of the angels, of the Virgin and of the heavenly Father. In his preface to the work Messiaen says: 'I followed the same idea, treating it a little differently and adding sixteen new "Regards".'

Messiaen's titles are not always easy to render into convincing English, but the sense of the word *regard* in this work involves contemplation as well as the more literal meaning 'gaze'. It is essentially a contemplation of the mysteries involved in the subject of each piece as well as of the child Jesus. The theme of the Nativity is not dealt with in a narrative sense. The distribution of the subjects throughout the work is partly governed by number symbolism.[13] The first piece—'Regard du Père'—relates to the first person of the Trinity and the other pieces relating to Persons of the Trinity are distributed in multiples of five throughout the work (five being the Indian number of Shiva who is the type of Christ—see Chapter 5, p. 41). The tenth movement, 'Regard de l'Esprit de joie', is dedicated to the Holy Spirit, the fifth movement, 'Regard du Fils sur le Fils', to Christ as the Son of God, the fifteenth movement, 'Le baiser de l'Enfant-Jésus', to Christ in the Blessed Sacrament, and the last movement, 'Regard de l'Église d'amour', to the Church as the Body of Christ. The number 'six' as the number of Creation is also significant. God made the world in six days through the Word 'without whom nothing was made' (John 1: 3); the sixth piece therefore relates to God the Creator—'Par Lui tout a été fait'—and the twelfth and eighteenth pieces to Christ as the Word of God—'La parole toute puissante' and 'Regard de l'Onction terrible'. 'Nine', as the number of Maternity (see Chapter 5, p. 42), occurs again in this work. The ninth piece—'Regard du Temps'—relates to Time— 'the mystery of the fullness of time; Time sees, born into itself, he who is eternal. . . .'[14]

As in *Visions de l'Amen*, Messiaen makes use of cyclic themes. The principal one is the *thème de Dieu* (or 'God-theme') which is stated in its complete form in the first piece, 'Regard du Père'. In this piece it is God the Father who contemplates the child Jesus: 'This is my beloved Son, in whom I am well pleased' (Matthew 17: 5); the tempo is extremely slow and the piece remains entirely static throughout, symbolizing the eternity of God. The *thème de Dieu* occurs again in 'Regard du Fils sur le Fils'. Here it is Christ as the Word of God, who contemplates God made man. A two-part rhythmic canon of chords (see Chapter 4, pp. 37–8) is superimposed on the cyclic theme, giving way to birdsong in the second half of each phrase. The Trinity is symbolized in the three-fold texture, and the two natures of Christ (God and Man) in the dual sonority of the canon and the main theme. Although the canon consists of two strands in two different dynamic levels (*pp* and *ppp*), they interact at the same register so that they tend to merge into each other, whereas both are sharply contrasted in all respects (including register) to the cyclic theme. Fragments of the *thème de Dieu* appear in 'Par Lui tout a été fait', 'Regard de l'Esprit de joie' and 'Première Communion de la Vierge', and it is used in a varied form in 'Le baiser de l'Enfant-Jésus'. It appears once again in its complete form in the coda of the last movement, where it is extended further to an ecstatic apotheosis. This is one of the most impressive moments in the work. The return of the *thème de Dieu* comes at the climax of a long and tur- bulent preparation, and when the composer's tempo indication ($\flat$ = 40) is taken as the point of departure for the performance of this section it achieves a power and intensity rarely equalled in any other of his works.

The second cyclic theme is the *thème de l'étoile et de la Croix* ('the theme of the star and of the cross'). This theme has a dual significance, symbolizing the star which heralded the birth of Christ and the cross on which he died.

It is stated in the second piece, 'Regard de l'étoile', and reappears in a different form in the seventh 'Regard de la Croix'. The number 'seven' represents for Messiaen divine repose and in this case symbolizes also the death of Christ on the Cross.[13] The other cyclic theme which Messiaen cites in the preface—the *thème d'accords* ('the chord theme')—has no symbolic significance and plays a purely decorative part, although a persistent one, in the work.

While *Vingt Regards* breaks no new ground as regards musical techniques, it nevertheless represents a development of processes already visible in earlier works. One of the most important developments for this work is the process called 'agrandissement asymétrique', which is the counterpart in terms of pitch of 'personnages rythmiques' (Chapter 4, pp. 35–6). Over the space of several repetitions of a theme or passage some groups of notes are transposed upwards and some downwards by steps of a semitone, while others remain unchanged.

Ex.49

'Par Lui tout a été fait'

2 1 1 1 3 3 1 1 1 3 3 1 1 1   1 – notes to be transposed upwards
(8 ...)   2 – notes to be transposed downwards
                             3 – notes remaining unchanged

The third piece, 'L'Échange', while of no thematic significance, is devoted entirely to this process of 'agrandissement asymétrique' which plays a role in the work as a whole similar to that of a cyclic theme. The first three pieces, therefore, are concerned with cyclic themes or processes important for the overall work.

Of the remaining seventeen pieces, the sixth, tenth and nineteenth present features of unusual or especial interest. The resemblance of the form of 'Par Lui tout a été fait', the sixth piece, was discussed in Chapter 4 (pp. 38–9). Messiaen describes it as a fugue, but it only resembles a fugue insofar as it has a subject and countersubject which appear simultaneously at the beginning and are treated in various canonic forms and other transformations at the 'middle entries'. The exposition itself presents successive transformations, rather than contrapuntal accumulations of the subject. After its initial statement it appears changed in rhythm and registers against a rhythmically compressed form in 'agrandissement asymétrique' (see ex. 49 above). Its inversion is then stated and transformed in the same way against a continuation of the 'agrandissement' on the original form of the subject. The most important features of the movement, however, are not so much those which are derived from fugue but the symmetrical, 'non-retrogradable' nature of the first section followed by the stretto and coda. The symmetrical first section represents the turmoil of Creation—'galaxies, photons, spirals in contrary motion, inverted lightning-flashes'[14] and is like a grand ritual incantation which, like creation, 'reveals to us the luminous shadow of his voice . . .'[14] (that is, the

voice of God). The whole of the first section and the stretto which follows it
lead up to a powerful climactic moment when the first phrase of the *thème de
Dieu* is sounded against thunderous rumblings representing 'the face of God
behind the flame'. In its essence this extraordinary piece anticipates the
surrealism of *Harawi* and *Turangalîla* and, in fact, bears a resemblance to the
sixth movement of *Harawi*, which is also an incantation leading up to a
'cosmic eruption'. It presents, at the same time, a remarkable contrast to the
pictorial and sometimes sentimental symbolism of other movements, such as
'Le baiser de l'Enfant-Jésus'.

Although Messiaen frequently changes mode during the course of a piece,
or superimposes different modes, the tonal centre, when present, rarely
changes at all. This applies whether it is a question of a modal 'final' (as in
the first movement of *Les Corps Glorieux*) or of a stronger sense of tonality
(as in such pieces as 'Regard du Père'). Some pieces present an ambiguous
sense of tonality, such as the fourth piece from *Vingt Regards* ('Regard de la
Vierge') which centres on F sharp at the beginning, yet C sharp emerges at
the end as the stronger modal tonic. Other pieces, such as the thirteenth
('Noël'), have no clear tonal or modal centre at all. The tenth piece, 'Regard de
l'Esprit de joie', on the other hand, is one of the few examples where Messiaen
creates a musical structure out of shifting tonalities, with a sense of modulation involved. The last three pieces of *Vingt Regards* present a similar pheno-
menon, but 'Regard de l'Esprit de joie' is probably the most striking example.
The modulations follow a consistent pattern of rising or falling major or
minor thirds, which are arranged in such a way that the music moves up or
down through successive thirds so that no intermediate key is touched on
more than once, as shown in the following plan:

Theme I *(thème de danse orientale)*	Theme II *(thème de joie)*
F sharp —	E flat — C — A . . . .
└———— falling minor thirds ————┘	

Transition to	Theme III *(air de chasse)*
(on the dominant of A)	A — D flat — F └ rising major thirds ┘

Theme II	Fragments of *thème de Dieu*	Theme II	Theme I and Coda
(F) — A flat — B . .	B — D —	B flat —	F sharp
└ rising minor thirds ┘	└————— falling major thirds —————┘		

The nineteenth piece, 'Je dors, mais mon cœur veille', is the closest that
Messiaen comes to a genuine mystical expression in his work. He describes it,

in fact, as 'a dialogue of mystical love', a contemplation of 'the sleeping Jesus who loves us in his "Sunday" and who bestows on us "l'oubli" ...'.[14] *Oubli* can mean forgiveness or oblivion, the 'Nirvana' of forgetfulness, the mystical union with God. The reference to 'Sunday', of course, evokes the day of rest after God had created the world. A portion of the *thème de Dieu* is used in this piece and is labelled *thème d'amour* in the score (this theme was also used in the coda of 'Par Lui tout a été fait'). The derivation of the 'love theme' from the 'God-theme' is, of course, appropriate, but it becomes of greater significance because of the fact that it also forms the basis of the *thème d'amour* from the *Turangalîla-Symphonie*.

Ex.50

'Love-theme' (bar 15 of the *thème de Dieu* in 'Regard du Père')

Beginning of *thème d'amour* from *Turangalîla*

Although the works that immediately follow *Vingt Regards* do not break new ground as regards their procedures, this work closes a phase in Messiaen's composition insofar as a specifically Christian symbolism gives way to a mythological one centring upon the 'Tristan and Isolde' myth. When he does return to Christian symbolism in *Messe de la Pentecôte* (1950) and *Livre d'Orgue* (1951), that symbolism has been greatly affected by the surrealism of the intervening works.

Notes on Chapter 8

1. *ROM* p. 63.
2. *ROM* p. 64.
3. *ROM* pp. 64–5.
4. The orchestration of *Poèmes pour Mi* does not affect this conception as no major changes are made in the accompaniment.
5. *ROM* p. 66.
6. The preface to the score.
7. Page 51, starting in bar two of the second system in the first piano and again on page 66, starting in bar two of the second system in the first piano. In both cases the rhythm is treated in three-part canon against the main theme (derived from the cyclic theme).
8. From Messiaen's sleeve note for the recordings of *Turangalîla*, first published in French for the original Véga recording and translated into English by Louis Biancolli for the RCA Victor recording. The translation given here is the author's own.
9. Large tuned cow-bells.

10. The sound of the Ondes Martenot (plural: Ondes Martenots) is synthesized electronically. Although it is equipped with a conventional keyboard, it is a monophonic instrument, incapable of sounding more than one note at a time. The pitch of a note may be varied slightly by the lateral movement of a key so that it can produce a vibrato, and in addition to the keyboard it has a horizontally stretched cord. A continuous variation of pitch can be obtained by the proximity of the player's hand to this cord.

11. In his note for the Erato recording of the work, Messiaen says: 'In spite of its surrealistic appearance (I was at that time an avid reader of Paul Éluard and Pierre Reverdy), it [the poem] embodies theological truths. . . '. In its conception surrealism was anti-Christian and politically anarchic, but Messiaen makes use of its artistic and symbolistic aspects while rejecting its ideology (see Chapter 9).

12. This symbolism of the number 4 is pointed out by Luc-André Marcel in his sleeve note for the early Ducretet-Thomson recording of the work.

13. *ROM* p. 109.

14. Messiaen's preface to the work.

9

Messiaen and the Tristan Myth

The three works written between 1945 and 1948—*Harawi*, the *Turangalîla-Symphonie* and *Cinq Rechants*—form a trilogy on the subject of love and death. In them Messiaen turns principally to the myth of Tristan and Isolde, and especially to Wagner's version of the story in which the symbolism of the Love-Death plays a large part. Although Messiaen abandons Christian symbols in these works, the concept of the Love-Death is nevertheless central to Christianity, in the sense that all true acts of love involve sacrifice, whether it be the love of God for Man through the sacrifice of the cross, or the love of man for God or for his fellow men, or the love of a man and a woman for each other. True love is at the same time self-consuming: 'a fatal, irresistible love, transcending everything outside itself, a love such as is symbolized by the love potion of Tristan and Isolde'.[1] There is a link between mythology and the surrealistic character of the Tristan trilogy: both are concerned with the workings of the subconscious, both use symbols of allegory to convey their message; but whereas mythology does this by means of a narrative, surrealism strives to do it more directly by invoking a world of dreams or nightmares in which objects which are not normally associated with each other in the physical world may be brought into stark opposition.

In allegorical terms death is symbolic of sacrifice, but it also symbolizes the transformation of the personality which accompanies an act of self-sacrifice. As Robert Donington points out in his book *Wagner's 'Ring' and its Symbols*, in commenting on the meaning of death in mythology: 'When St Paul (1 Corinthians 15: 31) cried in painfully difficult and anguished acceptance, "I die daily", he meant not physical death, but the necessary death of cherished illusions and outworn attitudes without which we can expect no growth of character, yet which however often repeated and manfully accepted never ceases to feel like shocking violence and distress of spirit.' The mythological meaning of the Love-Death, then, is the death or rejection of one's own desires for those of the loved one, and the awakening to a new life through the union of love.

In his earlier religious works Messiaen is concerned largely with a symbolism which is partly pictorial and partly dependent upon number. Tendencies towards surrealism are apparent in his religious music since *Poèmes pour Mi* (1936), but it is often difficult to draw a definite line between the strictly pictorial and the strictly surrealistic. On the one hand, there are the pieces such as 'Première Communion de la Vierge' (*Vingt Regards* XI), which arise primarily from a definite pictorial concept; and on the other hand, there is the more vivid and direct expression of such pieces as 'Par Lui tout a été fait' (*Vingt Regards* VI), where the concepts behind the music are essentially visionary. Many pieces, however, fall between these extremes and combine aspects of both.

The existence of a text, or a verbal explanation of the symbolism of the work (such as the composer supplies in the case of the recordings of *Turangalîla*), is useful as a focal point for its symbolism and in providing a stimulus to the imagination of the listener. It is in the nature of surrealistic symbolism, however, that these texts and verbal explanations themselves need to be interpreted—something which can only completely be brought about by the experience of, and the involvement in, the complete work (as listener or performer). No verbal explanation can fully replace this experience. Surrealism demands the total involvement in a work of art of the person with whom it is communicating. Although it delves into the subconscious for its symbolism, its message is to be accepted as a part of reality so that it is impossible to tell where fantasy ends and 'real' life—that is ordinary, everyday life—begins. In *Harawi*, Tristan and Isolde are not simply two characters who are the subject of the poems, nor do they merely symbolize everyman and everywoman; they *are* everyman and everywoman who become involved in the piece as listeners. They become part of the fantasy of *Harawi*, just as the fantasy of *Harawi* is to become part of their world of experience.

In his note for the recording of *Turangalîla*, Messiaen describes his 'Tristan trilogy' as being 'three aspects . . . of the Tristan and Isolde theme'. He has also described it elsewhere as three 'acts' of 'un grand Tristan et Yseult'; [2] this is a little misleading, as there is no dramatic continuity from one to the other, which is implied by this description. Each of the three works is self-sufficient and not necessarily intended for performance in the same programme.

The lack of dramatic content in the three works fundamentally distinguishes Messiaen's from Wagner's approach to the subject. Like the ancient Greeks, Wagner expresses mythology in terms of human drama. His characters are subject to the laws of time and continuity, although their actions may have a non-temporal or eternal significance. Messiaen, on the other hand, takes the Tristan myth out of the real world of human relationships into a surrealistic dream world, where time and causality do not exist. Here, the hopes, the fears and the aspirations of the mind are laid bare in a poetry and music which are more intense and immediate in their impact than is possible through the medium of human drama.

Harawi

Composed for soprano and piano and subtitled 'Chant d'amour et de mort', *Harawi* was the first part of the trilogy to be completed in 1945. It was about this time that Messiaen became interested in the writings of Béclard d'Harcourt on the folklore of the Andes,[3] and as a result he was influenced by Peruvian folklore and religion in his poems for the song-cycle. In order to intensify the Peruvian aspects of the work, much use is made in the poems of onomatopoeic and actual Quechua words, as well as symbols derived from Peruvian mythology.

The word 'Harawi' itself is also a Quechua word, meaning a love-song which ends with the death of the lovers—hence the subtitle: 'chant d'amour et de mort'. The woman is called Piroutcha and the man himself is not named, since it is he who frequently addresses the woman in the poems. As in *Visions de l'Amen* and *Vingt Regards*, Messiaen makes use of a cyclic theme but, as in earlier works, he also arranges the movements symmetrically around a central movement according to their musical and poetic characteristics, the first movement standing alone as an introduction.

The poem of the first movement, 'La ville qui dormait, toi', is ultra-symbolist. As in many other instances in *Harawi*, images of the external world are transferred to the beloved. She is the town which was sleeping ('La ville qui dormait')—as yet unawakened to a life of love; she is the grassy bank at midnight ('Le plein minuit le banc, toi')—the bank, that is, on which Tristan and Isolde recline in Act II (Scene 2) of Wagner's *Tristan und Isolde*; and again, she is the double violet—symbol of modesty ('La violette double, toi'). In the last line of the poem, her lover gazes at her steadily—he is the immovable eye, 'L'œil immobile, sans dénouer ton regard, moi'.

The second, seventh and last movements ('Bonjour toi, colombe verte', 'Adieu' and 'Dans le noir') form the pillars of the whole cycle around which the other movements gravitate. The vocal line of these movements consists of the cyclic theme, stated in the second movement and transformed by repetition, extension and juxtaposition of its phrases in the other two. The poems sum up the course of the whole cycle. All three are addressed to *colombe verte* ('green dove') which is the sacred Maya symbol of the beloved;[4] they suggest the transition from life, in the greeting of 'Bonjour toi', through the parting and death of 'Adieu' to the final eternity of 'Dans le noir'. The main sections of the cyclic theme are interspersed with short piano solos, reflecting the mood of the poems in the respective movements. In the second movement these consist of birdsong, symbolic of joy; in the seventh they suggest the funereal sound of bells; and in the last movement they consist of chord sequences in rhythmic canon, circulating continuously in an unchanging texture, symbolic of eternity (see Chapter 4, pp. 37–8).

The third movement, 'Montagnes', unites the symbols of death with the act of falling in love. The poem describes the vertigo experienced in looking down into great chasms from the mountain tops—'le chaos solaire du vertige. . . . Gouffre lancé partout dans le vertige'—the dizziness involved in the abandonment of the self to love, the dizziness of death.

The movements most closely related to the three 'cyclic' movements (the second, seventh and last) are the fourth, 'Doundou tchil' and the ninth, 'L'escalier redit, gestes du soleil'. Both these use thematic material based on the cyclic theme and both have the same tonality as the 'cyclic' movements: E flat. Each forms a pair with the one which follows it ('L'Amour de Piroutcha' and 'Amour, oiseau d'étoile') so that each pair is symmetrically placed before and after 'Adieu'. The title of 'Doundou tchil' is derived from the onomatopoeic words which are chanted in the introduction and coda of the song. The onomatope represents the sound of ankle-bells as used by Peruvian Indian dancers,[4] and the chant is accompanied by a piano part which simulates the sound of primitive drums. The whole of the poem and the music evokes a primitive dance, symbolizing the ritual of courtship.

The ritual of 'Doundou tchil' gives way to the love-song 'L'Amour de Piroutcha'. The key of this movement is G major—the key of desire (see Chapter 5, p. 43)—and the poem expresses as a dialogue between 'The young man' and 'The young woman' the lovers' desire for fulfilment. Like Tristan and Isolde in Act II of Wagner's music-drama, the lovers long for death as the seal on their relationship; but whereas in *Tristan und Isolde* the death-wish appears in quite long stretches of the love-duet, Messiaen expresses it very simply: 'Coupe-moi la tête, doundou tchil' ('Cut off my head, doundou tchil'), and 'Chaines rouges, noires, mauves, amour, la mort' ('Red, black, mauve chains, love, death'). The direct brutality of the first of the phrases anticipates the terrors and pain to come: the 'chains' are the mountain chains of the Andes as well as those of the Dauphiny, where Messiaen lived as a child. Their association here with 'love' and 'death' relates back to the third movement, 'Montagnes'.

The two movements which immediately precede and follow 'Adieu' are the most intensely surrealistic as well as ritualistic. The cataclysmic nature of the sixth movement, 'Répétition planétaire', heralds the approach of death; the opening cries and the following incantation, 'Mapa, nama, nama, tchil', call to mind a black magic ritual invoking the cosmic dissolution of the climactic final section. The cries from the opening of the movement now echo across the whole of eternity: 'Enfourche un cri noir, Echo noir du temps, Cri d'avant la terre à tout moment . . .' ('Bestride a dark cry, dark echo of time, a cry out of eternity, before the earth was formed . . .'). The lovers, passing up the 'winding staircase' from time to eternity, are caught up in a cosmic whirlpool which is like a planet, threatening to consume them: 'Escalier tournant, Tourbillon, Étoile rouge, Tourbillon, Planète mange en tournant.' Death is the dissolution of the physical world, the experience of which is nothing short of cataclysmic on a cosmic scale. For the lovers it is the pain of self-rejection necessary to their orgiastic entry into a new and more intense experience of their relationship.

Any act of self-sacrifice involves a sense of danger. This is symbolized in the eighth movement, 'Syllabes', by a musical and poetic enactment of the traditional Peruvian 'Dance of the Apes' (also found in Bâli). This is a ritual dance which commemorates an Inca prince who was once saved from great danger by the warning cries of the apes as they swung from tree to tree.[5] In both the original dance and in 'Syllabes' the cries of the apes are simulated by the repetition of the syllable *pia*.

The sixth, seventh and eighth movements are the core of *Harawi*. Their mythological ritual of death transforms the tentative experience of courtship in 'Doundou tchil' and 'L'amour de Piroutcha' into the full and ecstatic experience of love in 'L'escalier redit, gestes du soleil' and 'Amour oiseau d'étoile'. The ritual aspects of 'Doundou tchil' become intensely more ecstatic in the ninth movement, 'L'escalier redit', embracing the sky, the water, and the whole of time in the recurrent refrain: 'Du ciel, de l'eau, du temps. . . .' Love unites the lovers to each other and to the love of the whole world: 'Inventons l'amour du monde' ('let us find the love of the world'). They become one with the creative and evolutionary forces of nature as symbolized by the awakening of springtime: 'J'attends dans le vert étoile d'amour. C'est si simple d'être mort.' ('I wait in the green star of love, it is so easy to be dead.') In this phrase is compressed the whole symbolism of the Love-Death. 'Green' is not only the sacred colour of the beloved (*colombe verte*), but is also the colour of springtime; it is through the lover—'the star of love'—that the experience of love becomes a reality. The danger is passed, the sacrifice is made and the painful experiences of the past are forgotten in the experience of a new life.

The key of desire—G major—in 'L'amour de Piroutcha' becomes the key of mystical love—F sharp major (see Chapter 5, pp. 42–3) in its counterpart 'Amour, oiseau d'étoile'. The poem of this movement describes a surrealistic painting by Sir Roland Penrose,[6] which shows a man's hands outstretched from the bottom of the picture to the top, and a woman's head upside down, her neck merging into the sky and the stars. 'This picture,' says Messiaen, 'is the symbol of the whole of *Harawi*.'[5] It also provides the clue to the specific references to death found in 'L'amour de Piroutcha': 'Coupe-moi la tête, doundou tchil', and in the eleventh movement: 'Coupez ma tête, son chiffre roule dans le sang!'

In sharp contrast to 'Amour oiseau d'étoile' the eleventh movement, 'Katchikatchi les étoiles', recalls the cosmic cataclysm of the moment of death, balancing the anticipation of this moment in 'Montagnes'. The poem describes a surrealistic nightmare in which the lovers see the stars, the atoms and the whole cosmos jumping and dancing like grasshoppers (*Katchikatchi* is the Quechua word for 'grasshopper'):

> Katchikatchi les étoiles, faites-les sauter.
> Katchikatchi les étoiles, faites-les danser.
> Katchikatchi les atomes, faites-les sauter,
> Katchikatchi les atomes, faites-les danser.

The symbolic ritual-dance of the stars of 'Doundou tchil', 'Piroutcha te-voilà, ô mon à moi, la danse des étoiles, doundou tchil', becomes a reality in 'Katchikatchi'.

The last movement, 'Dans le noir', represents the eternal finality of death; the lovers rest 'far from love' ('loin d'amour'). The end of the movement recalls the beginning of the work: 'La ville qui dormait . . .', but now the 'toi' is omitted, the lovers are no more. In its intention, *Harawi*, like the great love stories of the past—'Orpheus and Euridice', 'Romeo and Juliet' and 'Tristan and Isolde'—is intensely tragic. Notwithstanding the mythological symbolism of death as the fulfilment of love through sacrifice, the love between man and woman is not the final goal, it must sooner or later pass away (perhaps to be replaced by the greater union of love between God and Man, but on this subject *Harawi* has nothing to say).

In the strength of its symbolism, *Harawi* outstrips previous works. In its musical aspects it breaks no new ground, but it has a more coherent overall unity than the long works which precede it. Sharngadeva rhythms, rhythmic canons and other typical rhythmic devices, as well as Messiaen's characteristic harmonies and modes, are all present. The piano plays an important role, assuming occasionally the character of a solo instrument. Even so, it does not altogether parallel Wagner's orchestra. For Wagner, the main thematic development takes place in the orchestra, whereas in *Harawi*, the main themes are retained in the voice, and the piano, when it plays on its own, provides commentaries in the form of birdsong, rhythmic canons and evocative chord-sequences.

Turangalîla-Symphonie

The composition of the *Turangalîla-Symphonie* occupied Messiaen for over two years, from the middle of 1946 to the end of 1948. It was commissioned by Serge Koussevitzky for the Boston Symphony Orchestra, who gave it its first performance under Leonard Bernstein on 2nd December 1949. Although Messiaen's musical language could not be described as symphonic in the traditional sense, there are aspects of *Turangalîla* which relate it to the symphony of the late nineteenth century. It consists of ten extensive movements, lasting altogether an hour and a quarter. Various cyclic themes are used in addition to others which are proper to each movement in which they occur. There are also be be found vestiges of traditional symphonic forms, such as the Scherzo (fourth and fifth movements), variations (ninth movement), and sonata form (last movement). Also, according to Messiaen's description, the eighth movement forms the 'development section' for the symphony as a whole.

The word *Turangalîla* is a combination of two Sanskrit words. *Lîla* means, literally, 'play', 'sport' or 'amusement'; it is a 'play' in the sense of divine action on the cosmos; that is, the acts of creation, destruction, reconstruction, and the play of life and death. It can also mean 'love'. *Turanga* signifies

' time', the time which runs like a galloping horse, or time which flows like the sand in an hourglass, as well as movement and rhythm.

The word as a whole, therefore, means 'a song of love', 'a hymn to joy', time, movement, rhythm, life and death. When Messiaen speaks of joy in connection with *Turangalîla*, he describes it as a superhuman, overflowing, dazzling and abandoned joy; and the love, signified by *lîla*, is a fatal, irresistible love, transcending all things, suppressing everything outside itself—a love which is symbolized by the love-potion of Tristan and Isolde.[7]

Messiaen cites four main cyclic themes in *Turangalîla*. In addition there are a number of others which are more or less related to the cyclic themes; these play a subordinate role in the work, but assume greater importance in *Cinq Rechants* and a number of later works (see Chapter 10, pp. 101–2). Three of the four main cyclic themes have a symbolic significance and are given names to identify them and to relate them to their symbolism. The first is the 'statue theme' which first appears loudly in the trombones and tuba near the beginning of the first movement. For Messiaen this theme recalls the heavy, terrifying brutality of old Mexican monuments: 'it has always evoked for me some terrible and fatal statue (for instance, the Venus d'Ille of Prosper Mérimée).'[7]

Ex.51

The second cyclic theme is called the 'flower theme' because of its tender, supple curve, like 'the tender orchid, the ornamental fuchsia, the red gladiolus, the supple corn-lily'.[7]

Ex.52

One can see in the entirely opposite character of these two themes the pure masculine element or *animus* of the 'statue theme' with its phallic symbolism and the feminine element or *anima* of the 'flower theme', tender and supple. In general, the 'statue theme' plays a more dominant role in the work than the 'flower theme'; it recurs more frequently and is transformed to become the new theme at figure 5 in 'Chant d'amour II' (the fourth movement), as well as forming material for the fifth movement, 'Joie du sang des étoiles'.

The third cyclic theme is the *thème d'amour* or 'love theme'. Both the masculine and feminine characteristics of the first two cyclic themes intertwine in the 'love theme', one transforming the other, to produce a new theme different in character from them both and symbolizing the union of Tristan and

83

Isolde. This theme occurs for the first time in its complete form in the sixth movement, 'Jardin du sommeil d'amour' (see ex. 58).

The fourth cyclic theme is the *thème d'accords*, which, like the 'chord theme' in *Vingt Regards*, has no symbolic significance; it associates itself with other motives, occurring sometimes in a fragmented form and sometimes extended.

Ex.53

Turangalîla uses a large orchestra consisting of triple woodwind, four horns, four trumpets, one cornet, three trombones and tuba, strings, piano, Ondes Martenot and a large percussion section. As in the *Trois petites Liturgies*, the pitched percussion and piano are grouped together to form the 'gamelan' (see Chapter 8, pp. 66–7), which, in this case, also includes the metal percussion—the triangle, cymbals, tam-tam and bells. The piano also functions on its own, having a number of cadenzas at various points in the work, usually preceding some important climactic point.

The movements are not arranged symmetrically as in *Harawi*, but they fall into three groups distinguished by particular common characteristics. The first group consists of the movements associated with the growth and development of love, as symbolized by the evolution of the 'love theme' in their main themes: 2—'Chant d'amour I', 4—'Chant d'amour II', 6—'Jardin du sommeil d'amour' and 8—'Développement de l'amour'. The second group comprises the third movement, 'Turangalîla I', the seventh movement, 'Turangalîla II' and the ninth, 'Turangalîla III'. These movements are brooding—one might almost say sinister—in character, recalling the pieces from *Harawi* most closely associated with death. The fifth movement, 'Joie du sang des étoiles', and the tenth, 'Final', are linked to form the third group. Both have the character of a scherzo and both conclude the respective halves of the symphony. The last movement is also related to the first group as it makes use of the 'love theme' and, like the second, sixth and eighth movements, makes use of the key of F sharp major.

The first movement, 'Introduction', stands on its own. It consists of two sections linked by a piano cadenza. The first section is devoted mainly to the statement of the first two cyclic themes along with other subsidiary material. The second section is one of the most complex examples of the superimposition of rhythmic patterns in Messiaen's music and, as such, is worth examining in detail. With its constantly repetitive motivic ideas and expanding and contracting rhythmic cells, it is strongly reminiscent of the 'Danse sacrale' from Stravinsky's *Le Sacre du Printemps*.

Four rhythmic pedals are superimposed on these varying rhythmic cells, two of which are Sharngadeva rhythms. 'Lackskmîça' (four durations) is combined with a chord-sequence in mode 6 (fourteen chords) in the wood-wind, and 'râgavardhana' (six durations) is combined with a chord-sequence in mode 4 (thirteen chords) in the strings. The two remaining rhythmic pedals are given to the cymbal and side-drum. The cymbal rhythm (which will be referred to as 'Tâla 4') consists of a chromatic sequence of values, alternately contracting and expanding in duration from seventeen semiquavers in length to seven. The side-drum rhythm ('Tâla 5') is a complex non-retrogradable tâla in which the values seven and seventeen again play a major part. The first cell is seventeen semiquavers in length and breaks down into three over-lapping sub-cells of seven semiquavers each:

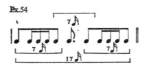

Each repetition of the complete tâla consists of this cell and three augmentations of it formed by the addition of values to the beginning and end, the last cell also having a value added in the centre. The symmetrical addition of these values gives rise to a sequence of larger, overlapping, non-retrogradable cells, spanning two statements of the tâla:

This technique of 'amplification at the extremes' or 'amplification at the centre' is Messiaen's usual method of developing non-retrogradable rhythms so that they retain their essential character; but it is the alternate addition of the four- and five-semiquaver durations to the extremes of each cell which creates the interesting counterpoint of non-retrogradable functions in this case. The immense rhythmic complexity of *Turangalîla* as a whole becomes compressed, not only into this section as a whole but also into the side-drum tâla. The total impression is one of relentless power, brought about by the inner complexity of rhythmic superimpositions and the effect is that of a ritual incantation, preparing for the play of life and death which is to follow.

'Chant d'amour I' begins with a tâla superimposed on its augmentations. The tâla is formed by the addition of values of two, three and one units in rotation, and its two augmentations are formed by the progressive addition of an arithmetical series of values to each duration in order:

	(+2)	(+3)	(+1)	(+2)	(+3)	(+1)	(+2)	
Tâla:	3 – 5 – 8 – 9 – 11 – 14 – 15 – 17							(Upper strings)
First augmentation:	4 – 7 – 11 – 13 – 16 – 20 – 22							(Upper woodwind)
Second augmentation:	5 – 9 – 14 – 17 – 21 – 26							(Lower instruments of all sections)
Values of augmentation:	1 – 2 – 3 – 4 – 5 – 6 – 7							

(values in semiquavers)

The values seventeen and seven once again play an important role, the first in defining the maximum limit of the tâla and the second in defining the maximum value of augmentation.

The form of the movement is the couplet-refrain form which was to become increasingly important in Messiaen's music. Both the refrain (figs. 4, 13 and 28) and the two couplets (figs. 9 and 18) are divided into two contrasting sections. Referring to the refrain, Messiaen says: 'It alternates two elements totally contrasted in tempo, nuance and feeling. The first element is a quick motive, strong and passionate, played by the trumpets. The second element is slow, soft and tender, played by the Ondes Martenot and strings.' [7]

The next movement in the first group, 'Chant d'amour II', is described by Messiaen as being a Scherzo with two trios.[7] It differs considerably from the classical scherzo, since the two trios follow on from one another and are then superimposed on each other. Altogether there are nine sections: (1) 'scherzo' theme, (2) bridge passage, (3) first trio, (4) second trio, (5) superimposition of the two trios (with interjections from the 'scherzo' theme), (6) bridge passage (repetition), (7) superimposition of the two trios, the 'scherzo' theme and ultimately the 'statue theme' in its original form, (8) cadenza for piano, (9) coda. The first trio takes the form of refrain and couplets, whereas the second trio is one continuous theme at its first appearance. In the fifth section, however, the second trio is broken up to be superimposed on the couplet sections of the first trio, while the 'scherzo' theme is broken up and superimposed on each of the refrains except the first. The seventh section builds up to considerable complexity, since all the subsidiary material which was originally superimposed on the 'scherzo' and trio themes also appears here. The 'scherzo' theme presents the chromatic Tâla 4 from the first movement, on cymbal and vibraphone [8] and Tâla 1 (see ex. 31) on the wood-block superimposed on it. From the twelfth bar a decorative passage on the piano and a chromatic figure on two double basses are added to make a five-part texture.

The two trios have nothing superimposed on them initially, but in section (5) birdsong in free rhythm is added on the piano together with the same melody on the vibraphone, broken up into short phrases in even semiquavers.

In the seventh section the five-part texture of the scherzo appears first, together with the birdsong from the fifth section in continuous, even semi-quavers, on celesta and glockenspiel. Tâla 5 from the first movement is used in the bridge passage (second and sixth sections) and is continued into the seventh section to make a total of seven parts at the beginning of the section. The two trio themes enter in the fifth bar (the first without its refrains) and the original version of the 'statue theme' in the sixteenth bar of the section, bringing the total of independent parts up to ten. The enormous accumulation of tension which gathers during this section is cleared by the piano cadenza, and the return of the 'flower theme' and the 'statue theme' in the coda marks the end of a phase in the work. In order to clarify the great complexity of this movement, its form is represented by the diagram on page 89.

The main thematic material of the 'Chants d'amour'—that is, the refrain of 'Chant d'amour I' and the scherzo theme of 'Chant d'amour II'—have varied affinities with the 'statue' and 'flower' themes. The two halves of the refrain from 'Chant d'amour I' are each related to one of the two cyclic themes; the first half, 'strong and passionate', is related to the masculine 'statue theme' and the second half, 'soft and tender', to the feminine 'flower theme'.

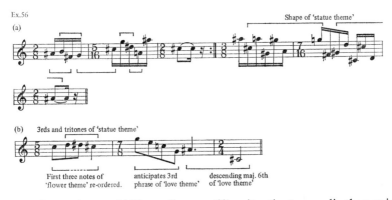

Ex.56

(a)   Shape of 'statue theme'

(b)   3rds and tritones of 'statue theme'

First three notes of   anticipates 3rd   descending maj. 6th
'flower theme' re-ordered.   phrase of 'love theme' of 'love theme'

The scherzo theme of 'Chant d'amour II' unites the two cyclic themes into the same melodic line, although they still remain distinct. The intervallic resemblance is also much closer than in 'Chant d'amour I'.

First four notes of 'love theme'

Ex.57

Notes of 'flower theme'   'statue theme'   'statue theme'

(N.B. The third group is the retrograde of the first four notes of the 'love theme').

The 'love theme' of the sixth movement evolves from these two themes as well as from the 'statue' and 'flower' themes; the first four notes are a re-arrangement of the four notes of the 'flower theme', although the upward ascent followed by a chromatic descent suggests the shape of the 'statue theme' with the third note displaced through an octave. There is also more than a passing resemblance of the opening of this theme, as it occurs here, to the opening of Wagner's *Tristan und Isolde*. Only the first interval is different (a major sixth instead of a minor sixth) and, of course, the harmonies.

Before discussing the sixth movement in detail, it will be necessary to look at the fifth, 'Joie du sang des étoiles', as it has strong affinities with the movements of the first group (the 'Chant d'amour' series). It follows the usual ternary form of a scherzo; the opening theme has two phrases, the first being a transformation of the 'statue theme' and the second being derived from the 'love theme'.

Messiaen makes a particular point of the rhythmic complexity of the middle section of this movement.[7] It is not the most complex in the symphony, but it is possibly the most typical as it consists of the statue theme treated in 'personnages rythmiques'. It appears first in the trombones and horns, divided into three rhythmic cells. The first two (of three notes each) augment and diminish respectively while the third remains unchanged. The complexity increases later in the section when this rhythmic pattern is transferred to the trumpets and cornet, while the trombones and horns have a retrograde form superimposed upon it. The rhythmic complexity and the turmoil of this section inject into the main theme, when it returns, a new force and a more ecstatic intensity. As in 'Chant d'amour II', there is a piano cadenza towards the end of the movement. Whereas the cadenza in the fourth movement had the effect of dissipating the tension accumulated in the climax which preceded it, that of 'Joie du sang des étoiles' heightens the excitement of what has gone before. It is as if the whole power of the orchestra had become invested in the solo piano, preparatory to the final triumphant return of the original 'statue theme' in the last nineteen bars. 'In order to understand the extravagance of this piece,' says Messiaen, 'it must be understood that the union of true lovers is for them a transformation, and a transformation on a cosmic scale.'[7]

The sixth movement, 'Jardin du sommeil d'amour', is totally contrasted to the ecstatic outburst of the fifth. Messiaen's description of the movement has itself a touch of surrealism: 'The two lovers are immersed in the sleep of love. A landscape has emanated from them. The garden which surrounds them is called "Tristan"; the garden which surrounds them is called "Isolde". This garden is full of light and shade, of plants and new flowers, of brightly coloured and melodious birds. "All the birds of the stars . . ." says Harawi.'[9]

Schematic diagram of 4—'Chant d'amour II'

(1) Scherzo theme _____

Tâla 4 (cym. & vib.) _____

. . . . . (b.5) Tâla 1 (block) _____

. . . . (b.12) Decorative figures (piano) _____

. . . . (b.12) Chromatic figure (double basses) _____

(2) Bridge passage _____   (3) Trio I: refrain and couplets ____   (4) Trio II

Tâla 5 (side-drum) _____

(5) Trio I: refrain – couplet – refrain – couplet – refrain – couplet – refrain ____

        Trio II ____   _____   _____

          Scherzo ____   _____   _____

          Tâla 1 ____   _____   _____

     Birdsong _____

(6) Bridge passage _____   (7) Scherzo _____

Tâla 4 (cym.) _____

Tâla 5 (side-drum) _____

               Tâla 1 (block) _____

               Decorative figures (piano) _____

               Chromatic figures (double basses) _____

               Birdsong (even semiquavers: cel. & glock) _____

               . . . . (b.5) Trio I (couplets only) _____

               . . . . (b.5) Trio II _____

               . . . . (b.16) 'statue theme'

(8) Piano cadenza _____   (9) Coda: 'flower theme', 'statue theme' refrain (Trio I) _____

Time flows on, forgotten, the lovers are outside time, let us not wake them. . . .'[7] Here we see the essential relationship between surrealistic symbols and the subconscious. The garden is Tristan, is Isolde, in the sense that it is their shared experience of love. It is not two gardens, but one, symbolizing their unity. The main theme of the movement, the 'love theme', is in ternary form and represents the lovers. As the garden emanates from the lovers, in Messiaen's description, so subsidiary themes on the flute and clarinet emanate from the main theme at the cadences. These gradually begin to overlap into the following phrases of the 'love theme' until, by the middle section, they follow an independent course. The first two of these subsidiary themes reflect aspects of the 'flower' and 'statue' themes, the first by its shape and the second by its dependence on thirds, related through a tritone or perfect fourth. They are also important because of their reappearance in later works (see Chapter 10, pp. 101–2).

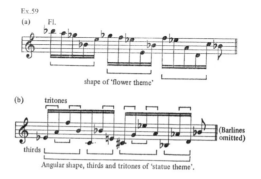

The birdsong on the piano, based on the songs of the nightingale, blackbird and garden warbler, is independent of the main theme, although its opening phrases reappear with the return of the first phrases of the main theme in the final section (fig. 7 in the score).

Beginning at the middle section of the movement (fig. 4), there are two tâlas in the percussion. One consists of two chromatic series of durations, one increasing from seven to thirty-seven semiquavers in duration (on low temple-block and cymbal) and the other decreasing from forty-eight to thirty-three, both by steps of one semiquaver (the last value is not counted in each case as it is cut short just before the end of the movement). According to Messiaen, the increasing values symbolize the flow of time into the future and the decreasing values convert the future into the past. 'Like Ligeia of Edgar Allan Poe, who overcame death—the heroine is something of a magician: "Her eyes travel . . . into the past . . . into the future. . . ."'[7] The two parts together represent the flow of time.

The other tâla, on celesta and glockenspiel, has a feature which is unusual in Messiaen's music, although it is an important device in the post-war generation of serialists. This is the substitution of silences (rests) for sounds in a rhythmic tâla. The left hand of the celesta part defines a non-retrogradable cell with some sounds replaced by silences and silences by sounds in the second half of the cell.

Ex.60

Barlines omitted

This is repeated with the values augmented to three times their length, repeated in its original form, and rounded off by a concluding motive on the glockenspiel.[10]

A further motive on the vibraphone forms a link between the essentially melodic and the purely rhythmic ideas of the movement. It occurs only in the first and last sections of the movement, taking the form of a melody in a non-retrogradable rhythm which, in the first section, is always forty-nine semi-quavers in length. Each statement is followed by a silence of equal duration so that it divides this part of the movement into equal durations of sound and silence. In the last section it undergoes symmetrical expansions and contractions (always remaining non-retrogradable); each repetition of the motive begins exactly ninety-eight semiquavers after the beginning of the previous one, so that the ensuing silences are contracted or expanded to balance the expansions or contractions of the motive.

Ex.61

Non-retrogradable 8   4   2 3   4   7   4   3 2 4   8 Barlines
rhythm: omitted

The remaining movement of the first group, VIII—'Développement de l'amour', is both a musical and symbolic development for the whole work. 'The love potion has united them for ever. But their passion increasing steadily into infinity is not the only significance of the title. It also refers to the musical development. In a work of ten movements, partial developments were insufficient. What was needed was a piece that *was* development.' All the cyclic themes are used, but the 'love theme' is the principal one to be developed. The main body of the movement is interrupted three times by increasingly longer and more ecstatic portions of the love-theme. These 'explosions of the love-theme', as Messiaen calls them, 'symbolize Tristan and Isolde transcended by Tristan-Isolde, and the climax of the whole symphony'.

The movements of the second group, or 'Turangalîla' series, are similar in character and are united musically by the use of important independent rhythmic structures assigned primarily to the non-pitched percussion. The third movement, 'Turangalîla I', and the ninth, 'Turangalîla III', both begin with themes which are similar in character and melodic shape. Both of these themes, as well as the main theme of the seventh movement (beginning at fig. 7), make use of *Klangfarbenmelodie*, dividing the notes or groups of notes between different instruments.

The form of 'Turangalîla I' is episodic. The first theme alternating between clarinet and Ondes Martenot is followed by a powerful contrasting theme in bassoon, trombones and double basses. The first theme returns on the strings with additional material superimposed on it and is followed by a third theme on the oboe. The complex rhythm of this oboe theme is very important as it not only supplies, in its retrograde form, the rhythm of the counter-melody in oboe and clarinet, but also forms part of a longer tâla ('Tâla 3', ex. 64), other parts of which are used in the first and last movements of *Cinq Rechants* and in *Cantéyodjaya* (p. 15, bar 13). The last main section of the movement superimposes the first theme on the second and is followed by a coda which resumes fragments of the third theme. The independent rhythmic structure, referred to above, takes the form of 'personnages rythmiques' extending throughout the fourth and fifth sections of the movement (the third theme and superimposition of the first and second themes). These 'personnages' are played on the bass-drum (values increasing from one to eight semiquavers, then decreasing), maracas (values decreasing from eight to one semiquavers, then increasing) and wood-block (non-retrogradable rhythm of five semiquavers, remaining unchanged). A fragment of this rhythm is resumed in the coda.

'Turangalîla II' is a less developed movement, musically, but forms an explosive contrast to the preceding movement, 'Jardin du sommeil d'amour'. Whereas the sixth movement is most intensely concerned with love, this movement expresses pain and death. From figure 7 in the score there is 'a terrifying rhythm, using the "chord theme" and the metal percussion instruments, giving a double sensation of enlargement and contraction, of height and depth, each rhythmic group ending in a tremendous stroke of the tam-tam. This recalls the double horror of the knife-shaped pendulum gradually approaching the heart of the prisoner, while the wall of red-hot iron closes in, as well as the unnameable, unfathomable depths of the torture pit in Edgar Allan Poe's celebrated story *The Pit and the Pendulum*'.[11] Like 'Turangalîla I', this movement is episodic. It begins with a piano cadenza, then follows the main theme in *Klangfarbenmelodie* (mentioned above). After two juxtaposed episodes (the first for percussion alone), this passage returns in retrograde form, leading straight into the third, or 'pit-and-pendulum' episode. A fragmentary passage, which includes a portion of the original 'statue theme', leads to the final statement of the main theme. Against the main theme there is a converging passage in the Ondes Martenot and trombones which Messiaen compares to the closing of a fan. When this passage occurs in retrograde form the fan opens. Here is the play of life and death, as signified by the word *lîla* and expressed in the words of the couplet in the second movement of *Cinq Rechants*:

'ma première fois terre terre l'éventail déployé
ma dernière fois terre terre l'éventail refermé . . .'

The independent rhythmic structure of this movement occurs first in the passage for percussion alone as the first episode and is finally superimposed on the last statement of the main theme. The values 1 to 16 semiquavers are distributed over three rhythms of different lengths and superimposed upon each other and upon their retrograde forms in the following way:

A	Triangle:	15	13	3	4	/15	13 ... etc.				
B	Wood-block:	12	14	1	2	7	8	16	/12	14 ... etc.	
C	Turkish cymbal:	5	6	9	11	10	/ 5	6 ... etc.			
A (retrograde) Maracas:		4	3	13	15	/ 4 ...					
B (retrograde) Chinese cymbal:	16	8	7	2	1	14	12	/16 ...			
C (retrograde) Bass-drum:	10	11	9	6	5	/10 ...					

'Turangalîla III' consists of variations on the opening theme. The variations appear simultaneously rather than consecutively; after two statements of the theme, three variations start simultaneously at figure 6 on the Ondes Martenot, piano and 'gamelan' (celesta, glockenspiel and vibraphone) and a fourth is added to the texture at figure 10 on the woodwind. In spite of Messiaen's interest in Eastern music, the resulting heterophonic texture is unusual for him. Between the first two statements of the theme, the independent rhythmic structure begins at figure 5 and continues throughout the rest of the movement. The arrangement is similar to that of 'Turangalîla II', but in this case the values 1 to 17 semiquavers are distributed throughout three different rhythms which are allotted to five different percussion instruments as follows:

Wood-block:	4	5	7	3	2	1	6	17	14 /	8	9	10	16	12	15
Tam-tam:	8	9	10	16	12	15 /	4	5	7	3	2	1	6	17	14
Cymbal:	(7)	11	13	11	13	11	13	(11)	14	17	6	1	2	3	7	5	4
Tambour:	(11)	14	17	6	1	2	3	7	5	4	(7)	11	13	11	13	11	13
Maracas:	(1)	15	12	16	10	9	8	(1)	15	12	16	10	9	8

(The values in brackets are rests)

After the second statement of the theme, the tâlas are 'coloured' by the addition of harmonies in the strings, following the same rhythmic pattern (thus anticipating a device to be used in *Chronochromie* twelve years later— see Chapter 13). At each repetition of the tâla each duration is preceded by an extra semiquaver value (one at the first repetition, two at the second). At the third repetition each duration is preceded by a shake or trill of five semiquavers' duration after which the tâlas stop and each instrument plays a continuous shake or trill until the end of the movement. There is no coda to this movement; the music ceases abruptly when the variations have worked themselves out.

The last movement, 'Final', is in sonata form. Although there is a tendency to be over-repetitious, the form is applied rather more successfully here than in 'Reflet dans le vent' from the *Préludes*. The only obvious reference to a cyclic theme in this movement is the use of the 'love-theme' as the second subject, transformed into the scherzo rhythm of the movement. The music, on the whole, carries with it a greater feeling of drive and momentum than the last prelude; and the first subject, when it returns in the recapitulation, is heightened by the addition of harmonic resonances in the strings, woodwind and piano leading up to a brief recalling of the falling fourths of the 'love-theme' at the end of each phrase. This accumulation of excitement carries through the recapitulation to the triumphant return of the 'love-theme' (as it appeared in the sixth movement) in the coda.

Because of the wealth of ideas and procedures in the *Turangalîla-Symphonie*, any analysis of it must necessarily be somewhat diffuse. The most important musical features to emerge from it are the various 'Turangalîla' motives which are to be considered in Chapter 10 (pp. 101–2), the consolidation of superimposed rhythmic structures (such as in the second section of the first movement) and the use of chromatic rhythmic series (i.e. rhythms where each value increases or decreases progressively by step). Chromatic rhythms were already a feature of *Vingt Regards* so that they are not in themselves new, but the method of distributing a chromatic series of values over a number of superimposed tâlas in 'Turangalîla II' and 'Turangalîla III' is an important anticipation of procedures found in later works. This is especially true of the first episode of 'Turangalîla II', where each of the values from one to sixteen semiquavers is found once only in the three basic tâlas on triangle, wood-block and Turkish cymbal. This, in fact, is Messiaen's first use of a rhythmic series.

With its complex superimposition of rhythmic, melodic and harmonic structures, *Turangalîla* was the logical outcome of Messiaen's development from 1935 onwards. Having reached this point of maximum complexity, further development in this direction became impossible; it is significant, therefore, that the works of the next few years are simpler in structure and contain new researches into the question of rhythm and duration.

Cinq Rechants

The last part of the Tristan trilogy, *Cinq Rechants*, was completed in December 1948. It is scored for three sopranos, three contraltos, three tenors and three basses. The work is not conceived as being for unaccompanied choir in the true sense, as all the voices are treated as soloists. Variety of weight and timbre is obtained by grouping the voices into the normal four parts, or dividing them into twelve solo parts, as well as varying the number that may be called upon to sing a single line. Messiaen also obtains a large variety of timbre by means of an invented language recalling the sounds of Quechua and Sanskrit. The words of this 'language' do not have an onomatopoeic function as in *Harawi*, but are chosen 'for the gentleness or violence of their attack; for their aptitude in giving prominence to the musical rhythms. They permit the smooth blending of the four elements: phonetic (timbres), dynamic (intensities), kinetic (accents), and quantitative (values)'.[12] It is as if Messiaen were orchestrating his voices by drawing systematically on the various qualities of vowel sounds and consonants for particular sections of the piece.

The term 'rechant' is derived from the *Airs* of Claude le Jeune, and it is used in homage of this composer's work *Printemps*, for which Messiaen has a great admiration.[13] In both *Cinq Rechants* and *Printemps*, 'rechants' are contrasted with 'chants' (or 'couplets' as Messiaen terms them), but Messiaen's treatment of his 'rechants' and 'couplets' differs in some detail from the 'rechants' and 'chants' of Claude le Jeune. In both composers the 'rechants' have the same text throughout each piece and basically the same music. The 'chants' of Claude le Jeune, however, have the same music but a different text for each repetition, whereas Messiaen's 'couplets' use the same text but the music is varied by the addition of new material, or by rhythmic expansions. In addition, Claude le Jeune uses only rhythms derived from the metres of Greek poetry, while Messiaen uses both Greek and Sharngadeva rhythms, as well as related ones of his own.

The exact layout of 'couplets' and 'rechants' is different in each movement of *Cinq Rechants*. Some movements have introductions, others not; some start with a 'couplet' after the Introduction if there is one, and others with the 'rechant'. The first four movements alternate 'couplets' and 'rechants', but the last has two versions of the 'rechant' in the middle with a 'couplet' on each side of it in an arch form.

A great deal of the material of *Cinq rechants* is derived from the subsidiary themes of *Turangalîla* and some from *Harawi* (see Table I, p. 99). According to Messiaen, the melodic style and spirit of the work issue from two sources: the 'Harawi' or 'Yaraví' of Peru and Ecuador, and the 'Alba' or medieval dawn-song of Western Europe. This takes the form of a warning to lovers that dawn is approaching and that the night of love is drawing to a close. He mentions the love songs of the troubadours Joufré Rudel and Folquet of Marseilles as examples, but most closely relevant to *Cinq Rechants* is Brangäne's warning from the tower to Tristan and Isolde in Act II of Wagner's music-drama. The second line of the text of the first movement refers to this warning, following a reference in the first line to the paintings by Marc Chagall in which 'the lovers surpass themselves and are carried away into the clouds': [12]

> 'les amoureux s'envolent
> Brangien dans l'espace tu souffle'

('the lovers fly away, Brangäne you breathe in space').

Here is the whole of the love-duet of *Tristan und Isolde* summed up in two lines: the lovers are only concerned for each other and are heedless of Brangäne's warning of the approaching dawn. Besides *Tristan und Isolde*, the first movement recalls several other love myths: Orpheus and Euridice—'l'explorateur Orphée trouve son cœur dans la mort' ('the explorer Orpheus finds death in his heart'), the crystal ball in which Hieronymus Bosch encloses his lovers —'bulle de cristal d'étoile' ('crystal ball of the star') and Bluebeard—'Barbebleue, château de la septième porte' ('Bluebeard, the castle of the seventh door').

The beginning of the second movement recalls the play of life and death:

> 'ma première fois terre terre l'éventail déployé
> ma dernière fois terre terre l'éventail refermé'

('my first time, earth, earth, the open fan
my last time, earth, earth, the closed fan')

The words are juxtaposed, not by the rules of syntax, but because of their sound in relation to the music; at the same time they evoke the various symbols associated with life and death. 'Ma première fois'—birth, 'ma dernière fois'—death, in association with 'terre'—the symbol of the physical as distinct from 'étoile', the symbol of the spiritual. Birth is also like the opening of a fan, and death is like its closing.

The third movement evokes the first fulfilment of love and the union of the lovers:

> 'ma robe d'amour mon amour
> ma prison d'amour'   (Introduction)

('my robe of love, my love, my prison of love')

> 'robe tendre
> toute la beauté paysage neuf'   (end of couplet)

('fond robe, all the beauty (of a) new landscape')

The 'new landscape' is that which has emanated from the lovers (Messiaen's note on 'Jardin du sommeil d'amour')—the garden of the sleep of love. The coda brings in a reference to the legendary love-potions and a version of the 'love theme' (ex. 62), and the ecstatic, wordless melisma in the solo soprano part which concludes the movement is the first subsidiary theme in the flute, starting in bar 3 of 'Jardin du sommeil d'amour' (ex. 59 (a)):

Most of the text of the fourth movement is artificial or incantatory. Fragments of French occur in the 'rechant':

> '. . . mon bouquet tout défait rayonne
> . . . les volets roses
> . . . amour amour du clair au sombre . . .'

('. . . my bouquet all disarranged radiates light . . . the pink shutters . . . love, love from the light to the dark . . .')

After the first experience of love, it endures ('du clair au sombre'), is renewed and rediscovered ('mon bouquet tout défait rayonne').

The last movement refers once again to the mythology of love and more particularly to its magical aspects. The 'Introduction' and 'Coda' recall that 'the heroine is something of a magician': [7]

'tes yeux voyagent dans le passé' (Introduction)
'. . . . . dans l'avenir' (Coda)
('your eyes travel into the past . . . into the future')

Messiaen emphasizes his use of Sharngadeva rhythms in *Cinq Rechants* as distinct from Claude le Jeune's use of Greek rhythms in his *Printemps*.[14] There are many isolated examples of these (see Table I). Sometimes they are decorated and sometimes superimposed on each other. The first 'couplet' of the first movement uses two Sharngadeva rhythms—'miçra varna' (26/2) and 'simhavikrama' (8)—both decorated, and the second 'couplet' superimposes 'laya' (106) and part of Tâla 3 (previously used in 'Turangalîla I'— see p. 92). The following example shows the treatment of the Sharngadeva rhythm in the soprano part:

Ex.63

Tâla 3 is an interestingly complicated rhythm, unusual in character for Messiaen, but still typical in its own way, particularly in its juxtaposition of very short and long values. It never occurs complete in any one context, but parts are used in 'Turangalîla I', the first and last movements of *Cinq Rechants* and in *Cantéyodjayâ* (pp. 15–16). Example 64 overleaf quotes it in full, while showing which portions are proper to particular contexts.

Some use is made of Greek metres in *Cinq Rechants*, besides the Sharngadeva rhythms quoted above. The one which opens the work (Aristophanian) is significant for its non-retrogradable outline—a characteristic of a number of other rhythmic patterns in the work.

The Tristan trilogy closes a period in Messiaen's development: a period of

Cantéyodjayâ (starting on p.15, b.8. L.H.)

Cinq Rechants V (Coda and part in the Introduction)   (C.R. V)   *Cinq Rechants* I (2nd Couplet)

(*Cantéyodjayâ*)

(C.R. I)

Turangalîla, 3rd movement (fig.6)

Turangalîla

(Rests or groups of demisemiquavers are substituted for certain values in different contexts.)

rhythmic development and consolidation of procedures. Although a change of direction became necessary after the complexity of *Turangalîla*, and although many of the ensuing works are less dependent on symbolism, Messiaen's musical thought remains basically unchanged, depending on collage structures of varying degrees of complexity. Rhythmic manipulation rather than superimposition becomes the important feature of the next few years, as is shown in the next chapter.

TABLE I

Thematic derivations and Sharngadeva rhythms in *Cinq Rechants*

Movement	Location of themes	Rhythms
I Introduction and Coda	————	————
Rechant (1–8) *	*T*.III (6) † (Ob.)	————
(10–12)	*Harawi* I (bars 5–6)	
(13–16)	*T*.VI (7)+2 (Fl./Cl.)	
Couplet (Contralto)	*T*.III (7) (Pno., Cel.)	Cp. 1 & 2 Sop.: 26/2 miçra varna
		Con.: 8 simhavikrama
		Cp. 2 Ten.: Tâla 3 ‡
		Bass: 106 laya
II Couplet	————	93 râgavardhana ⎫
		105 candrakalâ ⎬ Tâla 1
		88 lackskmîça ⎭
Rechant	*T*.II (5) and (7)	————
III Introduction	————	————
Couplet (11–13)	*T*.II (10)+6 (Fl., Bsn.)	————
Rechant (1–4)	*T*.VI (4)	33 turangalîla (retr.)
(5–9)	*T*.V (4)	
Coda (1–4)	'love-theme'	————
(7–10)	*T*.VI (Fl., from 3rd bar)	
IV Rechant	————	93 râgavardhana (retr.)
Couplet (4–5, Tenors)	*T*.VI (5) (Glock.)	————
Coda	*T*.II (9)+4 and (10)+4	————
	(Fl., Bsn.)	
V Introduction (1–4)	*T*.VI (5) (Glock.)	
(7–9)	*T*.III (7)+3 (Pno., Cel.)	
(10–12)		Tâla 3
Couplet (1–11)	*T*.III (6) (Pno., Cel.)	8 simhavikrama
(16–19)	*T*.II (12)+4 (Fl., Bsn.)	
Rechant	————	77 gajajhampa, 8 simhavikrama,
		105 candrakalâ, 93 râgavardhana

Notes:

* Bar numbers are given for the first appearance of each theme or rhythm only.

† The themes are located in *Turangalîla* as follows: *T*.VI (7)+2 + *Turangalîla*, sixth movement, starting two bars after figure 7.

‡ Although Tâla 3 is not a Sharngadeva rhythm, it is included because of its importance as a '*Turangalîla* rhythmic-motive'.

Notes on Chapter 9

1. Messiaen's sleeve note to the recording of *Turangalîla* (RCA SB 6761–2).

2. *ROM* p. 154.

3. *ROM* p. 149.

4. Rostand—*Olivier Messiaen*, Chapter 6.

5. *Ibid.*

6. *ROM* pp. 155–6. The original picture was painted by Sir Roland Penrose in 1938 and given to Max Ernst, who kept it in his house in France. It disappeared during the war, believed to have been destroyed by enemy action. The title of the picture was *Seeing is believing*, and the outstretched hands on the canvas were intended by the artist to represent a person looking at the picture, and to symbolize his involvement in it. This was a typically surrealistic touch, symbolizing that the subconscious world of the painting was to overflow into and become fully integrated with the world of experience; there was to be no sharp division between the physical world and the world of the painting. (Information supplied by the artist.) Messiaen himself never saw the original painting, but only a reproduction in the Swiss magazine *Forme et Couleur*.

7. From Messiaen's note for the recording of *Turangalîla*.

8. The ties in the second bar on p. 112 in the score, between the crotchet and minim, are apparently a misprint, as the vibraphone follows the rhythm of the cymbal exactly otherwise.

9. Quotation from 'Amour, oiseau d'étoile' from the song-cycle *Harawi*.

10. This is one of the 'Turangalîla' motives (see Chapter 10, pp. 101–2) and it occurs again as the initial theme in the fifth movement of *Cinq Rechants* as well as forming part of the refrain theme from the first section of *Cantéyodjayâ*.

11. In this extract from his note on the work, Messiaen compresses the events of the story somewhat.

12. Messiaen's note on the work for the Philips recording (ABL 3400).

13. *EOM* p. 147, *ROM* p. 176.

14. *ROM* p. 177.

10
The Experimental Period 1949=1951

A number of shorter works followed the composition of the 'Tristan trilogy' during the next three years. Three of these—*Cantéyodjayâ* for piano (1949), *Messe de la Pentecôte* for organ (1950) and *Le Merle noir* for flute and piano (1951)—have an affinity with the trilogy insofar as they make use of melodic and rhythmic material derived from it. The other two works—'Etudes de rythme' for piano (1949) and *Livre d'Orgue* (1951)—are particularly concerned with experiments in new rhythmic and modal procedures, experiments which also form part of the material of *Cantéyodjayâ* and *Messe de la Pentecôte*. A number of themes which form part of the trilogy, and especially many of the subsidiary themes from the *Turangalîla-Symphonie*, appear in subsequent works. These 'Turangalîla' motives are used to symbolize love in some contexts at least. In the fourth movement (entitled 'Communion') of *Messe de la Pentecôte*, for instance, there occurs the version of the 'love theme' which is to be found in the coda of the third movement of *Cinq Rechants* (ex. 62). Communion is, for the Christian, the consummation of divine love through the Eucharist, so, once again, the 'love theme' is employed to symbolize both human and divine love.

'Turangalîla' motives can also be found in *Catalogue d'Oiseaux*. Here the context is the operation of divine love in nature, or divine action on the cosmos through the evolution of life. In 'Rousserolle Effarvatte', some of the motives which reflect the undulating shape of the 'flower theme' from *Turangalîla* are associated with actual flowers in the score: 'yellow irises' (page 15, last line, and page 18, second line), 'purple foxgloves' (page 19, last line, and page 21, last line) and 'water-lilies' (page 25, fourth line).

Possibly the most important aspect of the Tristan trilogy from the purely musical point of view is the complex network of musical ideas which appear in two or more of the pieces of the trilogy and in later works. A rhythm may appear as a simple tâla on a percussion instrument, or be applied to melodies or harmonic sequences in other contexts. Similarly, a melody may appear in different transformations of rhythm, intensity or timbre, as well as being used on its own as a monody or with harmonic colouring, or appearing in combination with other material.

Ex.65

(a) *Turangalîla*, 2nd movement (fig.7)
Un peu lent, tendre.
col 8 . . .

strings p, Onde Mt. f
Harmony: sustained F♯ major chord.

(b) *Cinq Rechants* II (Rechant)
Vif, gai
ff
col 8 . . .
(No harmony)

(c) *Cantéyodjayâ* (p.16, b. 4–5)
(Presque vif)
mf
(Contrapuntal treatment)

(d) *Le Merle noir* (p.2)
mf
p

The underlying conception is one which treats rhythm and melody at least on an equal footing, the one setting the other off in different guises, with tempo, intensity, harmony and timbre assisting in this process of transformation.

Cantéyodjayâ (1949)

A notable feature of the *Turangalîla-Symphonie* is the wealth and variety of its musical material. In spite of the systematic repetition and transformation of its principal material, Messiaen's characteristic methods of working create a type of structure which depends on the principle of the *collage* rather than traditional symphonic methods.

Turangalîla still has its traditional elements in the use of cyclic times, but *Cantéyodjayâ*, with its more concise framework, displays the collage-structure developed to its ultimate extreme. In contrast to the economy of *Cinq Rechants*, where a minimum of material is used in each movement with much repetition and transformation, *Cantéyodjayâ* goes in the opposite direction of using a large variety of material, only about a quarter of which is repeated or transformed. It recalls the collage form of Debussy's *Jeux*, where contrasted and related ideas follow on from one another like a chain of different coloured beads. In spite of the fact that *Cantéyodjayâ* contradicts all traditional Western principles of composition in its wealth and non-development of material, it lacks neither continuity, shape nor climax. These partly arise from the common family relationship of much of its material with the cyclic themes of *Turangalîla*, but the general arrangement of musical ideas into the collage-structure is also governed by mood, tempo and dynamic so that the overall work has a clearly defined sense of shape. According to Messiaen the names printed in the score (including the term *Cantéyodjayâ*), other than those which refer to Sharngadeva's rhythms, are connected with Karnatic rhythmic theory, but this is comparatively unimportant for the work as a whole.

The form of the piece falls into three distinct sections, the first two being based on different types of refrain-and-couplet form and the third forming a coda to the whole piece. The first section begins with a refrain which is broken up and alternated with five different episodes. The second section is the longest and the most diffuse. It begins with three different refrains and is followed by three couplets, each longer than the previous one and each rounded off by one of the three refrains in turn. None of these couplets is related thematically, but each rises to a climactic point with material which is related in texture (homophonic), intensity (predominantly *ff* or *fff*) and type of rhythm (Sharngadeva rhythm becoming non-retrogradable in the third couplet).

Ex.66

In the first two couplets the climax is dissolved by a passage in chromatic rhythm leading to their respective refrains. The third couplet, on the other hand, is intensified towards the climax of the whole piece, with the interpolation of the first refrain of the second section and the fourth couplet of the first section before the reappearance of its own proper refrain.

Because of its thematic dependence on the Tristan trilogy, *Cantéyodjayâ* is largely a transitional work, but there is one new element in it which relates it decisively to the works of the experimental period. In the last couplet of the first section Messiaen uses a *mode de durées, de hauteurs et d'intensités* ('mode of durations, of pitches and of intensities'). Three groups of eight different notes are chosen, each being assigned a fixed register, duration, and intensity. These are then used freely as the basis of a three-part texture, one group being assigned to each part in which the characteristics of each note, as fixed by the mode, remain unchanged. The principle was to be extended further in *Mode de valeurs et d'intensités* (the second 'Étude de rythme'), in connection with which the implications of this mode will be discussed more fully.

'Etudes de rythme' (1949–50): (1) Neumes rythmiques

The four pieces which are collectively known as 'Études de rythme' do not form a 'cycle' in the same way as *Vingt Regards* or *Visions de l'Amen*. The first two pieces—*Neumes rythmiques* and *Mode de valeurs et d'intensités*—were written in 1949 and are quite separate from each other and from the two which followed in 1950: *Île de Feu I* and *Île de Feu II*.

In *Neumes rythmiques*, two distinct refrains alternate with lengthy strophes devoted to the 'rhythmic neums'. The first set of refrains is marked 'rythme en ligne triple: 1 à 5, 6 à 10, 11 à 15': three durations, short, medium and long, are expanded progressively by the addition of a semiquaver unit at each repetition of the refrain.

The second set of refrains is marked 'Nombre premier en rythme non rétrogradable' ('Prime number in non-retrogradable rhythm'). Here we see not only Messiaen's attraction for non-retrogradable rhythms but also for durations consisting of a prime number of units. These refrains also expand through a series of successive prime numbers: 41, 43, 47 and 53 semiquavers in duration and alternate with the first set of refrains.

The strophes which come between the refrains are marked 'neumes rythmiques, avec résonances et intensités fixes' ('rhythmic neums, with fixed resonances and intensities'). The term *neume* is derived from the short melismatic melodic groups found in plainchant. Here the term is applied to short rhythmic groups, each with characteristic pitch structure and intensity characteristics which, like their plainchant counterpart, combine together to form a coherent line in each strophe.

The rhythmic structure of the piece tends to grow out of the iambic rhythm at the beginning of the first strophe, by a process of augmentation of values combined with the addition of new values to form more complex rhythmic cells. Although the exact repetition of a melodic motive and rhythmic cell carries with it its own intensity-characteristic and harmonization or resonance, there is a great deal of manipulation of both motives and cells to form new groups of material. Groups of pitches may be transposed and have new resonances, dynamic envelopes and rhythmic patterns applied to them. Like *Cantéyodjayâ*, the structure is basically a collage, but the individual groups are simpler and more strongly linked, either by their pitch structure, rhythmic pattern or dynamic envelope, or by a combination of all three, as well as by their harmonization or resonance.

The pitch structure of many groups grows out of the major seventh at the beginning of the first strophe as well as out of the tritone which emerges in bar three of the first strophe. There are five basic dynamic-envelope patterns, with some variation of actual dynamic levels in each case. The same envelope pattern may be applied to different groups, just as the same melodic motive may appear in different rhythmic guises, with a new harmonic treatment and intensity characteristic.

(2) Mode de valeurs et d'intensités

As early as 1944, during the course of his discussions of Berg's *Lyric Suite* in his composition classes, Messiaen spoke out against the tendency of the second Viennese school to experiment exclusively with pitch structures while adhering to traditional conceptions of rhythm and form.[1] At the same time he cited the possibility of using a series of timbres, a series of intensities, and especially a series of durations. The beginnings of his use of a series of durations has already been noted in *Turangalîla* (Chapter 9, p. 94) and a move in the direction of a mode of durations and intensities occurs in *Cantéyodjayâ* (pp. 8–10 in the score). The first piece to make exclusive use of this principle, however, was the second 'Étude de rythme', *Mode de valeurs et d'intensités*.

To describe the piece as 'serial' is not strictly accurate, although it has many things in common with serial music. There are three twelve-note groups or series, each consisting of all the notes of the chromatic scale. Each note is fixed in register, so that the first group covers the upper range of the keyboard from top E flat down to B above middle C, the second group the middle range from the G above this to the second A below middle C, and the third group the middle to lower ranges from the second E flat above middle C to the lowest C sharp on the piano. There is therefore some considerable overlapping of ranges, although no note occurs in more than one group at the same register.

Each group is assigned a chromatic series of twelve durations—the first group from one to twelve demisemiquavers, the second from one to twelve semiquavers, and the third from one to twelve quavers. These durations, in ascending order of value, are assigned to the notes of each group in descending order. The lowest notes of the piano, which have the greatest sustaining power, are therefore the longest and the highest are the shortest. As some of the durations are inevitably common to more than one group (the quaver, for instance, occurs in all three), there are a total of twenty-four different durations. In addition, a series of seven intensities (*ppp, pp, p, mf, f, ff, fff*) and twelve attacks are distributed throughout the three groups. The distribution pattern of intensities is not a rigid one, but there is a tendency for notes of the same register to be grouped together under the same intensity or narrow band of intensities, regardless of which series they come from. The top two notes, for instance, are the only ones marked *ppp*, the next seven notes down in order vary from *mf* to *ff*, the four consecutive notes G, F, E flat and D (drawn from all three groups) are all *ff*, the chromatic series of notes from A flat above middle C down to the D below are either *p* or *pp*, while all those below (with one exception) range from *f* to *fff*. Some of the attacks are grouped in a similar way. The three groups interlock so that the greatest concentration of notes occurs in the middle register. All twelve notes in the octave above and including middle C are used, with a sparser layout above and below this octave.

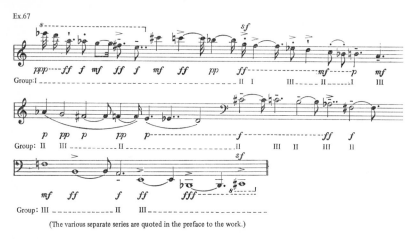

Ex.67

(The various separate series are quoted in the preface to the work.)

Unlike the pitches, durations and intensities, which have an absolute value in their own right, the attacks effectively have the function of modifying the intensity or duration of a note. The absolute duration between one note and the next is fixed by the duration series, but the effective length of a note may be shortened by means of a staccato or other shortening indication, so that a silence will follow for the remainder of a value. Similarly, the intensities can be modified by accents and sforzandi. Although Messiaen notates the attacks as in example 67 in the preface to the work, where he sets out the mode, he rationalizes the notation of attacks 2, 6, and sometimes 3, by writing the note-value shorter and following it by a rest in the context of the piece. Similarly the sforzandi of attacks 10 and 11 are incorporated into the dynamic markings so that they become *sff* and *sfff* respectively.

The most important feature is the fact that the characteristics of each note—its duration, dynamic and attack—are fixed for the whole piece. It is this fact which distinguishes the procedure from a true serial one. The traditional twelve-note row was essentially a series of intervals characterized by the pitch order. To interchange the order of the notes in a drastic way was to destroy the series. In *Mode de valeurs et d'intensitiés*, however, each note is characterized according to its place in the ranges of duration, intensity and attack, and not by its position in relation to other notes. It is this point which makes the system a 'mode' and not a series (or network of series), and enables the composer to choose freely from the notes in each group in the composition of the piece.

To sum up, in traditional serialism, the order of notes is fixed by the series (subject to the usual freedom of transposition, inversion, etc.), but its parameters are free. Conversely, in *Mode de valeurs*, the parameters of each note are fixed and its order in relation to other notes is free. Any number of notes, from two to twelve, can be selected from each of the three groups which comprise the mode, before repetitions occur. Only the traditional serial limitation against the simultaneous sounding of the same note in different octaves is preserved, and this is necessary in order to maintain the homogeneity of the three-part texture.

There is no trace of sectional form, which is so characteristic of Messiaen's other work, and there is no thematic working. Some note-patterns do tend to recur, however, especially descending sequences of different lengths from the top note of each series: this is common to all three strands. At eight points in the composition all twelve notes of one of the three groups appear in succession, but in only one part at a time. The notes of each group are permutated in a type of symmetrical order at each appearance, but in three cases the symmetry is slightly disturbed, apparently in order to avoid sounding a note at the same time as another part. The table overleaf shows the order of the notes in these eight groups, each note being indicated by its duration in the unit appropriate to the group (I = demisemiquavers, II = semiquavers, III = quavers). Numbers in brackets indicate those notes which are out of order.

Possibly the most serious limitation of the 'mode' of this piece lies in the use of the durations. Since each duration defines the interval between one note and the next in any given line, it is impossible to introduce rests or pauses in any part without lengthening the duration of a particular note beyond that allowed by the mode. In addition, chords are impossible, since each individual note of a chord would have to be succeeded by further sounds in order to characterize their duration, bearing in mind that the effective duration of a note is always to the beginning of the next sound. Because of the extreme limitations, this is the only piece in which Messiaen makes use of such a mode throughout. Like the modes of limited transposition, it constitutes for him a colour: 'The complete mode constitutes a colour . . . a colour of durations and intensities, the purpose of which is to vary the "greyness" of the sound-series and to create the search for other colourations.' [2]

In *Cantéyodjayâ*, as it has already been pointed out, he makes use of a 'mode of values and intensities', but only in one short episode of the piece, so that its characteristic colour is contrasted with the colours of the other material used in the piece. The mode is simpler in this work, consisting of three groups of eight notes each with a narrower range of intensities (*pp* to *ff*) and no series of attacks. A similar mode is used in *Île de Feu II* and another in 'La Chouette Hulotte' from *Catalogue d'Oiseaux*. These are the only instances (to date) of this kind of mode, although from *Livre d'Orgue* onwards there are many examples of the use of twelve-note pitch-rows in a fashion which is modal rather than serial (see *Livre d'Orgue* and *Catalogue d'Oiseaux* in particular). In spite of the limitations of *Mode de valeurs*, the broader conception of mode which it involves is very important in Messiaen's development, a conception which was to become broadened to an ultimate degree in later works, especially *Catalogue d'Oiseaux*.

TABLE II

1. Bars 24-28 (Group I)

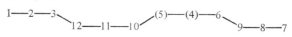

2. Bars 29-39 (Group II)

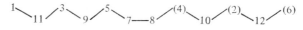

3. Bars 39-49 (Group II)

4. Bars 53-57 (Group I)

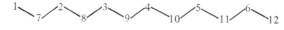

5. Bars 61-80 (Group III)

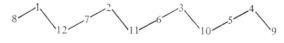

6. Bars 81-86 (Group I)

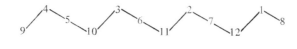

7. Bars 86-96 (Group II)

8. Bars 103-107 (Group I)

1—2—3—4—5—6—7—8—9—10—(12)—(11)

Île de feu I and II

These two remaining pieces from the 'Etudes de rythme' carry the dedication 'dédié à la Papouasie—1950' ('dedicated to Papua—1950'). Papua is now the south-eastern portion of the island of New Guinea, but the name was originally given to the whole island. The first piece is based on the cyclic theme which opens it. This is modified to become the cyclic theme of the second piece which is alternated with episodes based on a mode of 'twelve durations, twelve sounds, four attacks and five intensities'. Only a single group of twelve pitches is used, as distinct from three groups in *Mode de valeurs et d'intensités*, but this single group is used in octaves in two registers an octave apart, above and below middle C.

The use of symmetrical permutations of the twelve-note series was noted in *Mode de valeurs et d'intensités*. This principle is extended more systematically to the durations of *Île de feu II*, where the chromatic series of twelve durations (of the above mode) is permutated in a 'wedge' shape, starting from the middle and working outwards. In *Livre d'Orgue* Messiaen calls this process 'permutation in the form of an open fan', because of the sense of 'opening out' from the centre to the outside.

Durations of original series:	12	11	10	9	8	7	6	5	4	3	2	1
Permutation:			6	7	5	8	4	9	3	10	2	11	1	12

This produces 'Interversion I'. The same permutation order is then applied to 'Interversion I' to produce 'Interversion II', and then again to 'Interversion II' to produce 'Interversion III', and so on. Each successive pair of permutations is played together in the episodes of the piece: I/II and III/IV in the first episode, V/VI and VII/VIII in the second. The remaining pair, IX/X, is played against the final statement of the cyclic theme before the coda. The following table gives the complete series of permutations:

TABLE III

Initial series of durations:		12	11	10	9	8	7	6	5	4	3	2	1
Permutations ('Interversions'):	I	6	7	5	8	4	9	3	10	2	11	1	12
	II	3	9	10	4	2	8	11	5	1	7	12	6
	III	11	8	5	2	1	4	7	10	12	9	6	3
	IV	7	4	10	1	12	2	9	5	6	8	3	11
	V	9	2	5	12	6	1	8	10	3	4	11	7
	VI	8	1	10	6	3	12	4	5	11	2	7	9
	VII	4	12	5	3	11	6	2	10	7	1	9	8
	VIII	2	6	10	11	7	3	1	5	9	12	8	4
	IX	1	3	5	7	9	11	12	10	8	6	4	2
	X	12	11	10	9	8	7	6	5	4	3	2	1

An interesting feature of this permutation process is that it does not produce a complete cyclic series of twelve permutations (which one might expect when twelve objects are permutated cyclically amongst themselves). The reason for this is that two of the values—10 and 5—must inevitably change places throughout the cycle, so that the original order is restored when the remaining ten values have circulated. This is yet another example of the 'charm of impossibilities' of which Messiaen speaks in connection with his modes of limited transposition and non-retrogradable rhythms.[3]

The coda of the last piece is a wild dance, reminiscent of the opening of 'Regard de l'Esprit de joie' (*danse orientale et plainchantesque*). Whereas the latter is based on plainchant, the melody of the coda of *Île de Feu II* is derived from the melodic shape of various jâtis quoted in Lavignac's *Encyclopédie de la Musique*.[4] The particular jâtis used are 'naishâdi', 'ândhrî' and 'nanda-yantî'.

Ex.68

Île de Feu II p.8, b. 3.

Messe de la Pentecôte (1950)

Messe de la Pentecôte was written to accompany various parts of the Low Mass of Pentecost Sunday. Unlike the organ masses of the sixteenth century, its movements are not based on the Ordinary of the Mass (Kyrie, Gloria, Credo, Sanctus and Agnus Dei), but are designed to accompany the main actions of the Mass except for the Scripture readings. The actions concerned are the entry of the priest, the offertory, the consecration, the communion and the recessional.

Each movement carries a subtitle and, as in the case of the earlier organ works, a short quotation from scripture. The first movement, 'Entrée', is subtitled 'Les langues de feu', after the tongues of fire which came to rest on each of the disciples on the day of Pentecost (Acts 2: 3). The second movement, 'Offertoire', takes a phrase from the Nicene Creed as its subtitle, 'Les choses visibles et invisibles', and the third movement, 'Consécration' ('Le don de Sagesse') meditates on the gift of Wisdom, one of the seven gifts of the Holy Spirit. The fourth movement, 'Communion' ('Les oiseaux et les sources'), makes considerable use of birdsong, as the subtitle suggests. The meditation here is not specifically related to the feast, but to the mystery of Communion itself. The extract from scripture which precedes the movement is derived from the Canticle of the Three Young Men (Daniel 3), which is traditionally recommended in the Roman Missal as a meditation after Mass or Communion. The last movement, 'Sortie' ('Le vent de l'Esprit'), returns to the Acts of the Apostles for its source. It is a turbulent movement, invoking the 'great wind which filled the whole house where they [the disciples] were sitting' (Acts 2: 2). In the central section of the movement it expresses the joyful response of the disciples to the coming of the Holy Spirit by means of the ecstatic song of the skylark.

This work, more than any other of this period, brings together and integrates the various devices with which Messiaen was preoccupied at the time: rhythm, plainchant, birdsong, religious symbolism and some of the 'Turangalîla' motives (see pp. 101–2). The 'Offertoire' treats three Sharngadeva rhythms in 'personnages rythmiques'—'tritîya' (3), 'caturthaka' (4) and 'nihçankalîla' (6). The same movement includes a passage devoted to the permutation of five chromatic values (1 to 5 semiquavers) and the last movement superimposes the chromatic series of 4 to 25 semiquavers against the retrograde series 23 to 1. This forms an accompaniment to the song of the skylark mentioned above. The third movement ('Consécration') contains a number of strophes based on a free transformation of the Alleluia for Pentecost, *Veni sancte Spiritus*. These strophes alternate with two different refrains, one based on the rhythm 'simhavikrama' and the other on 'miçra varna' (8 and 26/2 in the table of Sharngadeva rhythms). The principal melody of these refrains is in the pedals, while the resonance harmonies on the manuals use a series of fixed timbres and intensities which vary with each note or group of notes in the melody.

The first movement contains a kind of rhythmic experimentation not hitherto found in Messiaen's work. A number of Greek rhythms are treated in 'irrational' values. Instead of being built up from a basic unit-value, these rhythms divide a longer duration into varying numbers of units which fluctuate in tempo one to another. The relationships may be simple ones, such as three in the time of two or five in the time of four, or more complicated, such as fifteen in the time of eight or twenty-one in the time of sixteen (see *Sept Haïkaï*, ex. 78, for examples of irrational values).

An example of the treatment of Sharngadeva rhythms in irrational values occurs in the second movement of *Livre d'Orgue*, although Greek rhythms, being based on simple 2:1 relationships, are more suited to this kind of treatment. A more extensive use of irrational values is to be found in *Sept Haïkaï*, in connection with which they will be discussed more extensively in Chapter 13.

Livre d'Orgue (1951)

The last work of Messiaen's 'experimental' period was *Livre d'Orgue*, in which he exploits Sharngadeva rhythms in combination with quasi-serial procedures applied to pitch.

There are seven pieces, arranged in an order which displays a cross-symmetry similar to that of *Les Corps Glorieux*. The first and last movements, 'Reprises par Interversion' and 'Soixante-quatre durées', are primarily concerned with particular compositional devices and have no explicit symbolism connected with them. The second and sixth movements are related by the use of the same set of pitch-series. Similarly, the third and fifth movements both make use of the same pitch-series, while the fourth movement forms the centrepiece of the work. A different set of relationships exists in parallel between the second and fifth, third and sixth, and fourth and seventh movements. Both the second and fifth movements are entitled 'Pièce en Trio', consist of three-part polyphony, and are symbolic of the Trinity. The third movement is called 'Les Mains de l'abîme' and the sixth 'Les Yeux dans les roues', and both are inspired by surrealistic concepts arising from Scripture. The fourth movement, 'Chants d'Oiseaux', and the last movement both make use of birdsong.

Generally speaking, *Livre d'Orgue* makes considerable use of Sharngadeva rhythms. In the first movement, 'Reprises par Interversion', and in the fifth, 'Pièce en Trio', they are treated in 'personnages rythmiques'. Three rhythms are used in the first movement—'pratâpaçekhara' (75), 'gajajhampa' (77) and 'sârasa' (103)—and two groups of three divided between the two manual parts in the fifth movement. The right hand plays 'laya' (106), 'niççanka' (119) and 'bhagna' (116) while the left hand has 'caccarî' (15), 'rangapradîpaka' (24) and 'sama' (53). In each case, the first rhythm mentioned is augmented, the second is diminished and the third remains unchanged. In addition, the order of the rhythms is changed at each repetition so that six different arrangements are possible. The first section of the first movement consists of all six arrangements of the three rhythms, and the duration of the fifth movement is determined by the time it takes to state all the arrangements of the rhythms in the left hand. The same permutation order is followed in each movement:

ABC – ACB – BCA – BAC – CBA – CAB

In addition to the permutation of the rhythmic cells in the first movement, Messiaen also applies a different permutation process to the individual notes of each cell. In the second section, notes or note-groups of the second half are alternated in retrograde with those of the first half in normal order. Messiaen describes this as a permutation in the form of a 'closed fan'. As each group of notes has a fixed intensity and timbre, these become permutated at the same time as the notes. The third section is a retrograde form of the second, so that the permutation process starts from the centre and works outwards. This is described as a permutation in the form of an open fan, and is the same operation as that which is applied to the duration series in *Île de Feu II* (see p. 109).

Ex.69

(a) 'Reprise par Interversions' – 1st section (beginning)

Timbre:
Récit (*R.*) – Bourdon 16', Hautbois 8', Cymbale
Positif (*P.*) – Prestant 4', Nazard 2²/₃',
Tierce 1³/₅', Piccolo 1'.

Grande orgue (*G.*) – Bourdon 16', 8', Flûte 4'
Pedal – Bombarde 16'

(b) 2nd section (beginning) — Permutation in the form of a 'closed fan'

The first movement ends with a retrograde form of the first section.

Twelve-note series are used extensively in *Livre d'Orgue* in all except the fourth and last movements. This does not imply that these movements are serial as, except in the fifth, Messiaen uses different arrangements of the notes for each successive twelve-note set. The process is therefore essentially a modal one, the general character of the piece being dependent upon a statistical equality which inevitably arises between all twelve notes of the chromatic scale.

In addition to the twelve-note series in the second piece, 'Pièce en Trio', a series of seventeen Sharngadeva rhythms is treated in irrational values. These are divided into two groups of nine, one being common to both groups, and are simply stated in numerical order throughout each group. The first group consists of 'simhavikrama' (8), 'gajalîla' (18), 'sama' (53), 'mallatâla' (64), 'vasanta' (73), 'pratâpaçekhara' (75), 'gajajhampa' (77) and 'lack-skmîça' (88). The second group has 'miçra varna' (26/2), 'vijaya' (51), 'sama' (53), 'manthîka 1' (55/1), 'dhenkî' (58), 'caturmukha' (78), 'râgavard-hana' (93), 'simha' (101), 'candrakalâ' (105) and 'bhagna' (116). The distortion of these rhythms by means of irrational values has, for the composer, a symbolic relationship to the quotation from scripture which precedes the piece: 'Now we are looking at a confused reflection in a mirror . . .' (1 Corinthians 13: 2).

The third piece, 'Les Mains de l'abîme' ('The hands of the abyss'), is preceded by a quotation from Habakkuk: 'The abyss has cried out! The depths have raised up their hands!' (3: 10). There is also a link, as Messiaen tells us,[5] with the Dauphiny mountains; the extremes of height and depth are suggested by the juxtaposition of long and short durations, and high and low registers in close proximity. In the middle section, a number of twelve-note sets are used as florid decorative figures, one of which (p. 9, bar 1) is to become the sole twelve-note row of the fifth movement.

113

The fourth piece, 'Chants des oiseaux', as the title suggests, is based mainly on birdsong. Hitherto Messiaen had used it mainly in a decorative or subsidiary way, but this piece, as well as 'Soixante-quatre durées' and the piece for flute and piano—*Le Merle noir*—(also written in 1951), is important in its anticipation of the larger 'bird-pieces' of the later 1950s. Besides the strophes of birdsong in 'Chants des oiseaux', there are four refrains which reflect the permutational treatment of the first movement. The material of the first refrain is based on the rhythm 'miçra varna', the second restates the first refrain in retrograde form, the third permutates the rhythmic cells in the form of a 'closed fan' and the last refrain permutates them in the form of an 'open fan'.

The second 'Pièce en Trio' (the fifth movement) is unique among Messiaen's output. It is his only piece to use a twelve-note row in a strictly serial fashion. Only one series is used, taken from the middle of the third movement,[6] and treated in the usual way with transpositions, inversions and retrogressions. The 'personnages rythmiques' of the manual parts, discussed above, form an accompaniment to a principal melody in the pedals in free rhythm. The note-row is distributed over all the parts simultaneously, and as long as the manual parts are on their own the order of notes in the row is strictly adhered to; the treatment becomes more flexible once the principal melody enters.

The rhythmic structure of this piece is entirely independent of the pitch structure. The rhythmic cells are also independent of each other, a point of which Messiaen makes especial mention in his conversations with Goléa: 'My greatest rhythmic achievement is probably the fifth piece, or "Pièce en Trio". It contains a melody of independent rhythmic structure . . . six Hindu rhythms, distributed in three "personnages rythmiques", that is to say, some augment progressively, others diminish progressively, while others do not change, but none of these functions come together at the same time.'[7]

The title of the sixth piece, 'Les Yeux dans les roux' (for Pentecost Sunday) recalls the eyes which the prophet Ezekiel saw in the wheels in his vision: 'And the rims of the four wheels were full of eyes all around . . . because the spirit of life was in the wheels' (Ezekiel 1: 18. 20). The turbulence of the vision is expressed by the *perpetuum mobile* semiquavers in the manuals and the force of the life-giving Spirit by the permutation of twelve pitches and durations ('sons-durées') in the pedals. The series of twelve pitch-rows from the second movement is used in the manuals. It is a characteristic of these rows that each begins on a progressively higher degree of the chromatic scale, starting on C. When all twelve have been stated, the cycle starts over again, symbolizing the wheels within wheels of Ezekiel's vision (Ezekiel 1: 16).

The tour de force of the whole work is the last movement, 'Soixante-quatre durées'. Sixty-four chromatic durations are arranged in groups of four to form a 'closed fan' (61, 62, 63, 64, 4, 3, 2, 1, 57, 58, 59, 60, 8, 7, 6, 5 . . .) against the retrograde form in 'open fan' (29, 30, 31, 32, 36, 35, 34, 33, 25, 26, 27, 28, 40, 39, 38, 37 . . .). The bird-song which forms the principal material of the piece is superimposed on these series. Each duration can be conceived as being 'coloured' in three ways—by timbre, by sustained chords (harmony) and by the birdsong. In this respect the piece anticipates the Strophe of *Chronochromie*, written nine years later, which Messiaen himself describes in just this way. The durations are not realized throughout by means of sustained chords; in certain places they give way either to a descending series of two-part chords, followed by a rest for the remainder of the duration, or to ascending arabesques having the character of birdsong. In one case, the durations are replaced by birdsong itself, which defines the missing values by means of its phrasing.

Other works of this period

Two minor works were written during this period—*Le Merle noir* (1951) for flute and piano, written for the Concours du Conservatoire National de Musique, and *Timbres-durées* (1952) for electronic tape, realized in the Paris 'Musique Concrète' Studios in collaboration with Pierre Henry. By Messiaen's own account, it was not a success [8] and, although he has since retained an interest in electronic music because of its new sonorities and its new conceptions of time and musical space, he has not composed anything further in this field.

Le Merle noir, although a short piece, is more significant, because it is symptomatic of his increased interest in birdsong as the principal material of a piece of music.

Notes on Chapter 10

1. *ROM* p. 247.
2. *ROM* p. 251.
3. *TLM* Chapter 1.
4. Vol. I—article on Indian Music.
5. *ROM* p. 209.
6. Page 9, second bar, second demisemiquaver group in the right hand.
7. *ROM* p. 211.
8. *EOM* p. 211.

11
Birdsong

'Among the artistic hierarchy, the birds are probably the greatest musicians to inhabit our planet,' says Messiaen in his conversations with Claude Samuel.[1] The impulse to write pieces consisting exclusively, or almost exclusively, of birdsong stems from his love of nature and from many years of research into the songs of many different species. He first began to note down birdsong when he was on holiday on a farm in the Aube district, at the age of about fourteen or fifteen,[2] although the first specific use of identifiable birdsong does not appear in his compositions until the *Quatuor pour la Fin du Temps* in 1941.

It was *Reveil des Oiseaux* which was to open a new period in his composition by making use of birdsong for all its material. This was followed by *Oiseaux exotiques* in 1956, *Catalogue d'Oiseaux* in 1958 and *Chronochromie* in 1960. In all these pieces it predominates as the main musical material.

Composition was inspired by Messiaen's journeys throughout the different regions of France for the purpose of gathering birdsongs. He made no use of a tape-recorder, the songs being notated directly onto manuscript paper 'like an exercise in aural training',[3] and the birds being identified with the aid of binoculars. On some of his journeys he obtained the help of eminent ornithologists: Jacques Delamain in the Charente district; Jacques Penot in the Camargue; Robert-Daniel Etchecopar on Ushant (Ouessant) island; on the moors of Hérault and the district of Pézenas, François Hüe; and in the eastern Pyrénées, Henri Lomont.[4] Knowledge of foreign birds and their songs was obtained from his visits to North America and Japan, and of others from gramophone records.

Allied to Messiaen's interest in birdsong is his love of nature in general. The sounds and rhythms of nature, such as the wind and the waves of the sea, feature in some of the 'bird' pieces, and the rhythm and chronology of birdsong itself often have an important influence on the flow and form of a piece. *Reveil des Oiseaux*, for instance, covers a period of time from 3 a.m. via the dawn chorus to the silence of midday, and in *Catalogue d'Oiseaux* the long middle movement, 'La Rousserolle Effarvatte', begins at midnight and ends

116

at 3 a.m. on the following day, thus covering sunrise and sunset and ending at the point where it began—in the dead of night.

In an article in *Le Guide du Concert* (3 April 1959),[5] Messiaen writes: 'In my hours of gloom, when I am suddenly aware of my own futility, when every musical idiom—classical, oriental, ancient, modern and ultramodern— appears to me as no more than admirable, painstaking experimentation, without any ultimate justification, what is left for me but to seek out the true, lost face of music somewhere off in the forest, in the fields, in the mountains or on the seashore, among the birds.' Although this quotation suggests that disillusionment has partly been the cause of Messiaen's escape back to nature, it has not been entirely an escape, as he has returned with a desire to communicate his discoveries in musical terms, in a way which is unique in the history of Western music. It is in any case a debatable point as to whether one should talk of an escape back to nature at all, as if this were some attempt to run away from the real world. The world of nature is no less real, and in fact is a more perfect reality than the artificial world of civilization which man has created.

One of the most problematical aspects of Messiaen's birdsong is the accuracy of his transcriptions. Some commentators have tended to exaggerate the accuracy with which Messiaen transcribes birdsong in his music, whereas Messiaen himself tends to be somewhat more cautious in his claims. In speaking of *Catalogue d'Oiseaux* to Claude Samuel, he says: 'I tried to copy exactly the song of the bird typical of a region, surrounded by the neighbouring birds of its habitat . . . I am personally very proud of the accuracy of my work; perhaps I am mistaken, because those who are truly familiar with birds cannot recognize them in my music. . . . Evidently it is I myself who listen and, involuntarily, I introduce something of my own style, my own way of listening, when interpreting the birdsongs.'[6] He goes on to describe the conscious modifications of birdsong which he has made in transcribing them for musical instruments: 'The bird . . . sings in extremely quick tempi which are absolutely impossible for our instruments; I am therefore obliged to transcribe the song at a slower tempo. In addition, this rapidity is allied to an extreme acuteness, the bird being able to sing in excessively high registers which are inaccessible to our instruments; I transcribe the song, therefore, one, two, three, or even four octaves lower. And that is not all: for the same reasons, I am obliged to suppress the very small intervals which our instruments cannot play. I replace these intervals of the order of one or two commas by semitones, but I respect the scale of values between the different intervals; that is to say, if several commas correspond to a semitone, then to the true semitone will correspond a whole tone or a third.'[7]

It is not surprising, with these modifications in mind, that the ear of an ornithologist, attuned to birdsong and probably not highly musical, cannot recognize what is familiar to him in the field. Accuracy is only relative and, while it is possible to pick faults from time to time in Messiaen's interpretations of birdsong, it is still possible for a musician to relate many of them to their natural counterparts. Further, one has to bear in mind that Messiaen achieves a more scientific accuracy in his rendering of birdsong than any composer had done before him.

In his works, Messiaen has treated birdsong in two basically different ways. In *Catalogue d'Oiseaux* his main concern is to create a portrait of a particular bird in each piece, at the same time giving an impression of its natural habitat by associating with it the songs of other birds to be found in the region and by evoking the sounds and colours of nature: sunrise, sunset, the sounds of the sea, and so on. In other works, such as *Oiseaux exotiques* or *Chronochromie*, he treats birdsong as a more flexible material and brings together the songs of birds of different countries, something which would not occur in a natural setting.

The development of birdsong in Messiaen's music

There are two ways in which Messiaen's birdsongs can be said to have developed since his earliest acknowledged use of them in the *Quatuor*. The first is in the extent and variety of his repertoire of birdsong, and the second is in the representation of its timbre.

It is significant that the two birdsongs to feature in the first movement of the *Quatuor*—the blackbird and the nightingale—are the two which predominate in subsequent works. Although when compared with later examples of these songs their realization is somewhat rudimentary in this work, their characteristic figures—particularly those of the nightingale—are already apparent.

In 'Regard des hauteurs' (*Vingt Regards*), Messiaen acknowledges in the preface to the work the songs of eight different birds. The treatment of their songs here is very primitive, and only two birds—the nightingale and the skylark—are named in the score. Of the remaining six birds, only one—the chaffinch—is readily identifiable by comparison with its appearance in later works, the identifying characteristics of the others being not yet fully developed. The following example compares the very simple treatment of this song in 'Regard des hauteurs' with its more developed form in *Chronochromie*.

Ex.71

(a) 'Regard des hauteurs'

(b) *Chronochromie* (Epode)

Messiaen admits that the major difficulty in representing birdsong in music is the faithful reproduction of its timbre.[8] No musical instrument is able to reproduce exactly the quality of birdsong, but this difficulty is partially overcome by the use of harmonies and harmonic resonances. The concern for timbre is the main development to be found in his birdsong from 1953 to

1958. In works before *Reveil des Oiseaux*, only the contours and melodic figurations of birdsong are reproduced, but in *Reveil des Oiseaux* itself the realization of timbre by harmonic means occurs for the first time in the songs of the song thrush and the golden oriole. Most of the other birdsongs in his work appear as single-line melodies or in octaves in the piano, and even the song thrush and golden oriole are very uniform in their harmonic treatment. In these cases the same harmonic resonance is reproduced over each note of the song. On the other hand, the harmonic treatment of these and other birdsongs in *Oiseaux exotiques* and *Catalogue d'Oiseaux* is considerably more varied.

Ex.72

The song of the Golden Oriole

(a) *Reveil des oiseaux*

(b) 'Le Loriot' (*Catalogue d'Oiseaux*)

In *Catalogue d'Oiseaux*, the harmonic interpretation of timbre varies from the single line of the garden warbler (fauvette des jardins) in 'Le Loriot', to the very rich harmonies of the black wheatear (traquet rieur) in the piece of that name. Again, birdsongs which are realized as a single melodic line in *Reveil des Oiseaux* can be found with harmonic colouration in *Catalogue d'Oiseaux*.

Although the principal function of harmony in connection with birdsong is to simulate the timbre of the original, for Messiaen, harmony also has colour associations. In certain cases the choice of particular chords is governed by the colour of the bird itself. In 'Le Merle de roche', for instance, from *Catalogue d'Oiseaux*, Messiaen literally paints a portrait of the whole bird; in his preface to the piece referring to the rock thrush, he says: 'Its song is bright orange, like its plumage!' and in a footnote on the page where the song of the rock thrush first appears (p. 9): 'The chords ought to have a sonority akin to a stained-glass window with orange dominating and complemented by specks of blue.' Similarly, in 'Le Merle bleu', the song of the blue rock thrush is marked (p. 3, l. 4) 'luminous, iridescent, with a blue halo'. Under these circumstances Messiaen resorts to the typical chords of his harmonic language; the harmonies associated with the rock thrush are fre-

119

quently derived from the 'chord on the dominant' by the addition of appoggiaturas in order to evoke the effect of a stained-glass window, as described in Chapter XIV of *Technique de mon langage musical*. In 'Le Merle bleu' and 'Le Traquet rieur', the song of the blue rock thrush is rooted strongly in A major, suggesting the association of this key with the colour blue, and in 'La Bouscarle' the blue-green flight of the kingfisher is suggested by chord-sequences in mode 3 of limited transposition. These associations, of course, are essentially subjective, but the devices themselves are nevertheless important in articulating the musical form.

Just as the choice of harmonies is normally governed by the question of timbre, so the rhythmic patterns of Messiaen's birdsong are derived from nature, allowing for a certain amount of slowing up of the original rhythms where the original song is extremely quick. The durations of phrases and the pauses between them also depend on the natural rhythm of birdsong, although there is often a certain amount of compression of the silences, particularly in the blackbird's song.

Before discussing the classification and characteristics of the different types of birdsong in Messiaen's music it will be useful first of all to glance at the two early bird-pieces: *Reveil des Oiseaux* and *Oiseaux exotiques*.

Reveil des Oiseaux (1953)

Reveil des Oiseaux is the only piece to make exclusive use of birdsong for all its material, both melodic and rhythmic. *Oiseaux exotiques* incorporates Greek and Indian rhythms as a counterpoint to the birdsong in the tuttis; *Catalogue d'Oiseaux* uses material derived from the sounds of nature; and all subsequent works employ various amounts of different kinds of material associated or juxtaposed with birdsong.

Reveil des Oiseaux carries three dedications: the first is to the memory of the ornithologist, Jacques Delamain, who assisted Messiaen in his studies of birds; the second is to Yvonne Loriod, who edited the piano part; and the third is 'to the blackbirds, thrushes, nightingales, orioles, robins, warblers, and all the birds of our forests'.

Like the later works for piano and orchestra, this piece comes close to being a concerto, not only because of the prominence of the piano part, particularly in the cadenzas, but also because of the important and difficult part given to other instruments, or groups of instruments. In this respect it calls to mind Bartok's *Concerto for Orchestra*, although there is no suggestion that this work has influenced Messiaen in any way. It is scored for a large woodwind section (piccolo, three flutes, two oboes, cor anglais, clarinet in E flat, two clarinets in B flat, bass clarinet and three bassoons), and small groups of brass, percussion and strings (two horns, two trumpets, four Chinese blocks, suspended cymbal, wood-block, tam-tam, celesta, xylophone and glockenspiel, eight first violins, eight second violins, eight violas, eight cellos and six double basses).

The form of the piece depends entirely on the programme underlying the work, which is based on the 'song-cycle' of the birds from midnight to midday. Although the exclusive use of birdsong renders the work thematically amorphous—that is, there are few *exact* thematic repetitions—a sense of symmetry and form is established in the work by means of relationships of timbre, texture and thematic morphology.

The arrangement of the material and its characteristics is such as to give the impression of two different forms—an arch, and a double binary structure—superimposed upon one another. The symmetry of the 'arch' is defined by the alternation of piano cadenzas and orchestral sections. The work begins and ends with a long piano cadenza which in each case is followed by a silence—the silence of the night and the silence of midday. The final silence (of midday) is broken only by brief calls from two chaffinches (violins), a blackbird (violin), the drumming of a woodpecker (wood-block) and the call of the cuckoo (Chinese blocks). The fragmentary nature of these calls helps to draw attention to the silence and to accentuate it, rather than to give the impression of a reawakening of new activity.

During the course of the work, four other cadenzas are arranged symmetrically around the central tutti of the dawn chorus and are interspersed with orchestral passages. The diagram overleaf illustrates this, and indicates the durations (in seconds) of each orchestral section as calculated from the composer's metronome markings. Although there is an asymmetry in the arch form insofar as the orchestral passages preceding the 'dawn chorus' are longer than those following it, the relative durations of these passages display Messiaen's highly developed sense of time in that those on the left of the arch are almost exactly three times the length of their counterparts on the right. This is all the more remarkable because of the large number of speed changes involved in each section.

The binary structure of the work is defined in one way by the long silences following the 'dawn chorus' and the final piano cadenza. Both of these sections make use of a large number of birdsongs, superimposed on one another in the 'dawn chorus' and mainly juxtaposed in the cadenza. No more than two birdsongs appear together at any one time in the cadenza, compared to the simultaneous superimposition of twenty-one songs and calls towards the end of the 'dawn chorus'. The orchestral passages preceding these sections do not have an identical structure, but there are sufficient similarities in the ordering of the material to give the second of the two passages the character of a shortened recapitulation. Both passages end with the same 'refrain' from the song thrush.

Another 'refrain'—two chaffinches, a woodpecker and a cuckoo—defines the binary structure in another way, so that the work almost resembles a sonata movement. This 'refrain' marks the end of an 'exposition' and the beginning of a central 'development' section, which culminates in the 'dawn chorus'. After the recapitulation of material mentioned above, the central 'development' is recalled in a smaller and less complex bird chorus, which

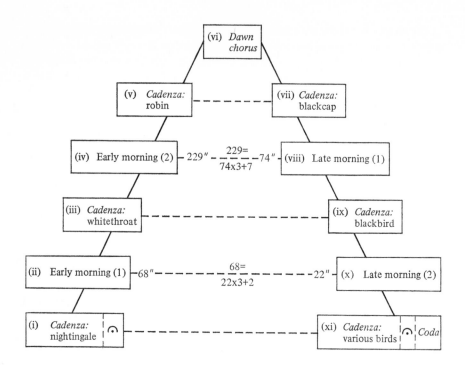

corresponds to the terminal 'development' of sonata form. After the final piano cadenza, this second 'refrain' is repeated with the woodpecker and cuckoo interchanged and a blackbird's song added (see Table IV, pp. 124–5).

Oiseaux exotiques (1956)

Whereas in *Reveil des Oiseaux* Messiaen chooses his birdsong material in order to provide a realistic sound-picture of a period of time in a natural setting, in *Oiseaux exotiques* birdsongs from countries all over the world—North and South America, India, China, Malaysia and the Canary Islands—are brought together and superimposed on each other in an abstract *collage* of sound.

The work is more clearly sectional than *Reveil des Oiseaux*. Due to the lack of traditional thematic relationships resulting from the use of birdsong material, the relationships between the sections depend entirely on timbre, morphology and texture (see Table V, p. 126).

In the two main tuttis, Greek and Indian rhythms, played on non-pitched percussion instruments, are superimposed on the birdsong. Unlike the Greek rhythms in the 'Entrée' of *Messe de la Pentecôte*, those in *Oiseaux exotiques* all appear in their original form. In addition to Sharngadeva rhythms, Messiaen also makes use of tâlas of the Karnatic system of Indian music: 'matsya-sankirna', triputa-mishra', 'matsya-tishra' and 'atatâla-cundh'. The rhythms

in the long central tutti are arranged into a 'strophe', which is played four times
and is divided into four sections which show similar patterns in the ordering
of the rhythms, intensities, and of the instruments to which they are assigned:

	Side-drum	Wood-block	Gongs and tam-tam	Temple-blocks
Section 1	Asclepiad	Sapphic	Nihçankalîla (6)	
	pp	p	p	
Section 2	Glyconic	Adonic	Gajalîla (18)	Lackskmîça (88)
	pp	p	p	mf
Section 3	Iambelegiac	Aristophanian	Matsya-Sankirna	Caccarî (15)
	pp	mf	mf	p
Section 4	Groups of five semiquavers		Candrakalâ (105)	Dactylo-epitrite
	pp		p	mf

Whereas the rhythmic strophes in the central tutti form an ever-present
counterpoint to the birdsong, their use in the final tutti is spasmodic, alternating with 'refrains' based on the calls of the Indian shama.

The songs (or calls) of the white-crested laughing thrush (garrulaxe à
huppe blanche) and the shama form the principal material of the central tutti.
The former occurs at the beginning and the end of the main section of the
tutti, in the manner of the opening and final ritornello in a Baroque concerto,
and has a close rhythmic relationship with the Greek rhythms at the beginning
of the section. Birdsong and rhythmic strophes develop independently in their
own separate ways from this point onward, although both retain the same
semiquaver unit throughout.

The interweaving of various birdsongs during the course of the tutti forms a
complex network of rhythmic and melodic material. All are united in their
tempo by the semiquaver unit, and some are interdependent in the way one
forms an anacrusis to another, or in the way they answer in dialogue.

During the course of the central tutti, one particular 'shama' call on the
piano begins to emerge. It first occurs independently of the other birdsongs
(9th and 10th bars after fig. 17) and again towards the end of the tutti, partially
integrated rhythmically with the songs of the laughing thrush and the white-
crowned sparrow (pinson à couronne blanche). During the final tutti, this
same call follows the shama refrains on the orchestra, and at their final
appearance becomes fully integrated with them.

Messiaen avoids potential monotony in these works, which depend heavily
on birdsong, by contrasts of timbre and texture. These nevertheless have their
limitations in providing variety within a work, and it is significant, therefore,
that in *Catalogue d'Oiseaux* he obtains contrasts within a movement by the
use of material other than birdsong.

TABLE IV

REVEIL des OISEAUX

Figs:	3		4	
Arch	CADENZA I (A)		TUTTI I (a)	
Binary I	A		B	
Binary II	////////		EXPOSITION	

Introduction CADENZA: nightingale ⌢ —	*Strophe* little owl, wryneck, Cetti's warbler, woodlark } (J)	*Refrain 3** nightjar	*Strophe* little owl, Cetti's warbler, woodlark } (J)
	(Superimposed birdsongs . . . . 3 blackbirds		chiffchaff robin

7		8		16		17		28

TUTTI II (b)				CADENZA III (C)	CENTRAL TUTTI	CADENZA IV (C)
////////	D	E (Ref.)		F (climax)		A
Refrain		CENTRAL DEVELOPMENT				////////
Refrain 2 2 chaffinches cuckoo woodpecker (J)	*Episode* various birds	*Refrain 1* song thrush (ex. 182)	CADENZA: robin	DAWN CHORUS	⌢ —	CADENZA: blackcap

35		39		44

TUTTI V (a)		CADENZA VI (A)		////////
D	E (Refrain)	////////		F (conclusion)
TERMINAL DEVELOPMENT		////////		Refrain
Episode Various birdsongs leading to a second 'chorus'	*Refrain 1* song thrush (ex. 182)	*Coda* CADENZA: various birds	⌢ —	*Refrain 2* 2 chaffinches } (S) blackbird woodpecker } (J) cuckoo

5				6
				CADENZA II (B)
				C
				////////
song thrush	*Refrain 3* nightjar	*Codetta* Cetti's warbler	2 chaffinches mistle thrush (S)	CADENZA: whitethroat
	· · · · · · · · · · · · · 3 blackbirds	· ·) 1 blackbird		

29	32	33		34
TUTTI IV (b)				CADENZA V (B)
////////	B			C
////////	RECAPITULATION			////////
Episode various birds	*Strophe.* wryneck little owl Cetti's warbler woodlark } (J)	*Refrain 3* (extended) nightjar	golden oriole	CADENZA: blackbird
	Various birdsongs superimposed, including blackbirds, robins and song thrush			

(J) = juxtaposed   (S) = superimposed

*The three refrains are numbered in order of importance, not in order of entry.

Note: Not all the material contributes to the definition of each formal structure (arch, binary I and binary II). The structure of the whole consists of the superimposition of these three forms. The first three rows of the table illustrate how each form is built up from the material (that which does not relate to a particular form is shaded out).

125

TABLE V

OISEAUX EXOTIQUES

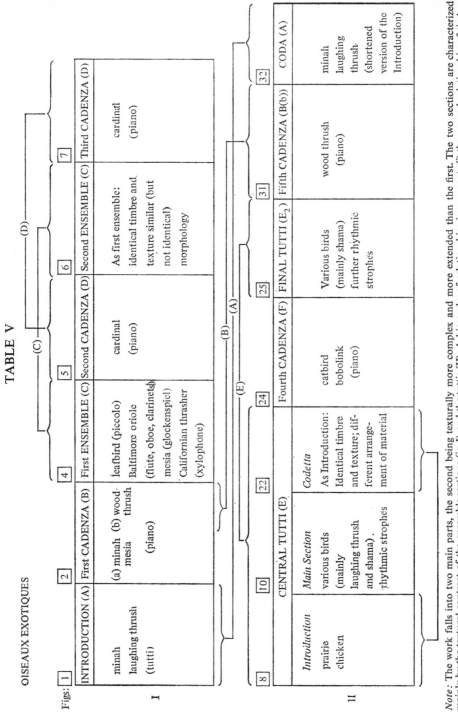

I

Figs:	1	2	4	5	6	7
	INTRODUCTION (A)	First CADENZA (B)	First ENSEMBLE (C)	Second CADENZA (D)	Second ENSEMBLE (C)	Third CADENZA (D)
	minah laughing thrush (tutti)	(a) minah mesia (b) wood-thrush (piano)	leafbird (piccolo) Baltimore oriole (flute, oboe, clarinets) mesia (glockenspiel) Californian thrasher (xylophone)	cardinal (piano)	As first ensemble: identical timbre and texture similar (but not identical) morphology	cardinal (piano)

II

Figs:	8	10	22	24	25	31	32
	CENTRAL TUTTI (E)			Fourth CADENZA (F)	FINAL TUTTI (E_2)	Fifth CADENZA (B(b))	CODA (A)
	Introduction prairie chicken	*Main Section* various birds (mainly laughing thrush and shama). rhythmic strophes	*Codetta* As Introduction: Identical timbre and texture; different arrangement of material	catbird bobolink (piano)	Various birds (mainly shama) further rhythmic strophes	wood thrush (piano)	minah laughing thrush (shortened version of the Introduction)

Note: The work falls into two main parts, the second being texturally more complex and more extended than the first. The two sections are characterized mainly by the textural contrast of the ensemble sections (in I) and the tuttis (II). A hierarchy of relationships is apparent: (i) the general relationship of timbre between the piano cadenzas and between the instrumental sections; (ii) a more specific relationship of timbre, texture and material between the two main tuttis; and (iii) a close relationship of timbre, texture and (to a certain extent) morphology (but not pitch structures) between other sections as indicated on the table by the brackets.

126

Notes on Chapter 11

1. *EOM* p. 95.
2. *EOM* p. 25.
3. *EOM* p. 29.
4. *EOM* pp. 107–8.
5. Quoted by André Hodier in his book *Since Debussy* (translated by Nigel Burch), p. 117.
6. *EOM* pp. 111–12.
7. *EOM* pp. 113–14.
8. *EOM* p. 113.

12

Catalogue d'Oiseaux

Catalogue d'Oiseaux is Messiaen's most important work of his 'birdsong' period and possibly his greatest piano work. It integrates birdsong in its fully developed form with the rhythmic and modal techniques of the post-war period, while incorporating some of the earlier modes of limited transposition and rhythmic devices.

His desire to treat each bird in a more individual way demanded an instrumental medium more homogeneous than the orchestra. The use of the piano was ideal for this purpose because the performer has at his disposal an instrument of great flexibility, dynamic range and expression. Indeed, because he is the only performer, he can give greater attention to the individual interpretation of each birdsong.

The work as a whole is symmetrically arranged into seven books. There are three pieces in each of the first and last books, one longer piece in the second and sixth, two in each of the third and fifth, and the longest standing alone as the central piece in the fourth book. Each piece is preceded by a short preface describing the habitat of the principal bird and those that are associated with it.

The first pieces in both the first and last books—'Le Chocard des Alpes' and 'La Buse variable'—are set in the mountains of the Dauphiny. The main feature of the first piece consists of three long sections of dissonant chords representing various mountain scenes: the ascent towards the Meidje glacier, the fallen logs around the warren of St-Christophe and the mystical stone circle of Bonne-Pierre 'with its huge rocks, lined up like phantom giants, or like the towers of a supernatural fortress'.[1] These three sections are described by Messiaen as 'Strophe', 'Antistrophe' and 'Epode' (see *Chronochromie*, Chapter 13, pp. 160–1) and they are interspersed with two couplets devoted to the cries of the alpine chough (chocard des alpes) and the raven (grand corbeau), and material representing the flight of birds. The scene of 'La Buse variable' is set beside Lake Laffrey, and it makes use of a number of birdsongs arranged into couplets, each followed by a refrain from the mistle thrush. A battle ensues between the buzzard (buse) and some crows (corneilles). These are rather like the 'personnages' of Messiaen's 'personnages rythmiques'—

the crows attack, while the buzzard is the one attacked and the red-backed shrike (pie-grièche écorcheur) comments as a passive observer.

The second piece, 'Le Loriot', is a very marked contrast to the dissonance of 'Le Chocard'. The scene is the Charente district in the early morning, the repetitive phrases of the golden oriole (loriot) dominating all the other bird-songs. In the last section of the piece, its song becomes stylized to represent the sun which 'resembles the golden rays of the oriole's song. . . .'[1] Significantly this stylized song is superimposed onto an extended version of the 'love theme' from the third movement of *Cinq Rechants* ('tous les philtres sont bus ce soir'—ex. 62).

The third piece, 'Le Merle bleu', the fourth, 'Le Traquet Stapazin' and the twelfth, 'Le Traquet rieur', are all set on the south coast of France in the Roussillon district. Each presents a different aspect of the sea and its birds. 'Le Merle bleu' is wild and exuberant, setting off the cliffs against the cries of the swifts (martinets noirs) and the song of the blue rock thrush (merle bleu) against the crashing of the waves which resemble Bâlinese gongs. The piece ends with a slow recollection of the blue rock thrush's song, 'very pure, like a choir of women's voices in the distance':[2] an echo of Debussy's *Sirènes*.

'Le Traquet Stapazin' presents a calmer aspect and turns more inland towards the moors and the terraced vineyards. Like its counterpart in Book VI—'Le Merle de roche'—it is programmatic, covering a period of time through dawn and sunset. The coda evokes a multicoloured sunset of red, orange and violet and incorporates two 'Turangalîla' motives, the first representing the sea (p. 24) and the second emerging from the colour chords of sunset (p. 26, ll. 3 and 4). These two motives are the first two subsidiary themes from 'Jardin du sommeil d'amour', the sixth movement of *Turangalîla* (ex. 59).

The two short pieces which comprise Book III—'La Chouette Hulotte' and 'L'Alouette Lulu'—both describe different aspects of night, the first sinister and frightening and the second mysterious and calm. 'La Chouette Hulotte' ('The Tawny Owl') is devoted to the different owls of the Orgeval wood in the Charente and 'L'Alouette Lulu' ('The Woodlark') contrasts two opposing songs—the liquid sounds of the woodlark singing high up in the darkness and the sharp tremolos of the nightingale replying from the wood.

'La Rousserolle Effarvatte' in Book IV is the longest, lasting about thirty minutes. Like 'Le Traquet Stapazin' it is programmatic, covering a period of twenty-seven hours from midnight through to 3 a.m. on the following day. A large number of different birdsongs and calls are used, but dominating them all are the swamp birds of the Sologne district (south of Orléans)—the reed warbler (rousserolle effarvatte), the great reed warbler (rousserolle tur-doïde) and the sedge warbler (phragmite des joncs). These birds all have highly varied songs which cover the long central strophes of the piece. The reed warbler also sings in the middle of the night, so it has two long strophes to itself in the introduction and coda, along with 'the music of the ponds' which opens the piece and the various other night-sounds from the swamp.

The piece is dominated by the character of these birdsongs, but they are also offset not only by the contrasted style of the other birds in the outer strophes but also by various 'Turangalîla' motives, derived from the 'flower theme' and representing various pond-flowers, which intervene between the various strophes.

The first piece of Book VI—'L'Alouette Calandrelle' ('The Short-Toed Lark')—is devoted to the various kinds of lark found in the Crau wilderness of Provence. It is followed by 'La Bouscarle' which is set alongside the River Charente. Mode 3 of limited transposition plays an important part in this piece; it appears at various points as a flurry of chords to represent the blue-green flight of the kingfisher and is used as the basis of the slow calm homophony representing the river. This provides the accompaniment to the blackbird's song and robin in the first strophes after the introduction, and later to the blackcap's song. These 'river' chords recall, in two places, the falling fourth of the 'love theme' from *Turangalîla*, harmonized by two added-sixth chords foreign to mode 3.

The 'programme' of 'Le Merle de roche' begins before dawn at the stone circle of Mourèze in the Hérault region; the moonlight reveals 'an immense stone hand, raised in a magic sign'.[2] The form of the piece is an arch; in the introduction we hear the sinister hoot of the eagle owl (hibou grand-duc). This is followed in the second section by the chatter of the jackdaws at dawn, and later, the chatter and song of the black redstart (rouge-queue tithys) mingling with the spiky chords and single isolated notes representing fantastic rock formations. The central section is devoted to the song of the rock thrush (merle de roche) in two strophes, separated by a passage of chords in a permutation of thirty-two chromatic durations representing a 'cortège of stone phantoms, carrying a dead woman'.[2] After the second strophe the black redstart returns again, singing among the rocks, this time joined by the rock thrush. At dusk—the jackdaws and finally once again the music of the introduction and the stone hand revealed in the moonlight. In spite of its forbidding aspect, this is one of the most impressive pieces in the work. It is particularly remarkable for its evocative use of silences—whether the long silences between the sinister hoots of the eagle owl, or those which break up the phrases of the rock thrush's song. Far from creating a hiatus, these silences add to the power and impact of the separate phrases of these birds.

After 'La Buse variable' in the last book, comes 'Le Traquet rieur' ('The Black Wheatear'), set again on the south coast of France. This piece has strong affinities with 'Le Merle bleu', not only in its setting; it also presents a joyful impression of the sea, but without the wild exuberance of the earlier piece. The song of the blue rock thrush occurs again, together with the swifts and herring gull, which both featured in 'Le Merle bleu'.

The last piece of the set is 'Le Courlis cendré'—a magnificent portrait of the curlew and the other sea-birds to be found on the bleak island of Ushant off the coast of Brittany. Unlike 'Le Traquet rieur', it presents a wild and desolate picture of the sea, with the doleful cries of gulls, terns, plovers and other sea-birds. Night and fog descend and out of the obscurity the last cries of the birds are heard, dominated by the lugubrious sound of the foghorn. Finally the cries of the curlew approach and recede into the night, leaving only the sound of the surf.

In spite of the fact that Messiaen would ideally avoid anthropomorphic terminology when speaking of birdsong,[3] it becomes clear from a study of *Catalogue d'Oiseaux* that he is concerned with a human world containing birds, rather than a 'bird-world' in its own right. The cries of the tawny owl in 'La Chouette Hulotte' are described as *lugubre et douleureux* and *vague et terrifiant* ('lugubrious and sad' and 'vague and terrifying'), both of which are human reactions to sounds which do not intrinsically have these essential implications. There is also a human reaction to nature in general in these pieces; 'Le Traquet rieur', for instance, begins with a passage marked *joie de la mer bleue* ('the joy of the blue sea'). It is not, of course, the sea which feels joy, but the person observing it. Again, in the middle of 'Le Merle de roche', we find anthropomorphic symbols in the formation of the rocks which suggest a *cortège de fantômes de pierre, transportant une femme morte* ('a cortege of stone phantoms, carrying a dead woman').

Thematic processes began to disappear in Messiaen's music after *Cinq Rechants,* and it has already become apparent, in *Reveil des Oiseaux* and *Oiseaux exotiques* (Chapter 11), that traditional thematic working is incompatible with birdsong, because of its essentially non-repetitive nature. The few calls and brief songs which do repeat exactly, or nearly so, are insufficient to bind the form of a piece together. It is true that the formal processes of *Catalogue d'Oiseaux* depend on the repetition and recall of particular birdsongs, but in the majority of cases these are different at each appearance. Some other formal criteria must be found in relating the wealth of material involved in these pieces and for this purpose all musical parameters—melodic shape or morphology, mode, register, texture, rhythm, timbre, intensity and tempo—must be taken into account. Bearing in mind all these factors, the musical material involved in any one piece presents a continuum of varying degrees of relationships from exact repetitions to the most general relationships of texture, with no formal preference for the few exact repetitions of material which there may be.

The first step in the classification of material in *Catalogue d'Oiseaux* is to distinguish between birdsong and other material not based on birdsong, since these often differ fundamentally in their characteristics.

The classification of birdsong in 'Catalogue d'oiseaux'

Birdsongs vary a great deal from one species to another, and some birds, such as the blackbird, have a considerable repertoire of different melodic formulae. As a result, Messiaen's interpretation of certain stereotyped songs—such as the chaffinch or yellowhammer—vary only slightly, while others are never precisely the same from one context to the next, even in the same piece. There is no characteristic 'blackbird melody' in Messiaen's music, just as no two blackbirds sing identically the same song in nature. In the case of both the original bird and Messiaen's transcriptions it is by the general shape, timbre, tempo and register of the melody that one identifies it as the song of the blackbird.

Messiaen's birdsongs can be divided into four main groups: I calls, II short repetitive song-patterns with slight variations, III varying declamatory or melodic song-patterns and IV rapid, 'chattering' songs, either continuous or broken up by short rests.

Those of group I are not strictly 'songs' at all. They are based on the calls of birds which do not sing, such as the tawny owl (chouette hulotte), swifts (martinets noirs), herring gull (goéland argenté) or raven (grand corbeau). The group can be subdivided into (a) brief calls (tawny owl, swifts) and (b) longer and more varied calls (herring gull, raven). In their developed form in *Catalogue d'Oiseaux* these calls are coloured by sharply dissonant and atonal harmony.

The song-patterns of group II vary from the simple repetitive song of the yellowhammer (bruant jaune in 'La Buse variable') to the more elaborate and varied goldfinch (chardonneret). The song of the goldfinch, in fact, as it appears in 'Le Traquet Stapazin' becomes more characteristic of group IV (see below) in the lengthy goldfinch 'duet' which appears in the reprise of the opening material (pp. 21–2 in the score).

The birdsongs of group III form the most important set in *Catalogue d'Oiseaux*. They fall into two distinct sub-groups: (a) those that are melodic in style, such as the blackbird (merle noir) and (b) those that are declamatory. Some of the principal birds of *Catalogue d'Oiseaux* fall into group III (a)— the blue rock thrush (merle de roche) and the black wheatear (traquet rieur). The blackbird, being common to most habitats in nature, makes its appearance in several pieces and is really too common to justify a piece on its own, since there is no special place or type of habitat in which it is found. The earlier piece for flute and piano which was devoted to the blackbird—'Le Merle noir'—is not really a 'portrait' in the sense that Messiaen means it in *Catalogue d'Oiseaux*, since there is no attempt to evoke the atmosphere of a habitat or region in this piece. The birds of group III (b) are important because of their appearance at crucial points in *Catalogue*. The two birdsongs which belong to this group—the nightingale (Rossignol) and the song thrush (grive musicienne)—have their own distinctly characteristic figures. In both cases, however, these are more stereotyped than the birdsongs of group III (a) and are less melodic in character. In nature, the song thrush tends to choose a prominent perch, and like some prima donna of the bird world gives tongue in a dominating and authoritative manner. Messiaen captures this quality well in his transcription of this bird so that, although its appearances in *Catalogue* are quite brief, it nevertheless automatically assumes an importance of its own by its character. In *Catalogue d'Oiseaux*, it only appears in two pieces: 'Le Loriot' and 'La Bouscarle', but it dominates the dawn chorus in *Reveil des Oiseaux* and has lengthy sections in the Antistrophes of *Chronochromie*.

The nightingale's motives are many and varied, but not as varied as those of the song thrush. There are three formulae which appear most frequently. The first consists of repeated notes, usually preceded and followed by a higher note or sound-complex. The second consists of a fairly quick or very rapid oscillation on two notes a major seventh or tritone apart. The third is what Messiaen calls the 'son lunaire', which he describes as being 'very distant and slow, which could be mistaken for the sound of another bird five hundred metres away, and which gradually draws nearer; this sound is then suddenly followed by two or three powerful notes back in a high register.' [4]

The birdsongs of group IV can be divided broadly into two categories: (a) those that have a pronounced 'dominant' note or notes and (b) those that do not. By 'dominant' in this context is meant a modal dominant, similar to that in plainchant, around which the melody tends to gravitate. The texture of these songs varies from a single line of the garden warbler (fauvette des jardins) in 'Le Loriot' [5] to the fuller texture of the swamp warblers (rousserolle effarvatte, rousserolle turdoïde and phragmite des joncs) in 'La Rousserolle Effarvatte'.

The degree of harmonic colouration of any of these birdsongs tends to vary with the context. In *Oiseaux exotiques* and later works, when two or more birdsongs appear simultaneously, they are not usually harmonized. On their own, however, they nearly always appear in at least a two-part homophony [6] or with added resonance. Both the birdsongs of group I (b) and group III (a) are usually accompanied by thick homophony (the blackbird is exceptional); whereas those of group I (b) are atonal in character, most of those of group III (a) have tonal as well as colour implications suggested by the plumage of the bird concerned (for example, the rock thrush—see Chapter 11, p. 119).

It must be emphasized that this classification refers to Messiaen's transcription of birdsong and the use he makes of them in his work. Because of this, the classification of a particular song might vary in one or two cases from one piece to another, or even within the same piece. The case of the goldfinch has already been mentioned and one could also cite the robin which usually has quite lengthy strophes in the style of group IV (a). In 'Le Loriot', on the other hand, Messiaen uses only a brief repetitive fragment as a refrain so that it is more proper to classify the robin as group II in this instance. The spectacled warbler presents an even more extreme case. It is used in 'Le Traquet Stapazin' and in 'Le Traquet rieur'; at the beginning of the former piece it sings short repetitive patterns in the style of group II, towards the end of the same piece the strophes become longer and gravitate towards a 'dominant' note (G sharp) like group IV (a), but in 'Le Traquet rieur' the 'dominant' disappears so that the song then has to be classified as group IV (b). This does not invalidate the classification, however, as these cases are exceptional. The following table gives a list of the birds used in *Catalogue d'Oiseaux*, the pieces in which they appear and their classification.

TABLE VI

Group I (a) characteristics: short calls, homophonic and dissonant, and usually atonal.

Bittern	7	Little ringed plover	13
Coot	7	Long-eared owl	5
Corncrake	9	Moorhen	9
Eagle owl	10	Pheasant	7
Green woodpecker	7	Quail	8
Hoopoe	9	Sandwich tern	13
Kestrel	8	Swift	3, 12
Kingfisher	9	Tawny owl	5
Little owl	5	Water rail	7

Group I (b) characteristics: longer and more varied calls, homophonic, and dissonant and atonal.

Alpine chough	1	Herring gull	3, 4, 12, 13
Black-headed gull	13	Jackdaw	10
Black redstart *	10	Little tern	13
Buzzard	11	Oystercatcher	13
Common gull	13	Raven	1, 4
Crow	11	Red-backed shrike *	6, (7)
Curlew	13	Starling	7
Guillemot	13	Turnstone	13

Group II characteristics: short, repetitive song-patterns.

Black-eared wheatear	4, 12	Ortolan bunting	4
Black redstart *	10	Redstart *	2, (7)
Cetti's warbler	9	Reed bunting	7
Chaffinch	9, 11	Robin *	2, (9)
Chiffchaff	2	Short-toed lark	8
Corn bunting	4	Spectacled warbler *	4, (12)
Golden oriole	2	White wagtail	7
Goldfinch *	4, 11	Wood lark	6
Great tit	6	Wren	2, 9
		Yellowhammer	11

Group III (a) characteristics: varied song patterns, melodic in style, often with tonal implications. Slower tempo than group IV.

Blackbird	2, 7, 9	Orphean warbler	4
Black wheatear	12	Redshank	13
Blue rock thrush	3, 12	Rock thrush	10
Mistle thrush	11		

Group III (b) characteristics: varied song patterns, declamatory in style.

Nightingale	6, 7, 9	Song thrush	2, 9

Group IV (a) characteristics: long strophes 'chattering' in style, continuous or broken up into shorter phrases. Tempo rapid. One or more notes tend to predominate as a modal 'dominant'.

Crested lark	8	Rock bunting	4
Goldfinch *	4, (11)	Skylark	7, 8
Melodious warbler	4	Spectacled warbler *	4, (12)
Redstart *	7, (2)	Theckla lark	3, 4
Robin *	9, (2)		

Group IV (b) characteristics: as group IV (a) except that there is no pronounced 'dominant'.

Blackcap	9	Sand martin	9
Garden warbler	2	Sedge warbler	7
Great reed warbler	7	Spectacled warbler *	12, (4)
Red-backed shrike *	7, (11)	Swallow	11
Reed warbler	7	Whitethroat	11

Not classified.

Grasshopper warbler	7	Yellow wagtail	9

(See Appendix III for the French names)

Note on the table: The numerals refer to the piece in which the birdsong appears under the particular classification given. Where a song appears in another piece under a different classification, this is cross-referenced in parentheses, and the bird is marked with an asterisk. In the case of the two birdsongs which are not classified, the grasshopper warbler is unique in simply consisting of a trill and the yellow wagtail's appearance is too brief to render it classifiable.

Classification of other material in 'Catalogue d'Oiseaux'

In *Livre d'Orgue*, Messiaen made frequent use of twelve-note sets in a fashion which was essentially modal and not serial (see Chapter 10, p. 113). The free permutation of such sets plays an important role in *Catalogue d'Oiseaux*. It is used for the purposes of describing the more colourless aspects of nature —the white of the Meidje glacier in 'Le Chocard des Alpes', or the grey of descending fog and the dark night in 'Le Courlis cendré', for example.[7] Whereas in *Livre d'Orgue* the note-sets of this mode usually remain distinct from one another without overlapping, in *Catalogue d'Oiseaux* they most frequently overlap in chain fashion, so that in homophonic passages such as the one at the beginning of 'Chocard des Alpes' it is impossible to determine a precise order of notes for each set. The main feature of the mode, however, remains intact. All the notes of the chromatic scale are treated equally so that no one predominates as a modal dominant or final.

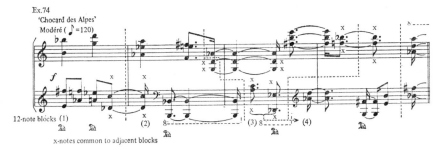

Ex.74
'Chocard des Alpes'
Modéré (♪ =120)

12-note blocks (1)   (2)   (3)   (4)

x-notes common to adjacent blocks

In conjunction with passages using this twelve-note mode, Messiaen occasionally makes use of Sharngadeva and Greek rhythms. In 'Chocard des Alpes' these are treated in 'personnages rythmiques', and in 'La Bouscarle' they appear in rhythmic canon. A different rhythmic treatment is used in 'Le Merle de roche', where permutations of thirty-two chromatic values are used in different arrangements and selections. The whole series of thirty-two values only occurs once—in the middle of the piece—in an arrangement which is identical to 'Interversion I' from *Chronochromie* (see Table VII, p. 177).

A modified mode of pitches, durations and intensities is used to evoke 'night' in 'La Chouette Hulotte'. Here, all the notes in the middle and lower registers of the piano are assigned a different chromatic duration. These increase progressively by demisemiquaver steps from the A above middle C (one demisemiquaver) to the bottom A on the piano (forty-nine demisemiquavers). The intensities are arranged in an equally 'chromatic' manner. All the As are marked, *fff* the notes on either side—G sharp and B flat—are *ff*, the next notes—G and B—are *f*, F sharp and C are *mf*, F and C sharp are *p*, E and D are *pp*, and finally D sharp is marked *ppp*.[8] The texture is arranged in three-part polyphony, as in *Mode de valeurs et d'intensités*; each of these parts covers a wide range, overlapping to a very large extent. The selection of notes from the mode is free, being determined neither by serial considerations nor by a desire to have all twelve notes sounded before any is repeated.

Modes of limited transposition are used in several contexts in *Catalogue d'Oiseaux*, and these are usually associated with particular colours in the score. In 'Le Merle bleu' mode 2 is used to represent 'the blue sea' (first appearance on p. 5), and in 'La Bouscarle' mode 3 is used to suggest the 'blue-green flight of the kingfisher' as well as 'the river' (first appearances on pp. 1 and 4). The change of colour-association according to other factors is illustrated in 'La Rousserolle Effarvatte'. Here, a set of chords of mode 2, different from those in 'Le Merle bleu', represents the pink and mauve of the sunrise (p. 11). They are tinted with added resonance in mode 3, marked 'orange' in the score. On page 13 the colours of the sunrise become mauve (chords in mode 4) tinted with gold (added resonance in mode 6). Later, similar chords in the same modes are used to represent the sunset. The mode 2 chords become more intense and are now 'red and violet' and the mode 4 chords become darker to represent violet only. They still retain their respective orange and gold resonances in modes 3 and 6.

Two other categories of non-birdsong material are used in *Catalogue*: 'Turangalîla' motives (see Chapter 10, pp. 101–2) and other colour-chords not belonging to one of the modes of limited transposition. These colour-chords are mostly drawn from the large repertoire of special chords to be found in Messiaen's earlier works.

These five groups of material can be summarized as follows:

Group I   Mode: twelve-tone. Rhythm: (a) Greek or Sharngadeva

                                                  (b) permutation series

                                                  (c) free

Group II   Mode of pitches, durations and intensities
Group III Modes of limited transposition
Group IV 'Turangalîla' motives
Group V Colour-chords other than those in groups I and III

The structure of 'Catalogue d'Oiseaux'

So far, the two distinct types of material involved in *Catalogue d'Oiseaux*—birdsong and non-birdsong—have been discussed without establishing any link between them. In spite of the fact that each has its own predominant characteristics, points of contact do in fact exist. The most important, and one to be found in all the pieces, is the use of colour-chords as a background to particular songs (the actual harmonization of birdsong, whether by genuine homophony, or by added resonance, is regarded as an integral part of the birdsong itself). This background resonance frequently consists of two or more chords, or occasionally a single chord, introducing a particular song and being sustained through it, as at the beginning of 'Le Loriot' and 'L'Alouette Calandrelle'.

As a method of integration, this is, of course, artificial, since it merely superimposes one type of material on another without necessarily establishing a structural relationship between them. A direct modal relationship between birdsong and other material is not usual, but it nevertheless exists. The use of colour-chords in connection with the rock thrush's song has already been cited. A closer integration comes about at the beginning of 'Le Merle bleu', which opens with a homophonic passage representing the cliffs by the sea. This consists of the rhythm 'râgavardhana' in a twelve-note mode, followed by the cries of the swifts which partially continue this mode. The second phrase consists of the rhythm 'candrakalâ', followed again by the cries of the swifts; this time their first chord completes a twelve-note set which is left unfinished in the previous chords. A later appearance of the swifts (on the second page of the piece, bar 2) is entirely in the twelve-note mode, this being preceded by a flurry of notes (again all twelve of the chromatic scale) representing the water. The musical integration of this passage has, of course, its pictorial counterpart, with the impression which it evokes of cliffs and the swifts flying over them with their shrill cries mingling with the breaking of the waves.

Although this example is not typical of *Catalogue d'Oiseaux* on the whole, it does suggest that the explanation of the remarkable coherence which undoubtedly exists in these pieces is to be found in a concept of mode. We have seen how it has been necessary to generalize the whole conception of mode in the development of Messiaen's music, from the modes of limited transposition, through the modal use of rhythm and the more complex melodic modes (represented by 'Antienne du silence' from *Chants de terre*), to the 'mode of pitches, values and intensities' in which all musical parameters play a part. If we dispense with the scale as the major characterizing factor in a mode and substitute the idea of shape or morphology (applied to pitch), rhythmic characteristics, texture, timbre, register, intensity and tempo as all playing a part (although not necessarily an equal part) in determining a mode, we arrive at a means of dealing with the varied material involved in *Catalogue d'Oiseaux* and a method of clarifying its structure. As it is no longer meaningful to use the term 'theme', a new word must be found to describe a musical unit which is characterized by any one of these musical parameters or a combination of them. Such a unit will be called a group.[9] The term may be applied to a short musical idea such as, say, the music representing the cliffs in 'Le Merle bleu', or it could be applied to a whole section of a piece, such as the opening Strophe of 'Chocard des Alpes', or even to a whole piece in which some particular modal characteristic tends to dominate, so distinguishing it from the other pieces.

Because of its simplicity of structure and economy of material, 'Chocard des Alpes' is an ideal illustration of the 'group' principle. The Strophe, Antistrophe and Epode form three groups, closely related in rhythmic structure, mode, texture, dynamics and in their use of almost the entire pitch-range of the piano. Their rhythms are derived from Greek and Sharngadeva sources and their mode is twelve-tone. The Strophe and Epode are most closely related to each other in having a polyphonic texture consisting of two layers of homophony in independent rhythms and a dynamic level of *f*. The Antistrophe is slightly differentiated from them in its single layer of homophony and dynamic level of *ff*.

In a sense these sections form refrains to the two couplets, in which two types of material are used: birdsong, consisting of the calls and cries of the alpine chough and the raven, and passages representing the flight of the alpine chough and the flight of the golden eagle. The couplet groups which have the closest links with the refrains are the flights of the alpine chough. Like the refrains, they use the twelve-tone mode, and although their range is more restricted to the middle register of the piano they do occasionally break out into the full range. In every other respect they are differentiated from the refrains; their dynamic range is variable (*pp* to *ff*) while that of the refrains is fixed, their tempo is more rapid and their rhythm is free and more uniform in its predominance of demisemiquaver figures. In dynamic range, predominantly restricted tessitura and free rhythm, they are more closely linked to the birdsong. Both the calls of the chough and the raven belong to group I (b) (see p. 134), but are differentiated in certain other details. The calls of the raven are in a quicker tempo and a lower range of the piano than those of the alpine chough; they are more closely linked to the flight-patterns of the chough in their frequent use of short demisemiquaver figures. The remaining group—'the flight of the golden eagle'—is most closely related to the flight of the choughs in its two-part homophonic texture and its use of a wide range of the piano, but it is sharply contrasted with it in its very slow tempo, and its slow graceful ascent from bass to treble.

With reference to any given parameter, it is possible to arrange these groups into a continuum of varying characteristics which will vary according to the parameter chosen. For instance, the material could be arranged according to its tempo (fast—slow), dynamic (loudest—softest), texture (most dense—least dense) or degree of dissonance. The various arrangements so produced will form a network of continuously varying characteristics, some or all of which may be significant in providing points of contact between otherwise contrasting material. In the case of 'Chocard des Alpes', there is one respect in which nearly all its groups are similar—that is in their dissonant and atonal style and their violence of character as represented by the frequent or continual use of loud intensities. Only the flight of the golden eagle does not quite fit in with these characteristics (although it is related to the flight of the choughs in its two-part homophonic texture), but it is too brief to prevent the other groups from forming the character of the piece as a whole. Because of its marked contrast, it has the function of breaking up each couplet into two distinct sections, thus providing a very important formal element in the piece.

Not all the pieces in *Catalogue d'Oiseaux* present the same homogeneity of material as 'Le Chocard des Alpes'. All depend on contrasts of some kind, but two in particular make a feature of opposing entirely unrelated groups of material. In 'La Bouscarle' these contrasts take the form of interruptions of the blackbird, robin or blackcap by the brusque and violent song of Cetti's warbler (bouscarle) and occasionally the harsh cries of the corncrake (râle de genets).

In 'Le Traquet Stapazin', the song of the principal bird—the black-eared wheatear—interrupts the calm flow of other material such as the chords representing the 'terraced vineyards' at the beginning, or the chords representing sunrise (pages 8–9 and 12–13). Other violent contrasts are reflected in the opposition of the dissonant, atonal cries of the raven and herring gull to the melodious songs of the ortolan bunting, spectacled warbler and goldfinch in the opening strophes. Both the birdsong and other material together form a broad continuum in this piece, ranging from groups with firm roots in E major, through groups of ambiguous tonality, to thoroughly atonal groups. The characteristics of the piece as a whole are partly defined by the E major characteristic of the tonal groups and partly by the oppositions of unrelated material drawn from opposite ends of the continuum. There is no attempt to unify the material under a single modal character as in 'Chocard des Alpes' and it is this very opposition of material, consistently applied throughout, which ensures the coherence of the piece.

We will end this chapter with a set of diagrams illustrating the group-structure and the form of each piece in *Catalogue d'Oiseaux*. For the sake of simplicity, only those characteristics are shown which contribute markedly to the mode of each piece.

The first diagram for each piece relates to its group-structure and the second to its form. Reading from left to right, the first diagram shows how the piece as a whole splits up into its constituent groups through the various characteristics which these have in common. Reading from right to left, it shows the synthesis and interaction of the material to form the mode of the piece as a whole. A dotted line without arrows between two boxes indicates a close affinity between the groups of material concerned with reference to a particular parameter; a dotted line with an arrow at each end indicates sharply contrasting characteristics.

The first diagram for 'Chocard des Alpes', for example, shows how the overall mode of the piece—'atonal, dissonant, violent'—is characterized by the freely atonal character of group I (b) birdsong and the twelve-note mode of most of the other material. Only the 'flight of the golden eagle' is strongly contrasted, but retains a link through its texture and a partial link through its dynamic to the 'flight of the choughs'.

The constituent groups of each piece, listed in the boxes on the extreme right, are each given a letter in order to identify them in the second diagram. Birdsongs have capital letters, other material—apart from that based on the flight of birds—has lower-case letters. As the flight material forms a category of its own, it is indicated by double letters. Since the vertical arrangement of these groups corresponds, as nearly as possible, to a continuum of one or more characteristics, close juxtaposition of letters far apart in the alphabet in the second diagram will usually correspond to contrast of material.

The following abbreviations are used:

H^v = homophony of variable density; H^2, H^3 ... = homophony consisting of two-part chords, three-part chords, etc.

P = polyphony (P^{2H} = polyphony consisting of two strands of homophony)

M = monody

M^r = monody with added resonance.

1. 'Le Chocard des Alpes'

(1) *Group structure*

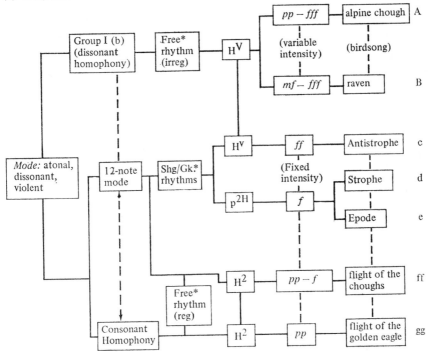

(2) *Form*

Strophe	Couplet I	Antistrophe	Couplet II	Epode
d	A — gg — B — ff — A — ff — A — ff	c	as Cp.I	e

*Note on the rhythms: Free rhythm (irreg.) = 'bird rhythm'
Free rhythm (reg.) = predominance of equal notes
Shg./Gk. rhythms = Shárngadeva and Greek rhythms

2. 'Le Loriot'

(1) *Group structure*

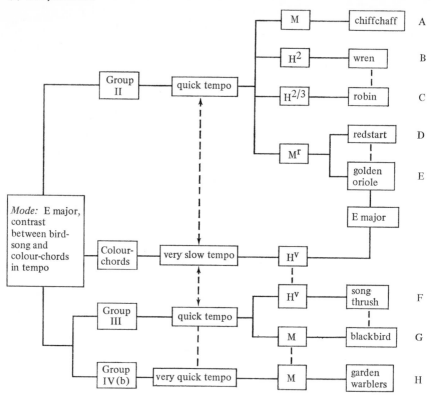

(2) *Form*

Couplet 1	Refrain	Couplet 2	Refrain	Strophes
E – D – B	C	G – D – B – F	C	H – H – H – E – A – E

Final section
E – E^{tr}* + Tur.motive – F – D – B – E

3. 'Le Merle bleu'

(1) *Group structure*

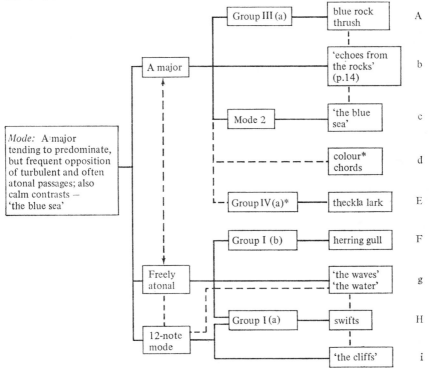

* The song of the theckla lark and the colour-chords do not define A major. On the other hand, they are consistent with it in so far as one of the 'dominant' notes of the former is A and the latter are associated with the blue rock thrush.

(2) *Form*

Introduction	1st Couplet	Refrain	2nd Couplet	Ref.
i/H/g/A	A+d/g	c	A + g	c

3rd Couplet	Ref.	4th Couplet	Coda
E − A/E + g − A+b/F − g − E − F	c	A+d/g − g	i/H/g/A

143

(1) *Group Structure*

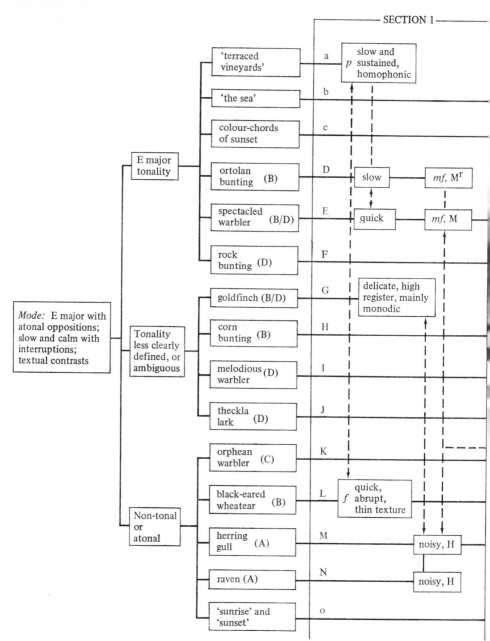

*Section 3 is omitted from the diagram as it repeats the contrasts and oppositions of Section 1 and some of those of Section 2.

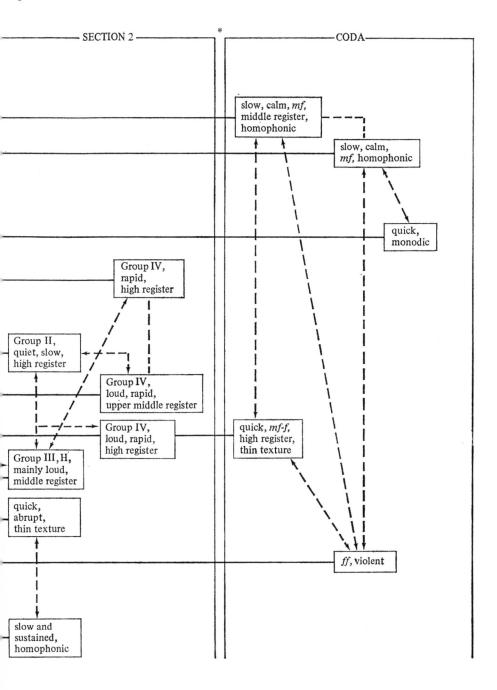

SECTION 2   *   CODA

slow, calm, *mf,*
middle register,
homophonic

slow, calm,
mf, homophonic

quick,
monodic

Group IV,
rapid,
high register

Group II,
quiet, slow,
high register

Group IV,
loud, rapid,
upper middle register

Group IV,
loud, rapid,
high register

quick, *mf-f,*
high register,
thin texture

Group III, H,
mainly loud,
middle register

quick,
abrupt,
thin texture

ff, violent

slow and
sustained,
homophonic

145

(2) *Form*

Section 1

Three Strophes (second and third expanded)	
a − L − D − E − M − N − E/G	(− K − M − E)*

*Third strophe only

Section 2

Two Strophes	
o/L − F − K − H − I	o/L − F − K/H − J

Section 3

Strophe	Episode	Coda
a − L − D − L − N − G − L	o − L − K − D − L	b/J − M − c/E − DLM⁺ − E

$^{+}$Fragments

146

5. 'La Chouette Hulotte'

(1) *Group structure*

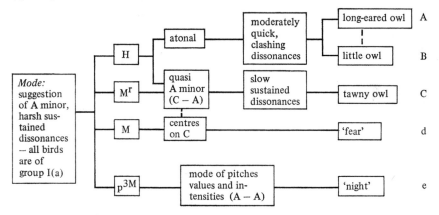

(2) *Form*

Refrain	Couplet 1	Refrain	Couplet 2
e	d – A – B – C – d – A – B – C	e	d – A – B – A – B – C

6. 'L'Alouette Lulu'

(1) *Group structure*

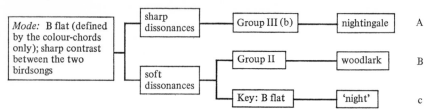

(2) *Form*

Introduction	Central strophes	Coda
B + c	Dialogue between A and B (+ c)	B + c

7. 'La Rousserolle Effarvatte'

(1) *Group structure*

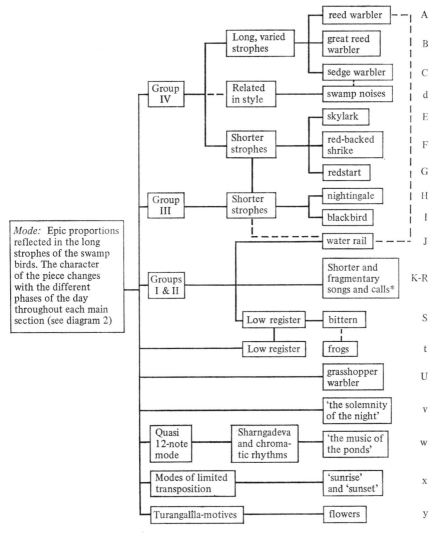

Mode: Epic proportions reflected in the long strophes of the swamp birds. The character of the piece changes with the different phases of the day throughout each main section (see diagram 2)

*pheasant(K), reed bunting(L), green woodpecker(M), starling(N), great tit(O), white wagtail(P), blackheaded gull(Q), coot(R)

149

7. 'La Rousserolle Effarvatte' (*continued*)

(2) *Form*

Introduction	Strophe 1	Refrain
w – t – S – A – v/d	x/I+F* – G* – x/I+F*	y ('yellow irises')

Strophe 2	Refrain
K – L – M – L – N – K – O – M – P	y ('yellow irises') – U

Strophe 3	Refrain	Strophe 4	Refrain
A – C	y ('purple foxglove')	A – C	y('purple foxglove')

Strophe 5	Refrain	Strophe 6	Refrain
B – C – A – Q – R	y ('water-lilies')	A – C – A – C – A	y ('yellow irises')

Strophe 6	Refrain	Interlude
A/C	y ('yellow irises') – U	R – E – t – E – t – J

Coda
x/S – H – x – v/H/S/d – A – t – w – S

* with colour-chords

150

8. 'L'Alouette Calandrelle'

(1) *Group structure*

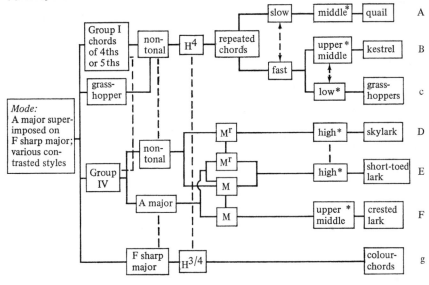

*register

(2) *Form*

Section 1	Section 2	Section 3	Coda
E+g − c − B − A − E+g	E+F − E+g	c − B − A − E+g	A − D − A − E

151

9. 'La Bouscarle'

(1) Group structure

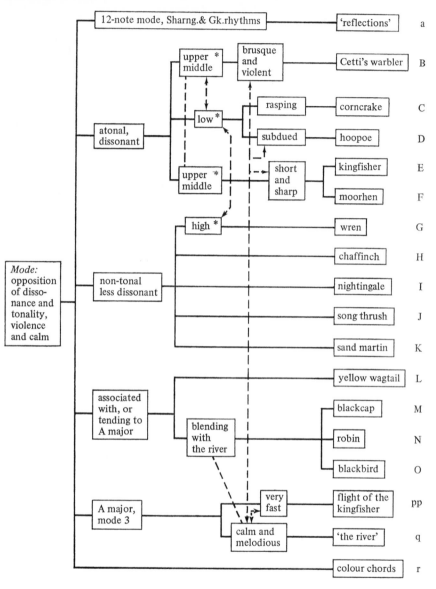

*register

152

9. 'La Bouscarle' (*continued*)

(2) *Form*

Introduction	Interlude	Strophe 1	
B — F — E — pp — E — B	a	q+O — B — pp — q+N	— B — C — J — G

Strophe 2a	
q+O — B — pp — q+N	— B — C — J — H — B — C

Strophe 2b		Strophe 2b		Strophe 2b
q+M — B — D — G		pp		q+N — C — L
	Interpolation		Interpolation	
	I		a — K — F — B	

Coda
pp — E — pp — B

10. 'Le Merle de roche'

(1) *Group structure*

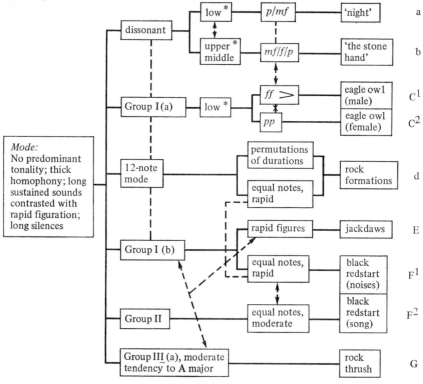

*register

(2) *Form*

Introduction	Strophe 1	Strophes 2-4	Strophe 5
a+b – C^1/C^2 – a+b – E – a+b	E – d/F^1/F^2	G – d – G	E/G/d/F^1/F^2

Coda
C^1/C^2 – a+b – C^1 – a+b

11. 'La Buse variable'

(1) *Group structure*

* register +General dynamic levels
f = louder than mf
p = softer than mf
$<$ = variable between
loud and soft

(2) *Form*

Introduction	1st Couplet	Refrain	2nd Couplet	Refrain
C – jj	E – F – D – F – D – C	D	F – G – E – F – D – F – D – C	D

3rd Couplet		Refrain	Interlude	Coda
H – F – G – E	B/A/C	D	I – F – G	C – jj

155

12. 'Le Traquet rieur'

(1) Group structure

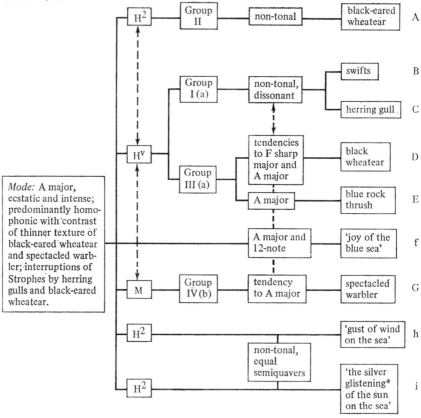

Mode: A major, ecstatic and intense; predominantly homophonic with contrast of thinner texture of black-eared wheatear and spectacled warbler; interruptions of Strophes by herring gulls and black-eared wheatear.

* *poudroiment*

(2) Form

Refrain	Strophe 1
f	D – C – E/D – A – E/D – A – D – B

Refrain	Strophe 2
f	E/D – A – D/E – A – E – A – B – C

Refrain	Strophe 3	Refrain
f	D – G – h – D – i – B – D	f

13. 'Le Courlis cendré'

(1) *Group structure*

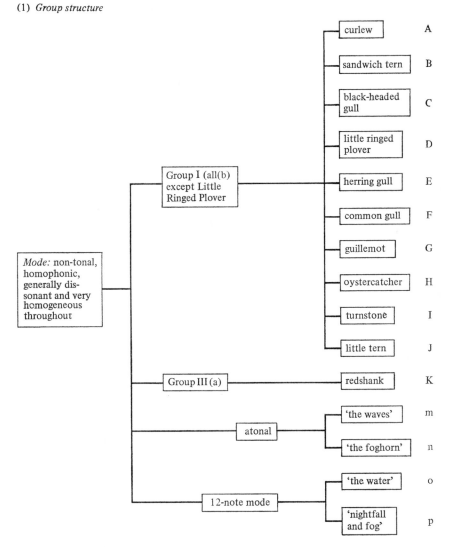

(2) *Form*

Introduction	Refrain	Strophe 1	Refrain
A	m	B – C – D – K – m/E	m

Strophe 2	Refrain	Interlude
F – G – K – G – K – H – K – I – H	m	o – p

Refrains and short strophes					Coda
n	E – B	n	D – C – E – J	n	K – E – K	A

Notes on Chapter 12

1. From Messiaen's preface to the piece.
2. A note on the score.
3. This point comes out in the conversation between Messiaen and Claude Samuel on page 102 of *Entretiens avec Olivier Messiaen*:

   Messiaen 'The nightingale [that is, the nightingale's song] changes suddenly from sadness to joy . . .'

   Samuel 'We would call it "sadness".'

   Messiaen 'Yes, you must forgive me for using words with human connotations, it is an old fault; I employ anthropomorphic terms in spite of myself. Let us say that the nightingale appears to pass suddenly from sadness to joy . . .'
4. *EOM* p. 102
5. In the more recent work, *La Fauvette des jardins*, the garden warbler's song appears with harmonic colouration. This would have hardly been possible in 'Le Loriot' as most of the middle section consists of a duet for two garden warblers.
6. The words 'monody', 'homophony' and 'polyphony' are used in the sense which Boulez uses them in his book *Penser la musique aujourd'hui* ('Boulez on Music Today'), to mean a structure consisting of single notes (whether melodic or not), a connected succession of chords (with or without melodic implications) and a combination of monodies, homophonies or both.
7. On page 251 of *ROM* Messiaen speaks of the greyness (*grisaille*) of the basic twelve-note series of the *Mode de valeurs et d'intensités*, without its durations, intensities and attacks. It appears evident, therefore, that any twelve-note row constitutes a neutral colour for him.
8. There is a misprint in bar 18 on page 1—the C sharp in the left hand should be *p*, not *pp*.
9. The term 'group' is used in mathematics to describe a very precise mathematical concept. The musical use of the word in this context is not intended to correspond to its mathematical use except in a very general way—to mean a set or collection of musical sounds having a defined structure with reference to a number of musical parameters (pitch-structure, rhythmic-structure, etc.).

13

The Works of the '60s and Early '70s

Following the composition of *Catalogue d'Oiseaux*, birdsong begins to play a slightly less important role in Messiaen's music, at least in its relation to nature. He had always perceived harmony in terms of colour, but this aspect begins to assume greater importance from the time of *Chronochromie* (1960) onwards, eventually playing a decisive role in the shaping of a work—as Messiaen claims in the case of *Couleurs de la Cité céleste*. *Chronochromie* is still heavily dependent on birdsong for its material, but in the works which follow it assumes a more balanced role alongside other material.

'Chronochromie' (1960)

Chronochromie was commissioned by Heinrich Ströbel and the orchestra of the Südwestrundfunk, and was first performed at Donaueschingen in Germany on 16 October 1960 under the direction of Hans Rosbaud. It is written for a large orchestra, including an entirely pitched percussion section. This includes instruments of definite pitch—a glockenspiel, xylophone, marimba and twenty-five bells—as well as those of relative pitch—three different sized gongs, two different sized cymbals and tam-tam. The work is unusual for Messiaen in using no piano.

The title, derived from two Greek words, *khronos* meaning 'time' and *khrôma* meaning 'colour', signifies 'The Colour of Time'. It was chosen to describe the fundamental musical process involved in the second and fourth movements (the Strophes), each of which is based on three superimposed permutations of thirty-two chromatic durations (values 1 to 32). These three permutations are 'coloured' in three different ways. In the first place, their unit value—the demisemiquaver—is defined by the superimposition of bird-song in the woodwind and pitched percussion. Although the rhythm of the various birdsongs is varied, they make constant use of the demisemiquaver value. The second colouration is by means of timbre. Each permutation is given to metal percussion instruments of contrasting timbre and pitch, and is assigned a different intensity. One line is given to the three gongs, played pianissimo, another to the bells, played forte, and the third to cymbals and tam-tam, played pianissimo. The third colouration is provided by the harmonies on the strings. Each rhythmic series is doubled by a series of chords of different structure and register, associated by the composer with, as it were, a different 'colour-scheme'.

The total number of permutations possible of thirty-two different values is astronomical; in order to limit them according to a system, Messiaen divides the thirty-two durations into five groups. The first group has one value (27), the second has three (19, 20, 21), the third has four (2, 8, 11, 28), the fourth has six (1, 3, 5, 7, 10, 26) and the fifth has eighteen (all other durations). The permutations in each group are rotated cyclically amongst themselves, giving a total number of permutations equal to their lowest common multiple—36 (see Table VII, p. 177).

The process is similar to the treatment of the twelve durations in *Île de Feu II*, but much more complex (see Chapter 10, p. 109).

At least part of three of these permutations appear in six of the seven movements of the work but, like Messiaen's earlier use of rhythms, they cannot be regarded as having a structural function, except in the Strophes where they are used throughout and define the duration of each movement. Even here, though, they do not govern the rhythmic shape of the birdsong.

The colouration of the durational series in the other movements—with one exception—is supplied by birdsong and timbre only. The exception occurs in the passages from figures 7 to 10 and 18 to 21 in the first movement, and from 129 to 132 in the last movement. Permutations 13, 14 and 15 are combined, and number 13 is realized by means of pseudo-birdsong figuration on the woodwind and pitched percussion.

Ex.75

The form of the work as a whole is modelled on the form of certain Greek choral lyrics—Strophe, Antistrophe, Epode. In Greek poetry, the Antistrophe had exactly the same form and metre as the Strophe. The Epode was different in structure and rounded off the form as a whole, or as Gilbert Murray says in *The Classical Tradition in Poetry*:[1] 'In the most complete form of choral lyric, besides the strophe and antistrophe we have a third stanza, or "Epodos", which puts a crown on the pair, much as the central figure in the pediment puts a crown on the two sides.'

In *Chronochromie* the Strophe and Antistrophe are repeated, and followed by the Epode. The whole is preceded by an Introduction and followed by a Coda. The two Strophes are closely related in structure, as are the two Antistrophes, but the only resemblance between Strophe and Antistrophe is in the use of three permutations of the durational series. The essential structure of the two pairs of movements is different, as the Strophes use the permuta-

160

tions throughout, whereas the Antistrophes use only part of them in their codas. The main body of the Antistrophes is taken up with the songs of the song thrush and skylark alternating on different groups of instruments, each section increasing its duration at each repetition.

The Epode is different in structure and timbre from the rest of the work, but not in material. Like the two Strophes, its texture consists of a polyphony of birdsong, but played on eighteen solo strings instead of woodwind and percussion. No other instruments are used and no rhythmic permutations are employed. Because it consists of a unified block of sound, varying little in quality and texture throughout, this movement creates special difficulties for the listener. These difficulties are attributed by Messiaen to the fact that the birdsong is taken out of its natural setting and transferred to the unexpected setting of the concert-hall: 'Insofar as I have obviously separated this extraordinary counterpoint from its context, it is this which has provoked a scandal!'[2]

It is evident, however, that Messiaen overlooked an important point in his explanation: the birdsongs are not only transferred from their natural surroundings to a foreign location, they are also transformed in timbre by being assigned to stringed instruments. It is not so much the sound of birds in the concert-hall which gives cause for scandal, but the sound of eighteen stringed instruments trying to sound like birds. At best, they play what is only a parody of the original songs, as it is impossible for musical instruments to reproduce exactly the timbre of a bird. This is not intended, however, to be a criticism of the movement. Once the transformation of birdsong into an artist's simulation of nature is accepted, the Epode becomes a 'colouration' of a long duration of time which balances the durations defined by the different 'colours' or 'modes' of the Strophes and Antistrophes. Just as a short duration can be defined by one single sound, so in the Epode a long duration (about $3\frac{1}{2}$ minutes) is defined by many sounds of the same texture and timbre.

Although it is in *Chronochromie* that Messiaen focuses attention on the colouration of time structures, the principle is nevertheless not a new one in his compositions. The work really sums up processes which have been developing in his music since his first systematic employment of rhythmic techniques in *La Nativité du Seigneur* in 1935, and the method of harmonic colouration adopted in the Strophes is anticipated in the ninth movement of the *Turangalîla-Symphonie* (see Chapter 9, p. 93).

It is not until he finally sheds the dependence of his technique on thematic processes in the late nineteen-forties and early 'fifties that 'the colour of time' becomes an all-important factor in his compositions.

Sept Haïkaï (1962)

In 1962, Messiaen visited Japan on a concert tour with Yvonne Loriod. The composition of *Sept Haïkaï* resulted from his contact with Japanese music and musicians, and with birdsongs collected during his visit. Although some of these had already appeared in *Chronochromie*, this was his first opportunity to study Japanese birds in their native habitat.

The word *Haïkaï* or *Haïku* means a short poem of three lines, having five, seven and five syllables to each line respectively. Its significance in connection with Messiaen's work is simply that the seven pieces which comprise it are short, like the poems.

In the introduction to her book *The Rhythmical Patterns in Gagaku and Bagaku*,[3] Eta Harich-Schneider describes the Japanese court music Gagaku as a mosaic of melody, rhythm and harmony, each capable of separate consideration. She also points out that the different instrumental groups are coordinated but no fusion is intended. The net result is a static music in contrast to the dynamic flexibility of Western music. This description could equally be applied to *Sept Haïkaï* as to Japanese Gagaku, and tendencies in this direction are already apparent in Messiaen's earlier orchestral works. Although the 'mosaic of melody, rhythm and harmony' of Gagaku resembles the *collage* structures of all his mature work, it would not be true to say that he does not intend a fusion between the different elements involved. Yet it is only a step from a work like *Chronochromie*, with its superimposed rhythms and birdsongs, to *Sept Haïkaï*, where the different layers of material stand out against each other in greater relief.

It is also characteristic of the Japanese influence in this work that a specific type of material is reserved for particular groups of instruments. In Gagaku, the three principal instruments—the ôteki (flute), the hichiriki (a double-reed instrument) and the shô (an instrument resembling a small pipe-organ, played with the mouth)—each have distinctive material. The hichiriki plays the principal melody, the ôteki a countermelody, and the shô provides a colourful background of dissonant harmonies. Although the functions of instrumental groups in *Sept Haïkaï* are generally more fluid than this, there is a marked tendency to associate certain instruments or instrumental groups with a certain kind of material, especially within the limits of a single movement (see Table VIII, pp. 178–9).

A similar functional disposition of the instruments is apparent in *Chronochromie*. In the Strophes and Antistrophes, the birdsong is reserved for the woodwind and pitched percussion, while, except in the codas of the Antistrophes, the strings support them with homophonic 'colouring'. The constant association of instrumental groups with particular 'blocks' of material in this and earlier works anticipates their extreme compartmentalization in *Sept Haïkaï*.

As in certain earlier works, Messiaen distributes the separate pieces of *Sept Haïkaï* symmetrically. The last piece, 'Coda', is a structural continuation of the first, 'Introduction', containing the second strophe of a violin melody which is begun in the first piece. This melody, however, is not the most important part of the texture. Unlike earlier works, such as *Turangalîla*, where complex rhythmic structures form the background to the principal melodic material, the melody in the first and last pieces of *Sept Haïkaï* is often marked at a lower dynamic level than the rhythmic tâlas on the other instruments so that its importance is relatively diminished.

Both the second and fifth pieces are musical paintings of Japanese temples. The second, 'Le parc de Nara et les lanternes de pierre', is an impression of the four Buddhist temples of Nara and the three thousand stone lanterns which huddle together as far as the eye can see; the fifth, 'Miyajima et le torii dans la mer', evokes the colours of the red and white Shinto temple of Miyajima with its large red gate or 'Torii' half-submerged in the blue sea. Behind them is a mountain covered in deep green Japanese pines and maple trees. The importance of colour in this piece is so great for Messiaen that he marks in the score the colours which he associates with the individual harmonies, timbres and resonances.

The third piece, 'Yamanaka-Cadenza', is related to the sixth, 'Les oiseaux de Karuizawa', in the use of piano cadenzas and the songs of Japanese birds. One bird in particular provides what is almost a thematic link between the movements: this is the *Uguisu*, or Japanese bush warbler (bouscarle de Japon). Its characteristic melodic shape, played on the trumpet, dominates the bird chorus of the second piece.

Ex.76

Uguisu (3rd movement)

(and similar melodic shapes)

Tpt. *ppp* ——— *f*

It also occurs on its own at the beginning of and at various points during the sixth piece, again on the trumpet, but this time coloured by the whole woodwind section.

The remaining piece, 'Gagaku', is based on the style and sonorities of Japanese court music, each of its characteristic instruments being replaced by a Western equivalent. The hichiriki is replaced by a trumpet, two oboes and a cor anglais all playing in unison (the principal melody), the ôteki becomes a piccolo and E flat clarinet (countermelody), and the mysterious strains of the shô are represented on the violins playing *sul ponticello* chords. In a footnote in the score, Messiaen describes the effect of the piece as 'hieratic, static—at the same time religious and nostalgic—slow and inexorable'.

A great deal of use is made of rhythmic tâlas of various kinds in this work. Permutations 4 and 5 from the permutation cycle of *Chronochromie* (see Table VII, p. 177) define the duration of the second piece, and a less rigid use is made in the fourth piece of permutations 19, 20 and 21, played by the cencerros, crotales and bells respectively.

In the first piece, the piano part consists of a tâla of six Sharngadeva rhythms—'sama' (53), 'vijaya' (51), 'simhavikrama' (8), 'gajajhampa' (77), 'lackskmîça' (88), and 'candrakalâ' (105), the whole tâla being superimposed in retrograde form in the woodwind. In the 'Coda' the roles are reversed, the woodwind having the original tâla and the piano the retrograde form. A typically Japanese rhythm is used on the brass and metal percussion instruments consisting of progressively accelerating values:

This is followed by 'simhavikrama' and 'lackskmîça' and augmentations of them.

The most interesting rhythmic feature of the first and last pieces is the use of a *metabole*—a practice derived from Greek poetry. This involves the metamorphosis of one rhythm into another by gradual stages—in this case, the transformation of 'simhavikrama' into 'miçra varna' in the xylophone and marimba.

In the second piece, Messiaen reverts to a rhythmic device which he had previously used only in the first movement of 'Messe de la Pentecôte'—the treatment of Greek metres in irrational values. Four metres—Cretic tetrametres, Phalacean, Pherecretean and Adonic—are modified in this way in the bass clarinet.

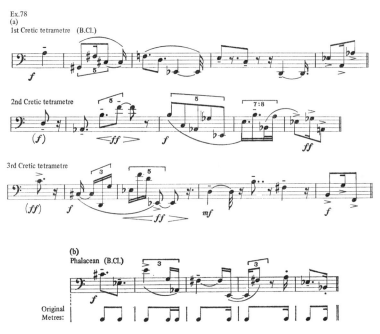

164

*The rhythm is indicated starting one note too soon in the score.

Against this, the other two clarinets weave a counterpoint in free, but more complex, irrational values.

In his own development of serial method in the 1950s, Stockhausen had already employed complex irrational values in such works as the *Klavier-stücke I–IV* and *Gruppen*. For Messiaen, of course, these rhythms do not arise from serial considerations, but their effect is similar insofar as they effectively define a series of different, but related, tempi, either in sequence or superimposed upon one another.

The third piece provides the best example of irrational values conceived in this way. The birdsong is accompanied by four independent tâlas on lower woodwind and percussion. The varying tempi are most clearly defined in the tâlas on the lower woodwind and cencerros, since these consist mainly of equal values. Each change of tempo can itself be regarded as defining a duration, and as the durations themselves are not of equal value, this adds to the complexity by defining yet another, slower rhythm.

Ex.79

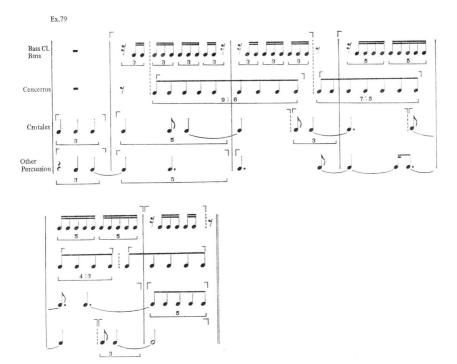

Messiaen himself has not hitherto developed these procedures further in his music, but it is possible to envisage the possibility of organizing most complex rhythmic structures consisting of the interaction of rhythms defined by blocks of changing tempi and the rhythms involved within each block.

Couleurs de la Cité céleste (1963)

Couleurs de la Cité céleste resulted from an unusual request by Dr Heinrich Ströbel for a work for three trombones and three xylophones. 'I agreed,' says Messiaen, 'but I was very unhappy because I could not think how to use these instruments. After long reflection it finally occurred to me that the trombones had an apocalyptic sonority; I therefore re-read the Apocalypse in search of texts. Then I was struck by the percussive sonority of the three xylophones, which enabled me to use birdsong provided that I could add a piano; always with birdsong in mind, I found that it was probably necessary to have several clarinets in order to vary the timbres and, with all these ideas in mind, I added to the three trombones a small trumpet in D, three trumpets and two horns in F, as well as a bass trombone. I transformed the three xylophones into a xylophone, a xylorimba and a marimba, I added the solo piano, and, finally, some metal percussion instruments: cencerros, bells, four gongs the three clarinets and two tam-tams.' [4]

Messiaen says of this work that it summarizes all his various musical preoccupations: Christian symbolism, plainchant, birdsong, rhythm and the colour-associations of sounds. Since the composition of *Livre d'Orgue* in 1951, the only work before *Couleurs de la Cité céleste* to be concerned with Christian symbolism was *Verset pour la fête de la Dédicace* (1960)—a short organ voluntary for the feast of the Dedication of a Church. *Couleurs de la Cité céleste* has a slight affinity with this work as both use the Alleluia for the Mass of the Dedication as part of their musical material.

The symbolism of the work is derived from the Apocalypse, suggested (as Messiaen points out in the above quotation) by the 'apocalyptic sonority' of the trombones. Five quotations from the book of Apocalypse are given in the Preface to the score (*Deuxième Note de L'Auteur*): (1) 'There was a rainbow around the throne. . .' (Apoc. 4: 3); (2) 'And the angels had seven trumpets. . .' (8: 6); (3) 'The star was entrusted with the key to the pits of the abyss . . .' (9: 1); (4) 'The light of the holy city was like crystalline jasper. . .' (21: 11); (5) 'The foundations of the city walls were adorned with all kinds of precious stones: jasper, sapphire, chalcedony, emerald, sardonyx, sardius, chrysolite, beryl, topaz, chrysoprase, jacinth and amethyst. . .' (21: 19, 20).

It is the first and last of these quotations in particular that give rise to the colour-associations of sounds (mainly homophonic chords) in this work. According to Messiaen, these colours dictate the form of the piece: 'The form of the work depends entirely on colours. The melodic or rhythmic themes, the combinations of sounds and of timbres, change in the manner of colours.' [5] The combination of different colours in the form of juxtaposed and superimposed blocks of sound is like the mosaic pattern of a stained-glass window.

Because of the importance of colours, and in order to communicate their associations in sound to the performers, Messiaen follows the practice adopted in the fifth movement of *Sept Haïkaï* of marking the names of the colours in the score: 'I have noted the names of these colours on the score in order to communicate the vision to the conductor, who will, in turn, transmit this vision to the players he is conducting; it is essential, I would go so far as to say, that the brass "play red", that the woodwind "play blue", etc. . . .' [6]

The whole question of colour association, of course, is a highly personal affair, but it is important at least in relation to the shape of the composition, because to each contrast of colour there corresponds a contrast of harmony or timbre, which in turn helps to define the form of the work.

Couleurs de la Cité céleste draws from plainchant sources more than any other single work before it. Four Alleluias are used, chosen from the 8th Sunday after Pentecost (*Magnus Dominus. . .*), the 4th Sunday after Easter (*Christus resurgens. . .*), Corpus Christi (*Caro mea. . .*) and the Feast of the Dedication of a Church (*Adorabo. . .*). All these Alleluias are relevant by the association of their verse text with the symbolic content of the work. The first and last refer to the Holy City of the Apocalypse, and the other two refer to Christ's redemption of mankind through death and resurrection, and through his Body and Blood. [7]

Each Alleluia is divided up and used in different portions of the work and treated in different ways. The Alleluia from the 8th Sunday after Pentecost is transformed melodically in the manner of the *Haec Dies* in 'Regard de l'Esprit de Joie' and appears in various different versions during the course of the work. The Alleluia for the 4th Sunday after Easter is also transformed melodically and its notes are divided among different instruments in the manner of *Klangfarbenmelodie*. Neither of the other Alleluias is altered melodically (an unusual procedure for Messiaen), but both are treated homophonically.

Both Sharngadeva and Greek rhythms make their appearance in the rhythmic structure of the work. A complete tâla consisting of seven of these rhythms is used during the course of the central section of the work (fig. 42), and is repeated at the end of this section (fig. 62) with one of its rhythms expanded (the Cretic) and another interpolated. These tâlas are broken up to appear elsewhere in connection with other material (ex. 80). They form the main rhythmic 'mode' of the piece, and interact with the other principal modes—the Alleluia melodies, the colour-chords and the blocks of instrumental timbre—to create the structure of the whole work. The choice of Sharngadeva rhythms in this work is governed by the symbolic implications of their names, as discussed in Chapter 5 (p. 44).

In his first preface to the work, Messiaen describes the melodic and rhythmic material, the complexes of sounds and of timbres, as evolving after the fashion of colours. He also adds: 'Again, one can compare these transformations to persons acting in several scenes superimposed on one another and

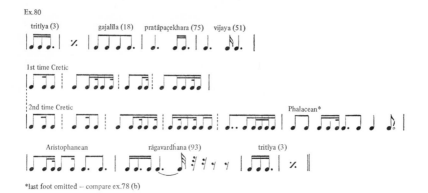

Ex.80

*last foot omitted – compare ex.78 (b)

simultaneously unfolding several different stories.' In musical terms, the form as Messiaen describes it here involves the interaction of the various groups of material, so that the characteristics of one are allowed to transform another. The tâla, for instance, does not remain a separate entity, but is broken up and applied to the Alleluia for the 8th Sunday after Pentecost in the last section of the work in place of its natural plainchant rhythm. Similarly, the colour-chords, which do not imply any particular rhythm in themselves, are stated first at figure 11 in the score in equal minims and continued at figure 13 using a section of the tâla. In addition, the homophonic texture of the colour-chords is applied to most of the Alleluia melodies at some point in the work, but principally to that of the 8th Sunday after Pentecost at figure 73.

There is also a continuum of timbre, of rhythm and of texture, the characteristics from opposite ends of each continuum being sharply opposed. The timbre varies from the essentially non-percussive but sustained quality of the woodwind and brass, then the comparatively sustained and percussive sound of the gongs and tam-tams, the more percussive and less sustained quality of the piano and bells, and finally the very percussive and dry xylophone, xylorimba and marimba. Although the wind instruments are not by nature percussive, they are used, in some passages, in a way which brings them closer to the quality of the less sustained percussion (for example in the Alleluia for the 4th Sunday after Easter). The texture of the work varies from monody to thick homophony, but this is at the same time affected by timbre and the degree to which chords are sustained. The impression of homophonic density is much greater when wind instruments are involved than when only percussion is used.

In the field of rhythm there is, on the one hand, the predominantly equal values of the plainchant and colour-chords (fig. 11) and, on the other, the complex mixture of durations in the tâla. Between these two extremes, there is a continuum of rhythms in which some of the characteristic cells of the tâla can be seen to emerge (ex. 81).

Although the birdsongs remain in themselves a distinctly separate class of material, in some sections long durations arising from the rhythmic structure of the birdsong itself are marked by the percussion, especially the cen-

168

Ex.81

1. *Colour-chords* (fig.11) – equal values

2. *Polyphony* (fig.8)

Tpt. in D.

(a)
(values 2:1)

Tpt.2.

(b)
(values 2:1)

cretic

Tpt.3.

(c)
(values 4: 2: 1)

Horns

(d)
(values 3:2:1)

Trbs.

(e)
(values 4:3:1)

Tpt.1.

Cretic   Cretic   tritīya   gajalīla

(f)
(irrational
values)

5   5   9:8

3. *Tāla* (see ex.80) and 'Interversion' series

cerros. These rhythms are not directly related to any others in the work but they have an affinity with the tâla in their general complexity. The following example occurs at figure 9 in the cencerros accompanying the phrases of the Bell-bird's song.

Ex.82

The interaction of the material is clarified by the sectional form of the work. It is divided into three main sections, preceded by an introduction and followed by a coda. The introduction consists of birdsong and the first statement of the Alleluia for the 8th Sunday after Pentecost. The first main section alternates strophes of birdsong (the New Zealand Bell-bird) with symmetrical arrangements of colour-chords and the same Alleluia melody. It ends with a refrain which includes the first phrase of the second Alleluia—that of Corpus Christi. The middle section includes more birdsong—chiefly the Brazilian Araponga bird which interrupts the refrain so dramatically—and the Alleluia for the 4th Sunday after Easter. The most important element is the rhythmic tâla (figures 42 and 62) which is superimposed on parts of permutations 13, 14 and 15 from the permutation cycle of *Chronochromie*. In the third section the main interactions of material take place. The Alleluia from the first section is juxtaposed in different treatments—first, as it appears in the introduction, second, with sections of the tâla applied to it, third, superimposed on the Alleluia for the Dedication, Sharngadeva rhythms and 'Turangalîla' motives, and fourth, in a very slow ecstatic version (fig. 73), harmonized with colour-chords and fragments of the tâla on the piano, forming upper resonances to the chords. The coda includes further strophes of birdsong, one of which has the tâla and another version of the Alleluia for the 8th Sunday after Pentecost superimposed upon it; the work ends with the refrain and continuation of the Alleluia melody which ended the first section.

Table IX, p. 180, shows the disposition and main interactions of material concerned in the work.

'Et exspecto resurrectionem mortuorum' (1964)

In its greater use of plainchant melodies at the expense of birdsong, *Couleurs de la Cité céleste* represents another turning-point in Messiaen's output. The work which follows, *Et exspecto resurrectionem mortuorum*, makes little use of birdsong, only two examples being used—the Uirapuru of Brazil and the Calandra lark of southern Europe. Two plainchant melodies are trans-formed: the Introit and the Alleluia of Easter Sunday, both being used in the fourth movement. Although these are the only actual plainchant melodies to be used, many of the themes from the other movements reflect something of the rhythmic flow and contour of plainchant.

The piece was commissioned by André Malraux, who was at that time the Minister of Culture, and was first performed in the Sainte Chapelle in Paris in May 1965, under the direction of Serge Baudo. In a note on the score, Messiaen says that the work was intended for large spaces: cathedrals, churches, and even in the open air and on high mountains. The orchestration has some unusual features, even for Messiaen. Piano and strings are totally omitted, replaced by a large woodwind and brass section (including a bass saxhorn). The constitution of the percussion section is typical of the works of this period in its use of metal percussion instruments, but is enlarged to include no less than three groups of cencerros, six gongs and three tam-tams, besides a set of tubular bells.

The work is divided into five movements, each of which are to be separated by a silence of about one minute in length. None of the movements have titles, but each is preceded by a quotation from scripture relating to the theological idea of the work—the resurrection of mankind, accomplished through the resurrection of Christ. The musical content of each movement is of the utmost simplicity, and yet because of this it is more powerful than any orchestral work since the *Turangalîla-Symphonie*.

The idea of Christ's resurrection is the subject of the second movement— 'Christ, risen from the dead, will die no more; death has no more power over him' (Romans 6: 9)—and is symbolized by the use of the Sharngadeva rhythm 'simhavikrama' (8) which means 'the power of the lion'. This rhythm also contains another Sharngadeva rhythm—'vijaya' (51)—which means 'victory'; it consists of fifteen unit-values or *mâtrâs*, the number of the Trinity (3) multiplied by the number of the Indian god Shiva (5). As we have seen (Chapter 5, p. 41), Shiva represents the death of death and is therefore a symbol of Christ, who conquered death on the Cross. Christ is also referred to in the Apocalypse as the Lion from the tribe of Juda who gained victory over death—hence the symbolism of the 'power of the lion' and of 'victory' in the rhythm 'simhavikrama'.

Ex.83

simhavikrama

The use of the song of the Uirapuru bird in the third movement is also symbolic. There is a legend among the natives of the Amazon, where the bird is found, that one only hears it sing at the moment of death. In a different sense, this bird becomes another symbol of Christ, relating to the quotation which precedes the movement—'The hour will come when the dead will hear the voice of the Son of God . . .' (John 5: 25).

There are three separate musical elements in this movement—the birdsong, four notes permutated on the bells, and a tremendous but brief crescendo on a repeated chord. This is followed by a further permutation of the bell-notes, now in the lower wind instruments. The orchestral crescendo is reflected in a tremendous roll on the lowest gong and tam-tam emerging from the last of the four wind notes and rising to the loudest point in the whole movement (marked *fffff* in the score).

On its own, a single tam-tam would not be regarded as being of great musical significance, yet with only the simplest of musical ideas associated with it Messiaen succeeds in producing one of the most powerful and impressive moments in the whole work. Further, in his use of such a simple *sound* as a complete musical idea in itself, devoid of melodic and rhythmic implications, he follows in the footsteps of that great pioneer of the twentieth century—Edgar Varèse, whom he regards as a very important figure.[8]

Simplicity of musical idea is also the mark of the next movement, which expresses the joy of the resurrection. Again, three separate ideas are used. The first consists of two plainchant melodies, together with the rhythm 'simhavikrama' on the gongs; this symbolizes 'the gift of light' (*le don de clarté*), one of the qualities of the risen body. The second is the song of the Calandra lark (alouette calandre), symbolizing joy and 'the gift of agility' (*le don d'agilité*). The third consists of three solemn strokes on the three tam-tams, symbolizing 'the call of the Trinity, the solemn moment of the resurrection and the distant melody of the stars'.[9] Like the tam-tam and gong roll in the previous movement, this remains a simple 'sound-element' which separates the different strophes of plainchant and birdsong. It returns more loudly each time until it eventually dominates the movement as its most significant and impressive feature. Although of extreme simplicity when compared with the other musical ideas, each statement lasts for about the same length of time as each strophe of birdsong or plainchant, so that a fairly equal balance in time is maintained between the different elements of the movement. After the climax of the movement, the tam-tam strokes return again quietly, twice in succession, but subtly transformed by the additional resonance of a pair of gongs to each stroke.

Apart from the explicit uses of plainchant in the fourth movement, the melodic style in other parts of the work, particularly the first and last movements, is reminiscent of the rhythmic shape and smooth melodic contours of plainchant, although Messiaen's use of much wider intervals than can be found in plainchant tends to disguise this relationship.

'La Transfiguration de Notre Seigneur Jésus-Christ' (1963–69)

In terms of length, plus vocal and instrumental forces employed, *La Transfiguration* is one of the largest works that Messiaen has written. It was commissioned by the Gulbenkian Foundation and first performed on 7 June 1969 under the direction of Serge Baudo. For this work, Messiaen requires a large orchestra of over 100 players, a mixed choir of 100 voices divided into 10 groups, and a group of seven soloists: piano, cello, flute, clarinet, vibraphone, marimba and xylophone. The text of the work (chosen by the composer) consists primarily of the Gospel narrative of the Transfiguration, with meditative movements drawing from the Psalms, the Wisdom of Solomon, Genesis, the Epistles of St Paul, the Roman Missal and the *Summa Theologica* of St Thomas Aquinas.

The work is divided into two 'Septenaries', or groups of seven pieces. The first and fourth in each group consist of settings of the Gospel text which describes the Transfiguration, and each of these is followed by two meditative movements which comment on each portion of the Gospel. Each Septenary ends with a Choral—that is, a piece in the style of a chorale, not an actual Lutheran chorale. In its alternation of Gospel narrative and meditative movements, as well as in the use of movements in the style of chorales, the shape of the work resembles the Passions of J. S. Bach. In addition, the role of the seven soloists in relation to the choir and orchestra recalls the role of the obbligato instruments in a Bach cantata. At this point, however, the resemblance ends; the work is completely typical of Messiaen in every other respect, in its use of plainchant,[10] melodies in plainchant style, birdsong, harmonic colours and resonances, Greek and Sharngadeva rhythms, 'Turangalîla' motives, and especially in the use of many of these musical elements to symbolize the various theological aspects of the narrative. Unlike Bach, Messiaen does not give the Gospel narrative to a solo voice, but to the men of the choir, or men and women together, singing in unison. Each of these movements is similar in its musical content, beginning with a passage for gongs and temple-blocks, and setting the text in a neo-plainchant style.

It is significant that Messiaen should have been drawn to this particular subject—the Transfiguration of Christ on the mountain—because of the fascination which mountains have always had for him. As in previous works, it is the familiar mountains of the Dauphiny on which he draws for his inspiration. In his note on the work he tells us that it was while looking at Mont Blanc, the Jungfrau, and the three glaciers of the Meidje in clear weather, that he understood the difference between the small splendour of the snow and the great splendour of the sun, and it was this that led him to imagine the extent to which the sight of the Transfiguration was awesome. It is appropriate therefore that, besides the many other birdsongs drawn from different countries, Messiaen makes particular use of mountain birds found in the Dauphiny region: the alpine chough, the alpine accentor, the peregrine and Bonelli's eagle.

In their different ways, both *Et exspecto resurrectionem mortuorum* and *La Transfiguration* display a monumental simplicity in the presentation of their material. *La Transfiguration* is less severe than the earlier work, however, but it is no less powerful in its impact. Its harmonic range is as wide as that of *Catalogue d'Oiseaux*, ranging from extreme dissonance to consonance and, in some places, to actual common-chord harmonies without added notes. Apart from the chorales themselves, there is a certain amount of quasi-chorale writing in other parts of the work, often contrasting with, on the one hand, the monodic passages in plainchant style and, on the other, birdsong.

Although *La Transfiguration* makes use of over eighty different birdsongs— more than any other work to date, including *Catalogue d'Oiseaux*—they are less important in relation to the work as a whole than in the 'bird' pieces of the 'fifties. There is, as has been pointed out, an association between certain birdsongs used and mountainous regions, but no symbolism is intended by the use of particular songs, as is the case with the Uirapuru's song in *Et exspecto resurrectionem mortuorum*. The material drawn from this source is, in the final instance, purely musical in its importance and content, taking its place alongside other material in the complete mosaic.

'Méditations sur le Mystère de la Sainte Trinité' (1969)

Following the completion of *La Transfiguration*, Messiaen has found the time to write two works, neither of which was commissioned, and both there-fore representing in their separate ways matters which he feels particularly involved with as a composer at the present moment. The first, *Méditations sur le Mystère de la Sainte Trinité*, is for organ—the first important work to be written for this instrument for eighteen years—and the second, *La Fauvette des jardins* for piano, is a successor to the *Catalogue d'Oiseaux*.

In the organ work, all the elements of his recent work are present—plain-chant, birdsong, religious symbolism derived mainly from the *Summa Theo-logica* of St Thomas Aquinas, and so on. There remains one new element in the work, and that is what Messiaen calls 'le langage communicable'. In discussing this aspect of the work in his note for the recording, Messiaen reveals some important points about his musical thought. He states, first of all, that music does not express anything directly, but that it can intimate, or give rise to a feeling, a state of the soul, or that it can touch the subconscious or increase the dream faculties. Without wishing to argue the point as to whether music is capable of expressing anything, suffice it to say that, in spite of what Stravinsky may have implied to the contrary, all the great musical traditions, Eastern and Western, have assumed that music, in some way or another, can do what Messiaen here describes. He goes on to cite the 'language' of Wagner's *leitmotivs* by which the music communicates to the listener, in its own way, the drama which is taking place on the stage. It is essential, however, for the listener to know these leitmotivs in advance. Further, he cites St Thomas Aquinas who, in his *Summa Theologica*, speaks of the direct telepathic communication between the angels, who are not subject to the restrictions of time and space. 'Overwhelmed by these grandiose examples,' says Messiaen, 'and without wishing to imitate the cabbalist who looks for hidden meanings behind the letters of words, or the numerical values of those letters—I have tried, nevertheless, as a game, and in order to give another form to my thinking, to find a kind of communicable musical language.'

In order to do this he takes the German musical alphabet as his basis: A, B (= B flat), C, D, E, F, G, H (= B natural) in order to 'translate' words into music. These eight notes are fixed in the octave beginning on the A above middle C. He then assigns the remainder of the alphabet to other notes, again in fixed registers, grouping them according to their quality of sound. In addition, each note is assigned a fixed duration as well as register.

Ex.84

Articles, pronouns, adverbs and prepositions are omitted in this 'language', and short melodic and rhythmic phrases are added before nouns and adjectives to represent the different cases. Two common verbs have their own complementary motivic formula—'to be' and 'to have', and the Divine Name of God is represented by its own melodic phrase which can exist also in retrograde form.

In order to understand the nature of what Messiaen is trying to do in this work, it is important to know the factors which led to its initial musical inspiration. At the time of Napoleon I, there lived in Messiaen's home town of Grenoble a scholar and linguist called Champollion, who was one of the few people of his day who could understand Coptic and decipher Egyptian hieroglyphics. During a campaign in Egypt, some of Napoleon's more cultured officers discovered a stone tablet at Rosetta, carved with Egyptian hieroglyphics. Since no one was able to decipher it, they sent it to Champollion. He discovered that there were circles around four words, which he therefore knew must be the names of kings. He was able to read these four words in Coptic, which enabled him to decipher, in consequence, the whole of the tablet. This feat of being able to decipher a whole tablet from clues supplied by only four words impressed Messiaen very much and led to his conception of the 'langage communicable' in his *Méditations*.[11]

In approaching this work, the listener is in the same position as Napoleon's officers when they discovered the tablet, in knowing that something is being communicated, but not knowing what. Messiaen supplies all the information for deciphering the message of the work in the score. Music, however, is to be heard and not read like a book so that, even when one knows the key to the language of the work, the message remains hidden and difficult to perceive, just as the Mystery of the Holy Trinity itself is hidden and difficult to comprehend. As Messiaen quotes elsewhere (*Pièce en Trio I* from *Livre d'Orgue*): 'Now we are looking at a confessed reflection in a mirror . . .' (I Cor. 13: 12), but, to complete the quotation, ultimately 'we shall see [the Trinity] face to face'.

'La Fauvette des Jardins' (1970)

Messiaen's latest work to date is in every respect a return to the world of *Catalogue d'Oiseaux*. It is a long piece, lasting about the same length of time as 'La Rousserolle Effarvatte' and is likewise programmatic insofar as the birdsongs and colours of the various times of day are represented. The location is once again the Dauphiny mountains, in particular Lake Laffrey and the foot of the mountain of the Grand Serre which featured in 'La Buse variable'. The season is the end of June and the beginning of July.

At the beginning of the piece, it is still night; towards 4.00 am the cry of the quail and the nightingale's song herald the dawn. The principal bird—the garden warbler—is heard as the sun rises. Different birdsongs are heard as the day progresses, but the garden warbler contributes its long and varied strophes at all times of the day. Late in the afternoon, the black kite (milan noir) climbs and descends, describing great spirals in the air. The calm of the lake is broken only by interjections from the yellowhammer, chaffinch and goldfinch. The sun sets with the song of the nightingale and finally, at 9.00 pm, the call of the tawny owl is heard—musically very similar to its appearance in 'La Chouette Hulotte'. Finally, night falls, leaving the lake faintly visible in the moonlight with the silhouettes of the alder-trees and the Grand Serre completing the landscape.

Although there are always differences in the realization of particular birdsongs, all those used in this piece fall into the same group classification described in Chapter 12. As in *Catalogue d'Oiseaux* there is a great deal of use of colour-chords, but phrases representing the lake at different times of the day are unusual in coming to a climax on a common chord without any added notes (a feature previously noted in *La Transfiguration*). Common chords do occasionally feature in *Catalogue* (for example, at the beginning of 'L'Alouette Calandrelle'), but never in a stressed context. The transformations which this phrase undergoes during the course of the piece recall the four paintings by Monet of Rouen Cathedral, in which he captures the play of light on the Cathedral at different times of the day. Its first appearance (p. 4) represents the pink reflections of the sun in the lake at dawn (climax chords—C major and B flat major). Late in the afternoon, the blue of the lake is evoked by chord sequences coming to rest in A major (representing blue, as in 'Le Merle blue' and 'Le Traquet rieur'). Above the final A major chord (p. 49) the yellowhammer's song is added almost like an upper resonance, bringing fresh colour to the chord.

In spite of the strong affinities that this work has with *Catalogue d'Oiseaux*, it retains its own unique character which is unlike any of the pieces in the earlier work. Only one new birdsong (or, more precisely, bird-call) is used— the black kite, but many of the birdsongs which appeared in different pieces in *Catalogue d'Oiseaux* are gathered together into the same piece in *La Fauvette des Jardins*.

Sufficient time has elapsed since the composition of *Couleurs de la Cité céleste* to make it clear that this work is yet another turning-point in Messiaen's output towards a more complete synthesis of all the main musical and symbolic elements in his previous work. *La Fauvette des Jardins*, on the other hand, is evidence that the use of birdsong to evoke impressions of nature is still as valid for him as its more symbolic use in other recent works.

To what extent the new ideas concerning language in *Méditations sur le Mystère de la Sainte Trinité* will be of significance for future work is impossible to determine at this stage. There is little doubt, however, that the work will become recognized as one of Messiaen's major compositions for organ.

Notes on Table VII. The table is divided into two halves (I—permutations 1–18; II—permutations 19–36). Each half is divided into six sets consisting of three permutations each. The permutations in each half of the table pair off (1 corresponding to 19, 2 to 20 and so on) such that the order of values in each pair is the same except for those belonging to group b (2, 8, 11, 28). Each pair of permutations is labelled A, B, C, D, . . . up to R. All pairs of permutations are represented in the work except for pair P and pair R. Of these, only the former has interesting potentialities as a rhythmic sequence as pair R corresponds to the original chromatic series which is to be permutated. The actual portion used of each set of permutations is bounded by a thick black line.

CHRONOCHROMIE

TABLE VII

			DURATIONS (to be permutated)	1	2	3	4	5	6	7	8	9	10	11	12	13	14	15	16	17	18	19	20	21	22	23	24	25	26	27	28	29	30	31	32	
I	1.	STROPHE I	I	3	28	5	30	7	32	26	2	25	1	8	24	13	15	16	17	18	22	21	20	19	4	31	6	29	10	27	11	15	14	12	13	A
			II	5	11	7	14	26	13	10	28	1	8	2	6	25	31	17	18	22	4	20	21	19	30	12	32	1	27	11	17	22	24	13	15	B
			III	7	8	26	23	10	9	1	2	3	5	28	32	29	12	18	22	4	30	21	19	20	14	24	13	3	27	2	2	17	31	6	25	C
	2.		IV	26	2	10	31	1	25	3	11	16	28	32	13	15	24	23	4	30	14	20	21	19	9	6	25	16	30	17	28	18	12	32	29	D
			V	10	28	1	12	3	29	5	7	26	11	9	30	24	15	6	4	14	23	20	19	21	31	32	18	25	18	22	11	22	24	13	15	E
			VI	1	11	3	24	5	16	7	28	2	2	8	25	17	32	30	14	23	31	20	21	19	13	29	12	13	22	26	8	4	6	9	16	F
	3.	ANTISTROPHE II	VII	3	8	5	6	7	16	26	11	1	28	22	29	18	13	14	23	31	12	21	19	20	24	9	15	4	10	27	2	30	32	25	17	G
			VIII	5	2	7	32	26	17	10	8	28	4	3	6	15	22	9	23	31	24	19	21	20	19	6	25	16	30	1	28	14	13	29	18	H
			IX	7	28	26	13	10	18	1	2	3	30	11	25	4	30	25	31	12	24	20	20	21	18	25	17	3	1	23	4	6	9	15	22	I
	4.		X	26	11	10	9	1	22	3	28	5	7	23	17	30	29	24	6	32	13	20	21	19	4	9	18	23	5	8	31	25	16	4	4	J
			XI	10	8	1	25	3	4	5	11	7	10	26	24	12	18	15	32	13	9	19	21	20	31	16	22	5	3	7	7	12	29	17	30	K
			XII	1	2	3	29	5	30	7	8	26	31	28	16	23	14	24	6	32	13	20	21	19	25	17	12	26	5	27	28	24	15	18	14	L
	5.	INTRODUCTION figs. 7-10, 18-21 CODA figs 129-132	XIII	3	5	7	15	14	13	26	28	12	24	4	31	17	32	32	13	9	25	21	19	20	18	22	30	24	10	27	11	6	22	23	23	M
			XIV	5	7	16	26	23	17	10	8	28	3	30	14	2	18	13	9	25	29	19	21	20	15	22	14	6	1	27	2	32	17	4	31	N
			XV	7	8	26	17	10	31	1	1	2	5	11	24	16	14	24	22	16	15	20	21	19	16	4	23	32	26	4	13	18	30	12	12	O
	6.		XVI	26	2	10	18	1	12	3	8	7	11	23	8	32	11	24	25	29	15	20	21	19	30	31	13	5	27	28	9	22	14	24	24	P
			XVII	10	28	11	22	3	24	5	4	3	2	26	4	8	31	32	30	16	17	20	21	19	18	14	12	9	1	25	7	4	23	6	6	Q
			XVIII	1	11	3	4	5	6	7	28	11	30	28	2	12	13	14	15	16	17	18	19	20	21	22	23	24	25	26	8	29	30	31	32	R
II	1.		XIX	3	8	5	30	7	32	26	11	25	1	28	24	16	17	18	22	21	19	20	21	20	4	31	6	29	10	27	11	15	14	12	13	A
			XX	5	2	7	14	26	13	10	8	1	8	2	6	25	31	17	18	22	4	20	21	19	30	12	32	1	27	11	16	23	24	9	9	B
			XXI	7	28	26	23	10	9	1	2	3	5	28	32	29	16	18	22	4	30	21	19	20	14	24	13	3	27	11	17	31	6	25	25	C
	2.	STROPHE II	XXII	26	11	10	31	1	25	3	28	16	7	32	13	15	24	23	4	30	14	20	21	19	9	6	25	16	30	17	18	18	12	32	29	D
			XXIII	10	8	1	12	3	29	5	11	26	8	9	30	24	15	6	4	14	23	19	21	20	31	32	18	25	18	22	28	22	24	13	15	E
			XXIV	1	2	3	24	5	16	7	8	2	2	28	25	17	32	30	14	23	31	20	21	19	13	29	12	13	22	26	27	4	6	9	16	F
	3.		XXV	3	28	5	6	7	16	26	11	1	28	22	29	18	13	14	23	31	12	21	19	20	24	9	15	4	10	27	11	30	32	25	17	G
			XXVI	5	11	7	32	26	17	10	7	28	4	9	6	15	22	9	23	31	24	19	21	20	19	6	25	16	30	6	8	14	13	29	18	H
			XXVII	7	28	26	13	10	18	1	28	3	5	11	25	4	24	25	31	12	24	20	20	21	18	25	17	3	14	23	2	23	9	15	22	I
	4.	ANTISTROPHE I	XXVIII	26	2	10	9	1	22	3	28	5	7	23	17	30	29	24	6	32	13	20	21	19	4	9	18	23	5	28	31	25	16	4	4	J
			XXIX	10	28	1	25	3	4	5	11	7	10	26	9	14	15	24	32	16	17	19	21	20	19	6	22	31	7	7	12	29	17	30	30	K
			XXX	1	11	3	29	5	30	7	8	26	31	10	16	23	16	24	6	32	13	20	21	19	25	17	12	26	27	28	24	15	18	14	14	L
	5.		XXXI	3	5	7	15	14	13	26	28	12	24	4	31	17	32	32	13	9	25	21	19	20	18	22	30	24	10	27	11	6	22	23	23	M
			XXXII	5	2	7	16	23	17	10	8	28	3	30	14	12	18	13	9	25	29	19	21	20	15	22	14	6	1	27	2	32	17	4	31	N
			XXXIII	7	28	26	17	10	31	1	2	5	5	11	24	16	24	24	22	16	15	20	21	19	16	4	23	32	3	3	13	18	30	12	12	O
	6.	INTRODUCTION figs. 4, 6 CODA figs 127-129	XXXIV	26	10	1	18	1	12	3	23	7	2	23	6	4	25	29	15	16	17	20	21	19	30	31	13	5	26	28	9	22	14	24	24	P
			XXXV	10	8	11	1	3	24	5	24	3	2	26	28	31	32	30	15	16	17	20	21	19	18	14	12	9	7	2	25	4	23	6	6	Q
			XXXVI	1	2	3	4	5	6	7	28	11	30	28	9	12	13	14	15	16	17	18	19	20	21	22	23	24	25	26	28	29	30	31	32	R

SEPT HAÏKAÏ

Movements:	I	II	III	IV
Woodwind piccolo flute 2 oboes cor anglais clarinet in E flat 2 clarinets in B flat bass clarinet 2 bassoons	Retrograde version of Tâla I (piano)	*clarinets only:* Florid melodies in irrational values	*treble wind:* birdsong *bass clarinet,* *bassoons:* Monody using irrational values	*piccolo,* *clarinet in* *E flat:* subsidiary melody *oboes, cor* *anglais:* principal melody
Brass trumpet trombone	Colouration of Tâla II (percussion)	[TACET]	*trumpet only:* birdsong (uguisu)	*trumpet only:* principal melody
8 violins	Melody (First Strophe)	Homophonic colouration of Permutation 5 (percussion)	[TACET]	Independent tâla (homo- phony)
Keyed *percussion* xylophone marimba	Tâla III	*marimba only* Monody (quasi- birdsong)	birdsong	[TACET]
piano	Tâla I	Polyphony in irrational values	birdsong	[TACET]
Non-keyed *percussion*	Tâla II ('rythme des 3 Shaktis')	*crotals:* Permutation 5 *bells:* Permutation 4	Three tâlas in irrational values	*cencerros:* Permutation 19 *crotals:* Permutation 20 *bells:* Permutation 21 *cyms, gongs,* *tam-tams:* Independent tâla in ir- rational values

V	VI	VII	Summary of instrumental functions
piccolo, flutes: Countermelody in irrational values *oboes, clarinets, bassoons:* Tâla in irrational values	birdsong	Tâla I	*Main function:* Various melodic material and birdsong *Secondary function:* Rhythmic tâlas
Tâla in irrational values	birdsong *(trumpet:* uguisu, *trombone:* hototoguisu)	Colouration of Tâla II (percussion)	*Functions:* 1. Rhythmic tâlas 2. Certain birdsongs (uguisu and hototoguisu)
Homophonic colouration of tâla on the bells	[TACET]	Melody (Second Strophe)	*Main function:* Rhythmic tâlas (homophony) *Secondary function:* The melody in movements I and VII
Monody (quasi-birdsong)	birdsong	Tâla III — retrograded	*Main function:* Birdsong and quasi-birdsong *Secondary function:* Rhythmic tâlas
Repeated rhythmic figures in irrational values	birdsong	Tâla I — retrograded	*Functions:* Tâlas, rhythmic figures and birdsong
triangle, crotals, cencerros: with piano *bells:* with Vlns (rhythmic tâla) *cyms, gongs, tam-tams:* with wind (tâla)	Various rhythms using irrational values	Continuation of Tâla II (movement I)	*Function:* Rhythmic tâlas

TABLE IX

Couleurs de la Cité céleste

	Introduction	
	Birdsong	A-P8
Timbre/Density of texture		3
Type of texture		P
Rhythm		2/3

1st section											
bellbird	CC	A-P8	CC	bellbird	A-P8	CC	A-P8	bellbird	CC	A-P8	CC
	4	2	4		2	4	2		4	2	4
	H	P	H		P	H	P		H	P	H
	1	2/3	1		2/3	1	2/3		1	2/3	1

Refrain			2nd section (2 strophes – second expanded)				
'The star which has the key to the abyss'	bird-song (piano)	A-C	: birdsong	'The abyss'	A-E4	tâla	:
		4		M	2	Mixed (mainly 1/2)	
		H		(+resonance)	M	P	
		1		1	1	4	

3rd section								
A-P8	A-P8	A-D+A-P8	A-P8	A-D+A-P8	A-P8	A-P8(CC)	A-P8	A-P8
3	2	4	2	4	2	4(1/2)	2	3
P	H	P	H	P	H	P	H	P
2/3	4	2/3	4	2/3	4	1/2/4	4	2/3

Coda					Refrain
bird-song (piano)	A-P8+birdsong+tâla		bird-song (piano)	'The abyss'	as before
	1			M	
	P			(+resonance)	
	1/4			1	

Notes on table IX

The scheme is somewhat simplified in order to illustrate the main interactions of material. The degree of rhythmic complexity is indicated by numbers 1 to 4, ranging from the simplest (1) to the most complex rhythm of the tâla (4)—see ex. 81. Textural density is indicated in the same way, taking into account the degree of sustaining quality involved. The colour-chords at fig. 11 are taken as a norm (4) and other figures indicate the degree of variation from this norm with respect to textural density and sustaining quality. (These considerations apply only to material other than birdsong.)

Abbreviations

H = Homophony, P = Polyphony
A-P8 = Alleluia for the eighth Sunday after Pentecost

180

A-E4 = Alleluia for the fourth Sunday after Easter
A-C   = Alleluia for Corpus Christi
A-D   = Alleluia for the Feast of the Dedication of a Church
CC   = colour-chords

Portions of the tâla applied to the colour-chords in the 1st section
1. (fig. 13)   Aristophanean—râgavardhana
2. (fig. 24)   Râgavardhana—tritîya

Portions of the tâla applied to the Alleluia in the 3rd section
1. (fig. 68)   (Gajalîla)—pratâpaçekhara—vijaya
2. (fig. 70)   (Aristophanean)—râgavardhana
3. (fig. 72)   Cretic
4. (fig. 77)   (Cretic)—Phalacean

(Incomplete rhythms are indicated in brackets)

Notes on Chapter 13

1. Oxford University Press, 1927, p. 116.

2. *EOM* p. 154.

3. *Ethno-Musicologica* Vol. III, E. J. Brill, 1954.

4. *EOM* pp. 164–5.

5. *Première Note de l'Auteur* in the score.

6. *EOM* p. 167.

7. The full texts of the Alleluia verses are:

   8th Sunday after Pentecost: 'The Lord is great and worthy of praise, in the city of God, in his holy mountain.'

   4th Sunday after Easter: 'Christ, rising from the dead, will die no more: death will have no more power over him.'

   Corpus Christi: 'My flesh is food indeed, my blood is drink indeed: he who eats my flesh and drinks my blood will remain in me and I in him.'

   Dedication of a Church: 'I will worship at your holy temple and I will praise your name.'

8. *EOM* p. 204.

9. Preface to the score.

10. Notably the transformation of the Alleluia for the Feast of the Transfiguration in the sixth movement of the second Septenary.

11. Information supplied by Messiaen.

14

Messiaen: a Historical Placing

At the beginning of the present century a number of different trends in music began to evolve. Two divergent ones in particular stand out as being of great importance in the light of musical developments since the Second World War. One, the serialism of the Second Viennese School, grew out of the symphonic tradition, although abrogating the tonal system on which it was based. The other trend, represented by Debussy and Stravinsky and, in America, Varèse, was more firmly opposed to the excesses of the late nineteenth century and its grandiose conception of the role of the symphony.

The Second Viennese School, while introducing important innovations, retained the classical attitude to rhythm, texture and form. Only Webern moved beyond this point towards some consideration of the relationship of rhythm, dynamic and timbre to the serial idea, but even he always worked from the basic assumption that everything was to be subordinated to pitch-structure. The main concern of the serialists—unity of idea—was the logical consequence of nineteenth-century symphonic practice.

In spite of the fact that Messiaen has occasionally drawn parallels between his own procedures and those of the symphonic tradition, he genuinely lies outside this tradition as a successor to Debussy and Stravinsky. As we have seen, the colouristic rather than functional conception of harmony which he inherited from Debussy led eventually to a rethinking of the relationships between, and relative importance of, pitch-structures (monody and homophony), rhythm, timbre and other parameters. In contrast to the Second Viennese School, his concern has never been for unity of idea, and the diversity of material on which he draws in any given work of length is one of the stumbling blocks which certain critics experience in his music.

It is the failure to recognize the extent to which Messiaen lies outside the symphonic tradition, and to appreciate that valuations of his music based on that tradition are irrelevant, that has misled some commentators to criticize his music for the wrong reasons. André Hodeir, for example, in his book *Since Debussy*,[1] compares the 'evolutive contemplation' of Bach's great organ chorales and Beethoven's Fifteenth Quartet to what he calls the 'frozen contemplation' of Messiaen's music. He regards this trait, derived from the

Far Eastern tradition, as an alarmingly retrogressive step, implicit in every one of Messiaen's ideas about music. The error embodied in this criticism is, of course, fairly obvious; criteria derived from the Western tradition are no more applicable to Messiaen than they are to the Far Eastern tradition, by which he is supposed to have been influenced (according to Hodeir). It would be truer to say that he arrives at a position which is analogous to Eastern music because of his attitude to harmony as a static element. A sense of time, marked by an evolving texture, is fundamental to Bach and Beethoven, but it has always been Messiaen's aim to suspend the sense of time in music (except in those works which are based on birdsong in relation to nature), in order to express the idea of the 'eternal'—in which time does not exist—as distinct from the 'temporal'. Viewed in this light, Hodeir's criticism becomes an inverted compliment, since he virtually complains that Messiaen has succeeded in doing exactly what he sets out to do. One may object in principle to the whole concept of 'timelessness' in music, but this becomes a philosophical objection rather than a musical one.

Another criticism which has been levelled against Messiaen's music is its dependence on sectionalized forms. The whole development of Western music since the end of the eighteenth century has involved a gradual breakdown of sectional working in both the symphonic and operatic fields. In the light of this tendency, Messiaen's early sectional structures appear to be retrogressive. It is certainly the case that in some of the early works the use of such forms is gratuitous: mere juxtaposition of different musical ideas which do not in themselves change or develop significantly is not of great value; compare, for instance, the moribundity of the Prelude 'Les sons impalpables du rêve' with 'Chant d'extase dans un paysage triste', which avoids this pitfalls. One of the most important developments in Messiaen's music, stemming from *Le Banquet céleste* and from 'Chant d'extase', was the introduction of a dynamic element into a sectional form so that extensions, variations or developments of material take place across the various contrasting juxtapositions. 'Fouillis d'arc-en-ciel, pour l'Ange qui annonce la fin du Temps' from the *Quatuor* is the archetypal piece in this form.

In later works, the dynamic cross-relationships of juxtaposed varying sections is provided by the various couplet and refrain forms, in which the couplet varies or is developed and the refrain remains unchanged, or merely undergoes internal rearrangements of its elements (as in 'Chants d'Oiseaux' from *Livre d'Orgue*), or rhythmic expansions (as in *Neumes rythmiques*). In other works, alternate contrasting strophes might undergo separate development or expansion, such as the alternating passages of song thrush and skylark in the Antistrophes of *Chronochromie*. In *Catalogue d'Oiseaux* the same formal principles are at work, but in a more intricate way.

The most significant formal development, however, comes about in *Couleurs de la Cité céleste*, where material is allowed to interact so that one idea can be modified by the characteristics of another to produce the 'stained-glass window' effect which is important to the idea of the piece. It is true that, for the composer, the form of this piece arises from his particular conception of 'sound-colour', an idea which is perhaps of no immediate importance to others; nevertheless, the musical interactions and transformations which take place as a result of this conception are of great importance, and are at the same time characteristic of post-war serial methods.

Messiaen is hardly influenced, of course, by the serialism of the younger generation, but comparison of his work with that of two of his foremost pupils—Boulez and Stockhausen—reveals important fundamental similarities in musical thought. Boulez was more immediately affected by Messiaen's music than Stockhausen. Having derived his own basic serial methods from a study of Webern's music and his cellular rhythmic procedures from Stravinsky, in his first *Structures* for two pianos (1952) he recognizes his debt to Messiaen by basing the work on the first of the three twelve-note series of the mode from Messiaen's *Mode de valeurs et d'intensités*. At the same time he extends his rhythmic procedures by the use of a chromatic durational series, applied to each note of a twelve-note row. *Structures* makes use of serial elements in a very rigid fashion, but subsequent works—*Le Marteau sans Maître*, *Improvisations sur Mallarmé* and the third Piano Sonata, for example—introduce a much greater freedom of working. By the time that the third Piano Sonata was written (1957) it was clear that Boulez had arrived at a conception of musical structure similar to that of *Couleurs de la Cité céleste*. The different musical elements—pitch-series, rhythmic groups, dynamic envelopes, tempo variations and timbres—are allowed to interact freely, one modifying the other in a continual variation of sound.

Stockhausen's musical thought and Messiaen's come close together in other respects. In his article 'Music and Speech' in Volume 6 of *Die Reihe*, Stockhausen says in the course of discussing his *Gesang der Jünglinge* (1955–1956) for electronic tape: 'At certain points in the composition, sung groups of words become comprehensible speech-symbols, words; at others they remain pure sound-qualities, sound-symbols; between these two extremes there are various degrees of comprehensibility of the word.' The point at which the text becomes a pure sound-symbol is the point where it makes contact with the electronic sounds. The text does not exist in opposition to the music, but forms part of the same continuum. Stockhausen sums up the procedure at the end of the article: 'The basic conception may have become clear: first of all to arrange everything separate into as smooth a continuum as possible, and then to extricate the diversities from this continuum and compose with them.' [2]

We have seen that the idea of the 'continuum' is not only relevant but also essential to the understanding of the musical and formal processes of *Catalogue d'Oiseaux* and *Couleurs de la Cité céleste*. The structure of these pieces depends on the degree to which different groups of material resemble or differ from one another in particular respects, so that formal relationships can be determined by resemblances of, say, texture or rhythmic shape, without the necessity for exact repetitions of material, or thematic development and variation.

Some characteristics, of course, induce stronger relationships than others, although any musical parameter can establish a relationship between different groups of material.

Similarities of melodic or rhythmic shape will always establish closer relationships than similarities of texture, and these in turn induce stronger links between groups than similarities of dynamic or timbre. It is nevertheless possible to create a formal link by having two blocks of material at different points in the composition which only resemble each other in the fact that they are both marked *ff*, or are allotted to the same group of instruments.

Although it would be rash to claim that Messiaen, Boulez and Stockhausen have always influenced each other, the similarities in their musical thought point to an important development in post-war European music which is not merely confined to instrumental and vocal music but which has had an impact on electronic music also. Indeed, Messiaen's conception of harmony as essentially integrated sounds is very relevant in the electronic field, where all sound-complexes are acoustically more integrated than they are in instrumental music. The modulation of one single pitch by another, for instance, can produce a sound in which the constituent pitches are not clearly audible. In ring modulation, in fact, they are totally suppressed and a new sound with a different character is produced.

In England, Alexander Goehr (a Messiaen pupil) and Harrison Birtwistle have both been influenced by Messiaen in their individual ways, although Goehr's music remains Teutonic and 'Schönbergian' in its actual sound quality and Birtwistle's has an individually English ethos. Peter Maxwell Davies, although he has expressed admiration for Messiaen, is more obviously influenced by the music of Italy, where he studied.

In some respects, an assessment of Messiaen's position and importance at this time must inevitably remain incomplete, but it is apparent that he has always undergone a development as a composer and that his music does genuinely embody new conceptions. Apart from stimulating the work of younger composers, since about 1950 he has been held in increasingly greater esteem by composers of many different outlooks as well as by the musical public. Controversy has raged, and still rages, among critics as to the value of his work, but this is merely the mark of a truly individual composer who has something to say which cannot be ignored.

Notes on Chapter 14

1. Translated by Noel Burch and published in England in 1961 by Martin Secker & Warburg.
2. Translated by Ruth Koenig.

Appendix I
Chronological List of Works

Date	Title	Instrumentation	Publisher
1917	*La Dame de Shalotte*	Piano	—
1921	*Deux Ballades de Villon* 1. Epître à ses amis 2. Ballade des pendus	Voice and piano	—
1925	*La tristesse d'un grand ciel blanc*	Piano	—
1927	*Esquisses modales*	Organ	—
1928	*Variations écossaises*	Organ	—
	Fugue en ré mineur	Orchestra	—
	Le Banquet céleste	Organ	Leduc
	L'hôte aimable des âmes	Organ	—
	Le Banquet Eucharistique	Orchestra	—
1929	*Préludes* 1. La colombe 2. Chant d'extase dans un paysage triste 3. Le nombre léger 4. Instants défunts 5. Les sons impalpables du rêve 6. Cloches d'angoisse et larmes d'adieu 7. Plainte calme 8. Un reflet dans le vent	Piano	Durand
1930	*Simple chant d'un âme*	Orchestra	—
	Trois mélodies 1. Pourquoi?	Soprano and piano	Durand

187

Date	Title	Instrumentation	Publisher
	2. Le sourire		
	3. La fiancée perdue		
	La Mort du Nombre	Soprano, tenor, violin and piano	Durand
	Diptyque	Organ	Durand
	Les Offrandes oubliées	Orchestra (also arr. piano)	Durand
	1. La Croix		
	2. Le Péché		
	3. L'Eucharistie		
1931	*Le tombeau resplendissant*	Orchestra	MS on hire —Durand
1932	*Hymne au St Sacrement*	Orchestra	Broude Bros. (New York)
	Thème et Variations	Violin and piano	Leduc
	Fantaisie burlesque	Piano	Durand
	Apparition de L'Église éternelle	Organ	Lemoine
1933	*L'Ascension*	Orchestra	Leduc

1. Majesté du Christ demandant sa gloire à son Père
2. Alléluias sereins d'une âme qui désire le ciel
3. Alléluia sur la trompette, alléluia sur le cymbale
4. Prière du Christ montant vers son Père

Date	Title	Instrumentation	Publisher
	Fantaisie	Violin and piano	—
	Messe	8 sopranos and 4 violins	—
1934	*L'Ascension*	Organ	Leduc

1, 2 and 4 as above
3. Transports de joie d'une âme devant la gloire du Christ qui est la sienne

Date	Title	Instrumentation	Publisher
1935	*Pièce pour le Tombeau de Paul Dukas*	Piano	*Revne musicale* May/June 1936
	Vocalise	Soprano and piano	Leduc (Hettich collection)

Date	*Title*	*Instrumentation*	*Publisher*
	La Nativité du Seigneur	Organ	Leduc

Book I 1. La Vierge et l'enfant
          2. Les bergers
          3. Desseins éternels
Book II 4. Le Verbe
          5. Les Enfants de Dieu
Book III 6. Les Anges
          7. Jésus accepte la souffrance
          8. Les Mages
Book IV 9. Dieu parmi nous

Date	*Title*	*Instrumentation*	*Publisher*
1936	*Poèmes pour Mi*	Soprano and piano	Durand

Book I   1. Action de grâces
          2. Paysage
          3. La maison
          4. Epouvante
Book II 5. L'Epouse
          6. Ta voix
          7. Les deux guerriers
          8. Le collier
          9. Prière exaucée

Date	*Title*	*Instrumentation*	*Publisher*
1937	*Poèmes pour Mi*	arr. orchestra	Durand
	O Sacrum Convivium!	Unaccompanied choir	Durand
	Fête des belles eaux	6 Ondes Martenots	—
1938	*Chants de terre et de ciel*	Soprano and piano	Durand

          1. Bail avec Mi
          2. Antienne du silence
          3. Danse du bébé-Pilule
          4. Arc-en-ciel d'innocence
          5. Minuit pile et face
          6. Résurrection

Date	*Title*	*Instrumentation*	*Publisher*
	Deux Monodies en quarts de ton	Ondes Martenot	—
1939	*Les Corps Glorieux*	Organ	Leduc

Book I   1. Subtilité des corps glorieux
          2. Les eaux de la grâce
          3. L'Ange aux parfums
Book II 4. Combat de la Mort et de la Vie

Date	*Title*	*Instrumentation*	*Publisher*

Book III 5. Force et agilité des corps glorieux
6. Joie et clarté des corps glorieux
7. La mystère de la Sainte Trinité

| 1941 | *Quatuor pour la Fin du Temps* | Clarinet, violin, cello and piano | Durand |

1. Liturgie de cristal
2. Vocalise pour l'Ange qui annonce la fin du Temps
3. Abîme des oiseaux
4. Intermède
5. Louange à l'Eternité de Jésus
6. Danse de la fureur, pour les sept trompettes
7. Fouillis d'arcs-en-ciel, pour l'Ange qui announce la fin du Temps
8. Louange à l'Immortalité de Jésus

| | *Chœurs pour une Jeanne d'Arc* | mixed chorus | — |

| 1942 | *Musique de scène pour un Oedipe* | Ondes Martenot | — |

| 1943 | *Rondeau* | Piano | Leduc |

| | *Visions de L'Amen* | 2 pianos | Durand |

1. Amen de la Création
2. Amen des étoiles, de la planète à l'anneau
3. Amen de l'agonie de Jésus
4. Amen de désir
5. Amen des Anges, des Saints, du chant des oiseaux
6. Amen du Jugement
7. Amen de la Consommation

| 1944 | *Trois petites Liturgies de la Présence divine* | Women's voices and orchestra | Durand |

1. Antienne de la Conversation intérieure
2. Séquence du Verbe, Cantique divine
3. Psalmodie de l'Ubiquité par amour

| | *Vingt Regards sur l'Enfant-Jésus* | Piano | Durand |

1. Regard du Père
2. Regard de l'étoile
3. L'échange
4. Regard de la Vierge

Date	Title	Instrumentation	Publisher

5. Regard du Fils sur le Fils
6. Par Lui tout a été fait
7. Regard de la Croix
8. Regard des hauteurs
9. Regard du temps
10. Regard de l'Esprit de joie
11. Première communion de la Vierge
12. La parole toute puissante
13. Noël
14. Regard des Anges
15. Le baiser de l'Enfant-Jésus
16. Regard des prophètes, des bergers et des Mages
17. Regard du silence
18. Regard de l'Onction terrible
19. Je dors, mais mon cœur veille
20. Regard de l'Eglise d'amour

1945	*Harawi*	Soprano and piano	Leduc

(Chant d'amour et de mort)
1. La ville qui dormait, toi
2. Bonjour toi, colombe verte
3. Montagnes
4. Doundou tchil
5. L'amour de Piroutcha
6. Répétition planétaire
7. Adieu
8. Syllabes
9. L'escalier redit, gestes du soleil
10. Amour, oiseau d'étoile
11. Katchikatchi les étoiles
12. Dans le noir

1946–8	*Turangalîla-Symphonie*	Orchestra	Durand

1. Introduction
2. Chant d'amour I
3. Turangalîla I
4. Chant d'amour II
5. Joie du sang des étoiles
6. Jardin du sommeil d'amour
7. Turangalîla II
8. Développement de l'amour
9. Turangalîla III
10. Final

Date	Title	Instrumentation	Publisher
1949	*Cinq Rechants*	12 solo voices	Salabert
	Cantéyodjayâ	Piano	Universal
	Neumes rythmiques	Piano	Durand
	Mode de valeurs et d'intensités	Piano	Durand
1950	*Île de Feu I and II*	Piano	Durand
	Messe de la Pentecôte	Organ	Leduc

    1. Entrée
    2. Offertoire
    3. Consécration
    4. Communion
    5. Sortie

1951	*Le Merle noir*	Flute and piano	Leduc
	Livre d'Orgue	Organ	Leduc

    1. Reprises par interversion
    2. Pièce en trio
    3. Les Mains de l'abîme
    4. Chants d'oiseaux
    5. Pièce en trio
    6. Les Yeux dans les roues
    7. Soixante-Quatre durées

1952	*Timbres-durées*	Musique concrète *	
1953	*Reveil des Oiseaux*	Piano and orchestra	Durand
1956	*Oiseaux exotiques*	Piano and orchestra	Universal
1956–8	*Catalogue d'Oiseaux*	Piano	Leduc

  Book I   1. Le Chocard des Alpes
             2. Le Loriot
             3. Le Merle bleu
  Book II   4. Le Traquet Stapazin
  Book III 5. La Chouette Hulotte
             6. L'Alouette-Lulu
  Book IV 7. La Rousserolle Effarvatte
  Book V   8. L'Alouette Calandrelle
             9. La Bouscarle

*Unpublished except for two pages published in *The Notation of New Music* by Karkoschka.

Date	Title	Instrumentation	Publisher
	Book VI 10. Le Merle de roche		
	Book VII 11. La Buse variable		
	12. Le Traquet rieur		
	13. Le Courlis cendré		
1960	*Chronochromie*	Orchestra	Leduc
	Verset pour la fête de la Dédicace	Organ	Leduc
1962	*Sept Haïkaï*	Piano and orchestra	Leduc

  1. Introduction
  2. Le parc de Nara et les lanternes de pierre
  3. Yamanaka-Cadenza
  4. Gagaku
  5. Miyajima et le torii dans la mer
  6. Les oiseaux de Karuizawa
  7. Coda

Date	Title	Instrumentation	Publisher
1963	*Couleurs de la Cité céleste*	Piano and orchestra	Leduc
1964	*Et exspecto resurrectionem mortuorum*	Orchestra	Leduc
1963–9	*La Transfiguration de Notre Seigneur Jesus-Christ*	Choir, 7 soloists and orchestra	
1969	*Méditations sur le Mystère de la Sainte Trinité*	Organ	Leduc
1970	*La Fauvette des jardins*	Piano	Leduc

Theoretical works

Date	Title		Publisher
1933	*Vingt leçons de solfège modernes* (only five lessons are by Messiaen)		Lemoine
1939	*Vingt leçons d'harmonie* (in the style of various composers from Monteverdi to Ravel)		Leduc
1942	*Technique de mon langage musical*		Leduc

In preparation—*Traité de rythme*

Appendix II
Table of 120 deçi=tâlas
according to Sharngadera

No.	Names of the tâlas	Notation
1	aditâla	♪
2	dvitîya	♪♪♪
3	tritîya	♪♪♪
4	caturthaka	♪ ♪ ♪
5	pañcama	♪♪
6	nihçankalila	♩. ♩. ♩ ♩ ♪
7	darpana	♪♪♩
8	simhavikrama	♩ ♩ ♩ ♪♩. ♩ ♩.
9	ratilîla	♪♪♩ ♩
10	simhalîla	♪♪♪
11	kandarpa	♪♪♪♩ ♩
12	vîravikrama	♪ ♪♪♩
13	ranga	♪♪♪♪♩
14	çriranga	♪♪♩ ♪♩.
15	caccarî	♪♪♪ ♪♪♪ ♪♪ ♪♪♪ ♪♪ ♪♪♪ ♪♪ ♪♪♪
16	pratyanga	♩ ♩ ♩ ♪♪
17	yatilagna	♪♪
18	gajalîla	♪♪♪♪
19	hamsalîla	♪.♪
20	varnabhinna	♪♪♪ ♩
21	tribhinna	♪♩ ♩.
22	râjacûdâmâni	♪♪♪♪♪♪♪♪ ♩
23	rangodyota	♩ ♩ ♩ ♪♩.
24	rangapradîpaka	♩ ♩ ♪♩ ♩.

194

Table of 120 deçi-tâlas

No.	Names of the tâlas	Notation
25	râjatâla	♩ ♩. ♬♩ ♪♩.
26	tryasra varna	♪♪♬♪♪
	miçra varna	♬♬♪ ♬♬♪ ♬♬♪ ♩. ♩ ♬♩ ♪♩
	caturasra varna	♩ ♪♬♩
27	simhavikrîdita	♪♩. ♩ ♩ ♩. ♩ ♪♩ ♩. ♪♩.
28	jaya	♪♩ ♪♪ ♬♩.
29	vanamâlî	♬♬♪♪ ♬♩
30	hamsanâda	♪♩. ♬♩.
31	simhanâda	♪♩ ♩ ♪♩
32	kudukka	♬♪ ♪
33	turangalîla	♪ ♪ ♬
34	çarabhalîla	♪♪ ♬♬♪ ♪
35	simhanandana	♩ ♩ ♪♩. ♪♩ ♬♩ ♩ ♪♩. ♪♩. ♩ ♪♪♪♪♪♪
36	tribhângi	♪♪♩ ♩
37	rangâbharana	♩ ♩ ♪♪♩.
38	mantha (1)	♪♪♩ ♪♪♪♪
	— (2)	♩ ♪♪♩. ♪♪
	— mudrita (3)	♩ ♪♪♪♪♪♪
	— (4)	♪♪♪♪♩ ♪♪
	[There are six other forms of mantha]	
39	kokilâpriya	♩ ♪♩.
40	nihsâruka	♪ ♪
41	râjavidyâdhara	♪♩ ♬
42	jayamangala	♪♪♩ ♪♪♩
43	mallikâmouâ	♪♪♬♬
44	vijayânanda	♪♪♩ ♩ ♩
45	krîdâ [and] candanihsâruka	♪ ♪

No.	Names of the tālas	Notation
46	jayaçrî	♩ ♪♩ ♪♩
47	makaranda	♫♪ ♪ ♪
48	kîrti	♪♩. ♩ ♪♩.
49	çrîkîrti	♪♪♩ ♩
50	pratitāla	♪♫
51	vijaya	♩. ♩ ♩.
52	bindumâlî	♩ ♫♫♩
53	sama	♪♪♩. ♪
54	nandana	♪♫♩.
55	manthikâ	♩ ♪♩.
—	[or]	♪. ♪
56	dîpaka	♫♪ ♪♩ ♩
57	udîkshana	♪♪♩
58	dhenkî	♩ ♪♩
59	vishama	♫♫. ♫♫.
60	varnamanthikâ	♪ ♪ ♫♪ ♫
61	abhinanda	♪ ♪ ♫♩
62	ananga	♪♩. ♪♪♩
63	nândî	♪ ♫♪ ♪♩ `♩
64	mallatāla	♪ ♪ ♪ ♪ ♫.
65	kankâla (1) pûrna	♫♩.♫♩ ♪
—	(2) khanda	♫♩ ♩
—	(3) sama	♩ ♩ ♪
—	(4) vishama	♪♩ ♩
66	kanduka	♪ ♪ ♪ ♪ ♩
67	ekatâlî	♪

No.	Names of the tâlas	Notation
68	kumuda	
	[or]	
69	catustâla	
70	dombulî	
71	abhanga	
72	râyavankola	
73	vasanta	
74	laghuçekhara	
75	pratâpaçekhara	
76	jhaîhpâ	
77	gajajhampa	
78	caturmukha	
79	madana	
80	pratimanthaka or kollaka	
81	pârvatilocana	
82	rati	
83	lîlâ	
84	karanayati	
85	lalita	
86	gârugi	
87	râjanârâyana	
88	lakskmîça	
89	lalitapriya	
90	çrînandana	
91	janaka	
92	vardhana	
93	râgavardhana	
94	shattâla	

No.	Names of the tâlas	Notation
95	antarakrîdâ	♪♪♪
96	hamsa	♪ ♪
97	utsava	♪ ♩.
98	vilokita	♩ ♪♪♩.
99	gaja	♪♪♪♪
100	varnayati	♪♪♪♪
101	simha	♪♪♪♪♪
102	karuna	♩
103	sârasa	♪♪♪♪♪
104	candatâla	♪♪♪♪♪
105	candrakalâ	♩ ♩ ♩ ♩. ♩. ♩. ♪
106	laya	♩ ♪♩. ♩. ♩. ♩ ♩. ♪♪♪
107	skanda	♩ ♪♩ ♪♪ ♩
108	addatâlî or triputa	♪♪♪
109	dhattâ	♪♪ ♪♪♪♩
110	dvandva	♪♪♩ ♩ ♩ ♪♩.
111	mukunda	♪♪♪♪♩
112	kuvindaka	♪♪♩ ♩.
113	kaladhvani	♪♪♩ ♪♩.
114	gaurî	♪♪♪♪♪
115	sarasvatîkanthâbharana	♩ ♩ ♪♪♪♪
116	bhagna	♪♪♪♪♪ ♪ ♪
117	râjamrigânka	♪♪♪ ♩
118	râjamârtanda	♩ ♪♪
119	niççanka	♪ ♩ ♩ ♩. ♩ ♩ ♩ ♪
120	çârngadeva	♪♪♩ ♩. ♩ ♩ ♪

Appendix III
Bird Names

Few published scores give the English names of the birds which Messiaen uses in his music from 1953 onwards. Since some of the birds which he cites are often mistranslated in programme notes and similar publications, and because dictionaries are frequently unreliable in supplying the accepted ornithological name for a particular bird the following list of birds, giving their Latin and standard ornithological English equivalents, has been appended. The first column gives the name in the language which Messiaen uses in his scores (French, Japanese, etc.—whichever is appropriate), the second column gives the Latin names of genus and species and, in special cases, subspecies (the name of the subspecies has been omitted when this is the same as the species). Identification of certain African and American birds is problematical. Where the Latin and English names are conjectural, they are given in brackets; where it has been impossible to identify the bird with any certainty, the Latin and English are omitted. Grateful thanks are due to Mr D. W. Snow of the British Museum (Natural History) for his assistance in identifying some of the more obscure birds.

The works in which particular birdsongs appear (from 1953 onwards) are identified in the lists as follows:

R = Reveil des oiseaux	Cc = Couleurs de la Cité céleste
E = Oiseaux exotiques	Ee = Et exspecto resurrectionem mortuorum
O = Catalogue d'Oiseaux	T = La Transfiguration
C = Chronochromie	M = Méditations sur la Mystère de la Sainte Trinité
	F = La Fauvette des jardins

I EUROPEAN BIRDS

Accenteur alpin	Prunella collaris	Alpine Accentor	T
Accenteur mouchet	Prunella modularis	Dunnock	R
Aigle de Bonelli	Hieraatus fasciatus	Bonelli's Eagle	T
Aigle royal *	Aquila chrysaetos	Golden Eagle	O

* Flight only, no song.

Alouette Calandre	Melanocorypha calandra	Calandra Lark	Ee
Alouette Calandrelle	Calandrella cinerea	Short-toed Lark	O
Alouette des champs	Alauda arvensis	Sky Lark	OCF
Alouette Lulu	Lullula arborea	Wood Lark	RO
Autour	Accipiter gentilis	Goshawk	T
Balbuzard	Pandion haliaetus	Osprey	C
Bergeronette grise	Motacilla alba (alba)	White Wagtail	O
Bergeronette printanière	Motacilla flava	Yellow Wagtail	O
Bouscarle	Cettia cetti	Cetti's Warbler	RO
Bruant des roseaux	Emberiza schoeniclus	Reed Bunting	O
Bruant fou	Emberiza cia	Rock Bunting	O
Bruant jaune	Emberiza citrinella	Yellowhammer	OCMF
Bruant mélanocéphale	Emberiza melanocephala	Black-headed Bunting	T
Bruant Ortolan	Emberiza hortulana	Ortolan Bunting	O
Bruant proyer	Emberiza calandra	Corn Bunting	O
Buse variable	Buteo buteo	Buzzard	O
Caille	Coturnix coturnix	Quail	OF
Chardonneret	Carduelis carduelis	Goldfinch	ROCTF
Chevalier gambette	Tringa totanus	Redshank	O
Chocard des Alpes	Pyrrhocorax graculus	Alpine Chough	OT
Choucas	Corvus monedula	Jackdaw	O
Chouette Chevêche	Athene noctua	Little Owl	RO
Chouette Hulotte	Strix aluco	Tawny Owl	OF
Chouette de Tengmalm	Aegolius funereus	Tengmalm's Owl	M
Circaète	Circaetus gallicus	Short-toed Eagle	T
Cochevis de Théckla	Galerida thecklae	Theckla Lark	O
Cochevis huppé	Galerida cristata	Crested Lark	O
Corneille noire	Corvus corone	Carrion Crow	ROF
Coucou	Cuculus canorus	Cuckoo	R
Courlis cendré	Numenius arquata	Curlew	O
Engoulevent	Caprimulgus europaeus	Nightjar	R
Etourneau-sansonnet	Sturnus vulgaris	Starling	RO
Faisan	Phasianus colchicus	Pheasant	O
Faucon crécerelle	Falco tinnunculus	Kestrel	O
Faucon pélerin	Falco peregrinus	Peregrine	T
Fauvette à lunettes	Sylvia conspicillata	Spectacled Warbler	O
Fauvette à tête noire	Sylvia atricapilla	Blackcap	ROCTMF
Fauvette babillarde	Sylvia curruca	Lesser Whitethroat	C
Fauvette des jardins	Sylvia borin	Garden Warbler	ROCTMF

Fauvette grisette	Sylvia communis	Whitethroat	ROC
Fauvette Orphée (1)	Sylvia hortensis hortensis	Orphean Warbler	O
Fauvette Orphée (2)	Sylvia hortensis orientalis	Orphean Warbler	T
Fauvette passerinette	Sylvia cantillans	Subalpine Warbler	T
Foulque	Fulica atra	Coot	O
Gelinotte	Tetrastes bonasia	Hazel Hen	T
Goéland argenté	Larus argentatus	Herring Gull	O
Goéland cendré	Larus canus	Common Gull	O
Gorgebleue	Cyanosylvia svecica	Bluethroat	C
Grand Corbeau	Corvus corax	Raven	O
Grive draine	Turdus viscivorus	Mistle Thrush	RO
Grive musicienne	Turdus philomelos	Song Thrush	ROCTM
Guillemot de Troïl	Uria aalge	Guillemot	O
Héron butor	Botaurus stellaris	Bittern	O
Hibou grand-duc	Bubo bubo	Eagle Owl	O
Hibou moyen-duc	Asio otus	Long-eared Owl	O
Hirondelle de cheminée	Hirundo rustica	Swallow	OF
Hirondelle de rivage	Riparia riparia	Sand Martin	O
Huîtrier Pie	Haematopus ostralegus	Oystercatcher	O
Huppe	Upupa epops	Hoopoe	RO
Hypolaïs des oliviers	Hippolais olivetorum	Olive-tree Warbler	T
Hypolaïs ictérine	Hippolais icterina	Icterine Warbler	C
Hypolaïs polyglotte	Hippolais polyglotta	Melodious Warbler	RO
Linotte	Acanthis cannabina	Linnet	RC
Locustelle tachetée	Locustella naevia	Grasshopper Warbler	O
Loriot	Oriolus oriolus	Golden Oriole	ROCTF
Martinet noir	Apus apus	Swift	O
Martin-pêcheur	Alcedo atthis	Kingfisher	O
Merle à plastron	Turdus torquatus	Ring Ouzel	M
Merle bleu	Monticola solitarius	Blue Rock Thrush	O
Merle de roche	Monticola saxatilis	Rock Thrush	OT
Merle noir	Turdus merula	Blackbird	ROCTMF
Mésange bleue	Parus caelureus	Blue Tit	R
Mésange charbonnière	Parus major	Great Tit	OC
Milan noir	Milvus migrans	Black Kite	F
Moineau	Passer domesticus	House Sparrow	R
Mouette rieuse	Larus ridibundus	Black-headed Gull	O
Perdrix bartavelle	Alectoris graeca	Rock Partridge	T
Petit Gravelot	Charadrius dubius	Little Ringed Plover	O

Phragmite des joncs	Acrocephalus schoenobaenus	Sedge Warbler	O
Pic épeiche	Dendrocopus major	Great Spotted Woodpecker	R
Pic noir	Drycopus martius	Black Woodpecker	M
Pic vert	Picus viridus	Green Woodpecker	ROF
Pie	Pica pica	Magpie	R
Pie-grièche à tête rousse	Lanius senator	Woodchat Shrike	T
Pie-grièche écorcheur	Lanius collurio	Red-backed Shrike	OF
Pigeon ramier	Columba palumbus	Wood Pigeon	R
Pinson	Fringilla coelebs	Chaffinch	ROCMF
Pouillot Bonelli	Phylloscopus bonelli	Bonelli's Warbler	R
Pouillot fitis	Phylloscopus trochilis	Willow Warbler	R
Pouillot véloce	Phylloscopus collybitta	Chiffchaff	ROC
Poule d'eau	Gallinula chloropus	Moorhen	O
Pygargue	Haliaetus albicilla	White-tailed Eagle	C
Râle d'eau	Rallus aquaticus	Water Rail	O
Râle des genets	Crex crex	Corn Crake	O
Rossignol	Luscinia megarhynchos	Nightingale	ROCTF
Rougegorge	Erithacus rubicula	Robin	ROCT
Rouge-queue à front blanc	Phoenicurus phoenicurus	Redstart	RO
Rouge-queue Tithys	Phoenicurus ochruros	Black Redstart	O
Rousserolle Effarvatte	Acrocephalus scirpaceus	Reed Warbler	O
Rousserolle Turdoïde	Acrocephalus arundinaceus	Great Reed Warbler	OF
Rousserolle verderolle	Acrocephalus palustris	Marsh Warbler	C
Serin cini	Serinus serinus	Serin	R
Sitelle	Sitta europaea	Nuthatch	RC
Sterne Caugek	Sterna sandvicensis	Sandwich Tern	O
Sterne naine	Sterna albifrons	Little Tern	O
Tichodrome échelette	Tichodroma muraria	Wall Creeper	T
Torcol	Jynx torquilla	Wryneck	R
Tournepierre à collier	Arenaria interpres	Turnstone	O
Tourterelle	Streptopelia turtur	Turtle Dove	R
Traquet rieur	Oenanthe leucura	Black Wheatear	O
Traquet Stapazin	Oenanthe hispanica	Black-eared Wheatear	O
Troglodyte	Troglodytes troglodytes	Wren	ROCMF
Verdier	Carduelis chloris	Greenfinch	RC

II ASIAN BIRDS

1. Japan (All occur in *Sept Haïkaï*; those marked * are also found in *Chronochromie* under their French names, where given)

Aka hara	Turdus chrysolaus	Brown Thrush
Aoji	Emberiza spodocephala personata	Black-faced Bunting (or Musked Bunting)
Binzui	Anthus hodgsoni	Indian Tree Pipit
Fukuro	Strix uralensis honoensis	Ural Owl
Hibari	Alauda arvensis japonica	Japanese Sky Lark
Hôaka	Emberiza fucata	Grey-headed Bunting
Hôjiro	Emberiza cioides ciopsis	Siberian Meadow Bunting
Hototoguisu *	Cuculus poliocephalus	Little Cuckoo
Ikaru	Eophona personata	Japanese Grosbeak
Iwahibari	Prunella collaris erythropygia	Alpine Accentor
Juichi	Cuculus fugax hyperthrus	Hawk Cuckoo
Kibitaki *	Muscicapa narcissina	Narcissus Flycatcher
Komadori	Erithacus akahige	Japanese Robin
Ko-mukudori	Sturnia sturnina †	Starlet
Kuro tsugumi (Merle japonais *)	Turdis cardis	Grey Thrush
Mejiro (Zosterops à lunettes *)	Zosterops palpebrosa japonica	Japanese White-eye
Misosazai	Troglodytes troglodytes fumigatus	House or Winter Wren
Nobitaki	Saxicola torquata steinegeri	Stonechat
Nojiko	Emberiza sulphurata	Japanese Yellow Bunting
Ôruri (Cyornis japonais *)	Muscicapa cyanomelana	Blue Flycatcher
Ô-yoshikiri	Acrocephalus arundinaceus orientalis	Great Reed Warbler
Ruribitaki	Erithacus cyanurus	Siberian or Red-flanked Bluetail
San kô chô (Gobe-mouches de Paradis *)	Terpsiphone atrocaudata	Paradise Flycatcher
Sendai mushikui	Phylloscopus occipitalis coronatus	Crowned Willow Warbler
Uguisu (Bouscarle de Japon *)	Cettia diphone cantans	Japanese Bush Warbler

(All English names taken from 'Birds in Japan' by Yoshimaro Yamashina—Tokyo News Service, Ltd)

2. India

Bulbul Orphée	Pycnonotus jocosus	Red-whiskered Bulbul	E

† Given as Sturnia philippensis in *Sept Haïkaï*

Garrulaxe à huppe blanche	Garrulax leucolophus	White-crested Laughing Thrush	E
Mainate hindou	Acridotheres tristis	Common Mynah	E
Shama des Indes	Kittacincla malabarica (or Copsychus malabarica)	Shama	ET

3. China

Liothrix de Chine	Leiothrix lutea	Red-billed Mesia	E

4. Malaysia

Verdin à front d'or	Chloropsis aurifrons	Lesser Green Leafbird	E

III AFRICAN BIRDS

Alouette hausse-col	Eremophila alpestris	Shore Lark	T
Barbu à tête rouge		Red and yellow Barbet	T
Bouvreuil à ailes roses	Chodopechys sanguinea	Crimson-winged Finch	T
Bruant striolé	Emberiza striolata	House Bunting	T
Bulbul	Pycnonotus barbatus	Common Bulbul	TM
Calao concolor	Lophocerus nasutus	Grey Hornbill	T
Cisticole à moustaches	Melocichla mentalis	Moustached Scrub Warbler	T
Cisticole du Natal	Cisticola natalensis	Great Grass Warbler	T
Dromoïque du Sahara	Scotocerca inquieta	Scrub Warbler	T
Fauvette à tête grise	(Eminia lepida	Grey-capped Warbler)	T
Grand Indicateur	Indicator indicator	Black-throated Honeyguide	T
Rubiette de Moussier	Phoenicurus moussieri	Moussier's Redstart	T
Serin des Canaries	Serinus canarius	Wild Canary	E
Spréo superbe	Spreo superbus	Superb Starling	T
Téléphone Tschagra	Tchagra senegala	Bush Shrike	T

IV NORTH AMERICAN BIRDS

Alouette oreillarde	Eremophila alpestris (= European and African Shore Lark—see above)	Horned Lark	E
Ani à bec lisse	Crotophaga ani	Smooth-billed Ani	CT
Bobolink	Dolichonys oryzivorus	Bobolink	ET

204

Bruant renard	Passerella iliaca	Fox Sparrow	E
Cardinal rouge de Virginie	Richmondena cardinalis	Cardinal	ET
Carouge noir	Molothrus ater	Brown-headed Cowbird	T
Chouette de la Louisiane	Strix varia	Barred Owl	ET
Chouette des terriers	Speotyto cunicularia	Burrowing Owl	T
Colin de Californie	Lophortyx californica	California Quail	E
Colin de Gambel	Lophortyx gambeli	Gambel's Quail	E
Dindon sauvage	Meleagris gallopava	Common or Wild Turkey	E
Doliconyx (=Bobolink)			
Engoulevent criard	Caprimulgus vociferus	Whip-poor-will	E
Engoulevent de la Caroline	Caprimulgus carolinensis	Chuck-will's-widow	T
Grive d'Alice	Hylocichla minima aliciae	Grey-cheeked Thrush	T
Grive de Californie	Toxostoma redivivum	California Thrasher	E
Grive des bois	Hylocichla mustelina	Wood Thrush	E
Grive ermite	Hylocichla guttata	Hermit Thrush	E
Grive rousse	Toxostoma rufum	Brown Thrasher	E
Grive de Swainson	Hylocichla ustulata	Olive-backed Thrush	ET
Grive de Wilson	Hylocichla fuscescens	Veery	E
Gros-bec à tête noire	Hedymeles melanocephalus	Black-headed Grosbeak	E
Guiraca à poitrine rose	Pheucticus ludovicianus	Rose-breasted Grosbeak	ET ET
Hibou oreillard	Bubo virginianus	Great Horned Owl	T
Long-bec a collier châtain			T
Merle migrateur	Turdus migratorius	American Robin	E
Merle de Swainson (= Grive de Swainson)			
Moqueur polyglotte	Mimus polyglottus	Northern Mockingbird	E
Oiseau-chat	Durnetella carolinensis	Catbird	ET
Pape indigo	Passerina cyanea	Indigo Bunting	ET
Pape lazuli	Passerina amoena	Lazuli Bunting	E
Pinson à ailes baies	Pooecetes gramineus	Vesper Sparrow	E

Pinson chanteur d'Amérique	Melospiza melodia	Song Sparrow	E
Pinson à couronne blanche	Zonotrichia leucophrys	White-crowned Sparrow	E
Roselin pourpré	Carpodacus purpureus	Purple Finch	E
Rougegorge bleue d'Amérique	Sialia sialis	Common Bluebird	T
Stournelle à collier	Sturnella magna	Meadowlark	E
Stournelle des prés de l'Ouest	Sturnella neglecta	Western Meadowlark	CcT
Tangara écarlate	Piranga olivacea	Scarlet Tanager	ET
Tangara de la Louisiane	Piranga ludoviciana	Western Tanager	E
Tangara rouge	Piranga rubra	Summer Tanager	ET
Tétras Cupidon des prairies	Tympanuchus cupido	Prairie Chicken	E
Troglodyte de la Caroline	Thryothorus ludovicianus	Carolina Wren	E
Troupiale de Baltimore	Icterus galbula	Baltimore Oriole	ET
Troupiale des vergers	Icterus spurius	Orchard Oriole	E
Viréo à front jaune	Vireo flavifrons	Yellow-throated Vireo	E
Viréo gris-olive	Vireo gilvus	Warbling Vireo	ET
Viréo à tête bleue	Vireo solitarius	Blue-headed Vireo	E
Viréo aux yeux rouges	Vireo olivaceus	Red-eyed Vireo	E

V MEXICAN BIRDS

Ani (see North American list)			
Attila	Attila spadiceus	(Bright-rumped) Attila	C
Cassique de Mexique	Cassiculus melanicterus	Yellow-winged Cacique	T
Grive de Gray	Turdus grayi	Clay-coloured Thrush	C
Moqueur bleu	Melanotis caerulescens	Blue Mockingbird	CT CT
Moqueur des Tropiques	Mimus gilvus	Tropical Mockingbird	CT
Oropendola de Montezuma	Gymnostinops montezuma	Montezuma Oropendola	CT
Saltator grisâtre	Saltator coerulescens	Greyish Saltator	CT

Solitaire ardoise	Myadestes unicolor	Slate-coloured Solitaire	CT
Troglodyte à poitrine tachetée	(Thryothorus rutilus	Spot-breasted Wren)	T
Troglodyte strié			T

VI SOUTH AMERICAN BIRDS

(The names marked * are those of Brazilian birds given in Portuguese)

Arapaçu *	(Campylorhamphus falcularius	Black-billed Scythebill)	Cc
Araponga *	Procnias nudicollis	Bare-throated Bellbird	Cc
Benteveo	Pitangus sulphuratus	Great Kiskadee	Cc
Cassique Cela	Cacicus cela	Yellow-rumped Cacique	Cc
Colombe Talpacoti	Columbina talpacoti	Ruddy Ground-dove	T
Corococho *	(Ampelion?	Cotinga?)	Cc
Engoulevent à collier blanc	Nyctodromus albicollis	Pauraque	Cc
Engoulevent roux	Caprimulgus rufus	Rufous Nightjar	T
Evêque bleu du Brésil			T
Grive à ventre roux	Turdus rufiventris	Rufous-bellied Thrush	CcT
Guaxo *			Cc
Hornero	Furnarius rufus	Rufous Ovenbird	Cc
Merle gris du Brésil	(Turdus nigriceps	Slaty Thrush)	T
Moqueur à tête noire	Donacobius atricepillus	Black-capped Mocking-thrush	T
Moqueur de Venezuela (= Moqueur des Tropiques, see Mexican list)			
Rouxinol do rio negro *	(Microcerculus marginatus	Nightingale Wren)	T
Sabiá-coleira *	Turdus albicollis	White-necked Thrush	Cc
Sabiá-polyglota *			T
Sabiá-verdadeiro *	Turdus fumigatus	Cocoa Thrush	T
Saltator cendré (= Saltator grisâtre, see Mexican list)			
Sporophile à joues blanches	Sporophila palustris	Marsh Sandeater	T
Tarin de Magellan	Spinus magellanicus	Hooded Siskin	T
Toucan	Ramphastos dicolorus	(Red-breasted) Toucan	Cc
Troglodyte barré	Campylorhyncus nuchalis	Stripe-backed Wren	Cc
Troglodyte à long bec	Thryothorus longinostris	Long-billed Wren	Cc

Troglotye mignon   T
Uirapuru   Leucolepis modulator Musician Wren   Ee

VII AUSTRALASIAN BIRDS

1. *New Zealand* (Couleurs de la Cité céleste)

Mohoua à tête jaune	Mohoua ochrocephala	Yellowhead
Nestor de Nouvelle-Zélande	Nestor meridionalis septentrionalis	South Island Green Kaka
Oiseau cloche	Anthornis melanura	Bellbird
Râle Takahé	Notornis mantelli	Takahe
Tui	Prosthemadera novaeseelandiae	Tui (or Parson Bird)

2. *Australia* (La Transfiguration)

Grive grise	Colluricincla harmonica	Grey Thrush (or Grey Shrike-Thrush)
Koel	Eudynamys scolopacea	Koel
Loriot vert	Oriolus viridis	Olive-backed Oriole
Melliphage à joues blanches	Meliornis nigra	White-cheeked Honeyeater
Rhipidure de Willie	Rhipidura leucophrys	Black and White Fantail (Willie Wagtail)
Siffleur à ventre roux	Pachycephala rufiventris	Rufous Whistler
Siffleur doré	Pachycephala pectoralis	Golden Whistler

Bibliography

Bibliography

Books and articles on Messiaen

CLAUDE ROSTAND *Olivier Messiaen* (Ed. Ventadour, 1952).
An introductory study of the composer.

ANTOINE GOLÉA *Rencontres avec Olivier Messiaen* (Julliard, 1960).

CLAUDE SAMUEL *Entretiens avec Olivier Messiaen* (Pierre Belfond, 1967).
These two books take the form of conversations with the composer. Goléa's book contains much commentary besides actual conversation, and the author tends to put forward interpretations which do not always represent Messiaen's own point of view. Samuel's book is more useful in revealing the composer's attitude to theology, birdsong, symbolism and other topics.

ROGER NICHOL *Olivier Messiaen* (Oxford University Press, 1974).
A short introductory study useful to the listener and concert-goer.

DAVID DREW 'Messiaen—a provisional study' (*The Score*, Dec. 1954, Sept. 1955, and Dec. 1955).
Three articles, the first comprehensive study of the composer to be published in English.

OLIVIER MESSIAEN Lecture in Brussels (*Conférence de Bruxelles*, 1958; Leduc).
A lecture on aspects of rhythm and nature in music, published in French, English and German.

TREVOR HOLD 'Messiaen's Birds' (*Music and Letters*, April 1971).
A critical study of Messiaen's use of birdsong.

DAVID DREW 'Modern French Music'. (*European Music in the Twentieth Century*, Ed. Hartog, Penguin books, 1957).

BRIAN DENNIS 'Messiaen's *La Transfiguration*' (*Tempo*, XCIV Autumn 1970), 29–30.

BENNETT GARDINER 'Dialogues with Messiaen' (*Musical Events*, XXII October 1967), 6–9.

RICHARD FRANKO GOLDMAN 'Review of Records' (*Musical Quarterly*, LIII April 1967), 290–293.

PAUL GRIFFITHS 'Poèmes and Haïkaï: A Note on Messiaen's Development' (*Musical Times*, CXII September 1971), 853–855.

OLIVIER MESSIAEN and BERNARD GAVOTY   'Who Are You, Olivier Messiaen?' (*Tempo*, LVIII Summer 1961), 33–36.

ROGER SMALLEY   'Debussy and Messiaen' (*Musical Times*, CIX February 1968), 128–131.

NICOLAS ARMFELT   'Emotion in the Music of Messiaen (*Musical Times*, November 1965), 856–858.

LEONARD BURKAT   'Turangalîla-Symphonie' (*Musical Quarterly*, XXXVI April 1950), 259–268.

CHOU WEN-CHUNG   'Asian Concepts and Twentieth-Century Composers' (*Musical Quarterly*, LVII 1971), 211–229.

NORMAN DEMUTH   'Messiaen and His Organ Music' (*Musical Times*, XCVI April 1955), 203–206.

— 'Messiaen's Early Birds' (*Musical Times*, CI October 1960), 627–629.

BEVERLY DECKER ADAMS   'The Organ Compositions of Olivier Messiaen' Ph.D. dissertation, University of Utah, 1969.

PIERRETTE MARI   *Olivier Messiaen* (Paris: Éditions Seghers, 1965).

Other books and articles cited in the text

LAVIGNAC   *Encyclopédie de la Musique et Dictionnaire du Conservatoire*, Vol. I (Delagrave, 1924).
    Containing articles on Greek and Indian music which are relevant to Messiaen.

ANDRÉ HODEIR   *Since Debussy* (trans. Noel Burch; Secker & Warburg, 1961).

BOULEZ   *Boulez on Music Today* (trans. Susan Bradshaw and Richard Rodney Bennett; Faber and Faber, 1971).

BOULEZ   *Relevés d'apprenti* (Éditions du Seuil, 1966).
    Article: '*Stravinsky Demeure*'—an analysis of 'Le Sacre du Printemps' based on Messiaen's own analysis for his composition classes.

STOCKHAUSEN   'Music and Speech' (*Die Reihe*, Vol. VI, Theodore Presser Co. in association with Universal Edition).

Indexes

Index of Works by Messiaen

In the case of major works, the main references are shown in bold type. Except in the case of *Catalogue d'Oiseaux*, reference to individual movements is only made when these occur outside the main sections dealing with the work as a whole; they are listed under the title of the work from which they come. Figures in *italics* refer to places where the movement or movements discussed fall within the main section of the work.

Index of Names and Works by other Composers

General Index